Effective Business Communication

Principles and practice for the information age

Richard Blundel

FINANCIAL TIMES
Prentice Hall

An imprint of **Pearson Education**

Harlow, England · London · New York · Reading, Massachusetts · San Francisco
Toronto · Don Mills, Ontario · Sydney · Tokyo · Singapore · Hong Kong · Seoul
Taipei · Cape Town · Madrid · Mexico City · Amsterdam · Munich · Paris · Milan

Pearson Education Limited
Edinburgh Gate
Harlow
Essex, CM20 2JE
England

and Associated Companies throughout the world

Visit us on the World Wide Web at:
http://www.pearsoneduc.com

© Prentice Hall 1998

Typeset in $9\frac{1}{2}$ Melior
by PPS, London Road, Amesbury, Wilts.

Printed and bound in Great Britain by
T.J. International Ltd

Library of Congress Cataloging-in-Publication Data

Available from the publisher

British Library Cataloguing in Publication Data

A catalogue record for this book is available from
the British Library

ISBN 0–13–742701–8

---

10 9 8 7 6 5 4
04 03 02 01 00

Contents

▮▮ Appendices

Foreword

In the world of work, communication skills have always been important. However, today's technologies have transformed the old techniques of collecting, handling and sharing information into a *key* source of competitive advantage. Over two short decades, the computing and telecommunications revolutions have generated many serious challenges, alongside the much hyped opportunities. Managers, for example, have always been encouraged to write short reports; given today's limitless oceans of data, we have to be *obsessively* concise and focused.

This book provides a wide-ranging and much-needed primer on the most productive ways to communicate. Theory is complemented by a mass of practical, down-to-earth advice. The 'real world' flavour is continued in a variety of case studies, including a profile of my own company. Above all, the book raises some thought-provoking questions about the ways that we may share information and ideas in the future.

I hope that you find this book a useful and stimulating guide to this vital area of business management. Welcome to the 'Information Age'!

Russ Nathan CBE

Russ Nathan is the founder and Chairman of Romtec plc, a specialist market research and direct marketing company serving the computing and telecommunications industries. He is Chairman of the Business Link Network Company and of the Thames Valley Economic Partnership. Russ is also a Board Member of The Marketing Council with special responsibility for SMEs and a Director of Thames Valley Enterprise.

Preface

This book is designed to meet the needs of those studying for degrees and diplomas in business management, marketing and related subjects. It covers relevant underpinning knowledge for Management Charter Initiative / BTEC NVQs in management at levels four and five, and is also sufficiently accessible to be of value to Advanced GNVQ students. Practising managers, in public, private and voluntary sector organisations, should find the material useful, including those who are moving from a technical specialism (e.g. accountancy, engineering, medicine) into a broader management role.

Objectives and approach

The primary objective is to help you become a more effective communicator at work. The book considers principles and practice in a range of challenging and realistic business contexts, including: report writing, questionnaire design, running business meetings, organising exhibitions and giving presentations. A variety of 'real world' case studies and exercises help you to test and apply your learning at each stage. Most exercises are designed for group or individual use, catering for the independent learner and for class-based tuition.

This is not simply an instructional manual. Some time is spent on the 'key essentials', where there are broadly 'right' and 'wrong' ways of doing things. However, the emphasis throughout is on matching practical skills (i.e. how to construct a business report, agenda, etc.) with consistent underlying principles. The principles are there to help you generalise from specific experiences; they should also encourage you towards more flexible and creative solutions when new and unexpected challenges arise in the future.

Layout and use

The opening chapter is a **General Overview** of the whole book. It introduces the communication process, defines some essential terms and outlines the main themes to be developed later on. Be sure to read this chapter thoroughly, before proceeding. After Chapter 1, the rest of the book is divided into two inter-related parts:

- **Part I Principles of communication** This provides the essential groundwork, introducing a number of broad concepts that can be applied in a variety of business situations using different media and channels.
- **Part II Communication in practice** This deals with the practical application of the processes covered in Part I. It shows how to select the appropriate media and 'mix' of channels to deliver a particular message, whether you are in a meeting, making a presentation or preparing advertising copy.

Each chapter includes **exercises** and **case studies**. These are designed to confirm your understanding, and to provide practice in applying what has been learnt. The chapters in Part I ('principles') build on one another and are therefore best studied in sequence. Those in Part II ('practice') are entirely self-contained, and can be worked through in any order, depending on your current interests and needs. This flexible format allows you to explore the links between principles and practice by alternating between Parts I and II.

Skill and performance

Like tennis or piano playing, effective business communication is about the skilful application of knowledge. Just as in sports or the arts, you can also improve your performance by questioning and challenging established methods. With a positive, self-critical approach and a constant, determined focus on the **receiver**, you can become a more effective business communicator.

Student and tutor feedback

The key learning point in this book is that communication is a **two-way** process. In this spirit, I welcome your comments and suggestions which can be sent via the publisher.

How to use 'Effective Business Communication'

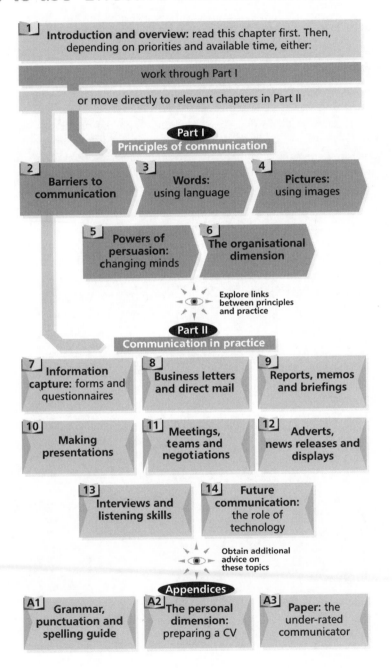

1 Introduction and overview: read this chapter first. Then, depending on priorities and available time, either:

work through Part I

or move directly to relevant chapters in Part II

Part I
Principles of communication

2 Barriers to communication

3 Words: using language

4 Pictures: using images

5 Powers of persuasion: changing minds

6 The organisational dimension

Explore links between principles and practice

Part II
Communication in practice

7 Information capture: forms and questionnaires

8 Business letters and direct mail

9 Reports, memos and briefings

10 Making presentations

11 Meetings, teams and negotiations

12 Adverts, news releases and displays

13 Interviews and listening skills

14 Future communication: the role of technology

Obtain additional advice on these topics

Appendices

A1 Grammar, punctuation and spelling guide

A2 The personal dimension: preparing a CV

A3 Paper: the under-rated communicator

Acknowledgements

I am very grateful to Julia Helmsley, Christopher Glennie and their colleagues at Prentice Hall for kind words of advice and encouragement throughout the joyous process of authorship. Many thanks to Alice and Ken Blundel, Anne Felton, Bryn Griffiths, Mary Hall, Dan Herbert, Sandy Gordon, Colin Mills, Allister Mitchell, Anne Rix, Anna Robinson, Ina Taylor, Keith and Jenny Walley, plus several anonymous reviewers who commented on earlier drafts. I am also indebted to all those who provided case study material, including Birgitte Baltzer-Nielsen (IKEA), Lianne Bradbrook (RDC), Phillipa Butters (BT), Craig Farmer (Quartz Presentations), Mark Foster (Royal Mail), Mark Graves (CBSO), Julie Hoyland (In Touch Research), Sam Magee (Oxfam), Diana Miall (Department of Transport) Russ Nathan (Romtec), Carla Phillips (Town & Country PR), Malcolm Thomas (Friends House).

Lastly, I should like to thank my inimitable colleagues at Harper Adams College who, along with many un-named students, friends and business contacts, have helped to bring this book to life. Any responsibility for errors and communication failures in the following pages is, of course, entirely mine.

Richard Blundel
Shropshire
Summer 1997

Chapter one

Introduction and overview

*The human mind is like an umbrella,
it works best when open*

Walter Gropius, architect and designer

Objectives

- To establish the importance of effective communication, in business life and more widely (1.1–1.2)
- To introduce some key concepts in communication theory, and build up a comprehensive model of the communication process (1.3–1.5)
- To show how general principles can be applied to inform and enhance business practice (1.6)
- To emphasise the importance of approaching the subject of communication with an open mind and a willingness to understand the needs of each audience (1.7)
- To provide an overall framework for the remainder of the book, which comprises Part I ('Principles') and Part II ('Practice') chapters

1.1 ▪▪ Introduction

This book looks at the ways we communicate at work and shows how improved communication enables individuals and organisations to deal with one another more successfully. The opening chapter introduces a model of the communication process that will be developed and re-applied throughout the text. It also highlights some essential terminology, explaining the concept of 'noise' and the differences between 'messages', 'media' and 'channels'. But before this, there are two more fundamental questions to consider:

- Why is communication such a critical issue for businesses?
- Why is it so difficult to communicate effectively?

1.2 ▪▪ Communication is about people

Human beings are social animals. In a complex technological society, our quality of life, even basic survival, depends on countless successful interactions with other people. Without this intricate, and largely unseen, network of communication our commercial markets, public services and cultural institutions would collapse and die. Of course, this has not stopped individuals, tribes and nations from seeking simpler solutions to their problems, usually through violence or avoidance. True communication is generally more difficult than these 'fight or flight' alternatives. This is because it requires each party to make a genuine effort to **understand** the other. However, though it may sometimes appear the more trickier option, effective communication is rewarding. For example, it can result in:

- Satisfied, repeat customers instead of disgruntled ex-customers
- Motivated employees instead of a costly industrial dispute
- An enhanced public reputation instead of a consumer boycott of your products
- A successful international alliance instead of a diplomatic incident or war

Many of the communication issues dealt with in this book will be similar to those you face every day, dealing with family and friends. However, once inside a business, there are some additional obstacles to overcome. These include:

- Organisation structures and procedures
- Cultural differences between departments
- Power and status differences between employees
- Unfamiliar communication techniques (e.g. interviewing, giving presentations)
- Financial and time pressures

As a result, communicating at work is often an uphill struggle. However, making that *extra* effort to understand the people you deal with is almost always worthwhile. As well as being an enjoyable and humanising thing to do, it is also the key to business success.

The challenges of effective communication are suprisingly similar, whether your 'business' is in the private, public or voluntary sector. For this reason, the book seeks to address the major communication issues affecting today's organisations, irrespective of size, structure or mission. The case studies and exercises range from small businesses to national charities and large international companies.

1.3 ■■ 'To communicate' – origins and definitions

What does the verb 'communicate' actually mean? Its roots in the Latin language are '*com*' and '*munis*', translating literally as 'with the people'. There are two closely related words, 'communion' and 'community', which emphasise that key idea of bringing people together. By contrast, present-day definitions are less helpful. For example, '*to transmit or pass on by speaking or writing*' (Concise Oxford) is rather narrow, ignoring the many non-verbal forms of communication which are covered in Chapter 4. Similarly, whilst one aim of communication is, '*to succeed in conveying information, evoking understanding*' it is also essential to persuade and motivate your audience; this is the subject of Chapter 5. So, rather than begin with someone else's words, it may be more useful to create a working definition of your own. How would you describe an 'effective communicator'?

EXERCISE 1A

'Effective communicators?' – assessing strengths and weaknesses

(a) At the top of a new page, write down your description: 'An effective communicator is . . .' Try to sum up the main characteristics in a sentence or two.

(b) Below this description, divide the page into two columns and use them to list YOUR 'Top Five' communication strengths and weaknesses. What do you do well, and where can you see room for improvement? How are you at letter writing, using the telephone, giving presentations, being interviewed, 'socialising' informally and so on? Try to be as comprehensive (and honest!) as possible.

Ask a friend or colleague to review your description and the 'Top Five' lists. Do their views agree with your own? Keep this exercise on file and refer to it again at the end of the course, noting how far your personal 'strengths' develop and 'weaknesses' are overcome.

If studying in a **group**, discuss the differences between your images of 'an effective communicator'. Try to draft a concise statement that embraces each person's ideas. Finally, add together the ranking scores from each person's 'Top Five' list and calculate averages. Where does the group see its main strengths and weaknesses? Use a whiteboard or flipchart to present your results.

1.4 ■■ Towards a model of human communication?

Since earliest times, men and women have been speculating on the basic mysteries of human existence:

- Where did I come from?
- Where am I going to?
- Why – in the meantime – am I so misunderstood?

Over the years, great philosophers, theologians and artists have done their best to answer these questions, but it is only within the last century or so that the mysteries of human communication and understanding have been investigated systematically. Scientific research, conducted by psychologists, sociologists, anthropologists and others, has contributed important insights. Later chapters consider some of these findings in more detail. However, the first step is to build a workable model of the communication process. The one that is most widely used today arose out of research

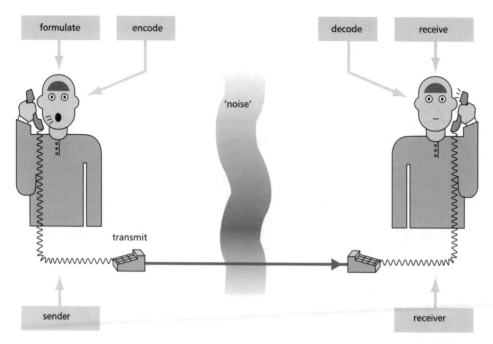

Figure 1.1 Communication model (i) 'one way' tranmission. (Adapted from Shannon and Weaver (1949))

into the ways that people used the telephone. Though the original work is largely forgotten, the terminology survives. In its simplest version, the model describes a 'one-way' process with two people – a 'sender' and a 'receiver' – who are connected via a telephone line (Figure 1.1):

- **From sender to receiver** The communication process starts when a message is *formulated* in the sender's brain. It is then *encoded*. In this case, encoding means that the message is turned into a series of spoken words. The encoded message (i.e. the words) are then *transmitted* along the telephone line. When the message is received by another person, it has to be *decoded*. The meaning behind those words must be interpreted by the receiver before it can be absorbed by *their* brain and finally *received*. This process continues, with the positions of 'sender' and 'receiver' reversed. Hence, a conversation takes place.

- **Trouble on the line?** Between the encoding and decoding, a transmitted message may be affected by '*noise*'. In the original research this word referred – literally – to the random electrical crackle affecting early telephone connections. The meaning of the term 'noise' is now much wider, including *anything that interrupts or distorts an encoded signal and, as a result, the message it contains*. Consider the following varied examples of 'noise' as experienced in a typical work situation. Try to add your own examples, based on events at work or when studying:

poor quality photocopying of a faxed invoice, resulting in the figures being misread by an accounts clerk and an over-payment being made.

heavy lunches and an over-heated meeting room, causing conference delegates to doze off in the afternoon (the so-called 'graveyard slot').

a badly organised filing system, leaving a sales executive unable to locate vital customer data that the sales director wants 'right now'.

1.5 ▪▪ Introducing feedback

The 'one-way' model (Figure 1.1) can be enhanced by adding a *feedback* loop. The term 'feedback' originated in cybernetics, the study of control systems. A simple application of feedback is the thermostat; it regulates the temperature of a building by switching the central heating system on and off when it reaches a pre-set level. In communication theory, feedback refers to *the receiver's response to a message*. It is important to realise how this kind of feedback differs from the smooth, automatic reaction of a thermostat. Human responses are variable and often

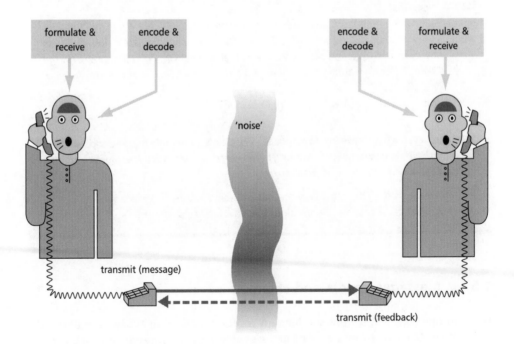

Figure 1.2 Communication model (ii) 'two way' with feedback.

unpredictable. Two apparently 'similar' individuals can respond to an identical message in a variety of ways. As an experiment, try smiling across a room at two colleagues; one might smile back at you, whilst the other frowns or appears to ignore you. Because there is no **automatic** feedback 'loop' in human communication, a dotted line is used in the model (Figure 1.2).

The unpredictable responses of human beings certainly make life more interesting. They are, for example, the basis of most stand-up comedy routines. However, confused feedback gets in the way of mutual understanding, with disastrous results. Consider this exchange between two colleagues, which appears to start promisingly:

EXERCISE 1B

Nicola and Brian – misreading the feedback?

NICOLA (Walking into office with a smile, waving report) *Well, Brian, the Sales Report certainly looks a lot better this month.*

BRIAN (Jumps up from a paper-strewn desk) *And what do you mean by that?*

NICOLA (Folding arms) *Hang on a second, Brian, there's no need to get all aggressive about it!*

BRIAN (Leaning back on desk) *I knew it. You're at it again, Nicola, aren't you? Ever since that . . .*

NICOLA (Gesturing with hands) *WHAT? Look, all I said was . . .*

BRIAN *Alright. Look, just forget it Nicola. You know, I'm just completely sick . . .* (Turns away from Nicola and picks up a ringing telephone) *Oh, hello Jim, how was the skiing?* (Laughs loudly) *Yeah, I bet you did! . . . anyhow, what can I do for you, my old mate?*

NICOLA (Storms out of office, muttering) *Chauvinist pig!*

Messages, even when delivered 'face to face', are clearly vulnerable to noise and incorrect decoding! What do you think was getting in the way of the *intended* messages contained in Nicola and Brian's short conversation?

(a) Draw up a list of the most likely causes of their unsuccessful exchange.
(b) Suggest how Nicola and Brian might have avoided this outcome.

1.6 ■■ Messages, media and channels

How do messages get from a sender to a receiver, and what types of material do they convey? In this section, we look at the contents and coding of a typical message, and describe the ways that it might travel from one brain to another.

MEDIUM This term is used to describe the way that messages are encoded. Almost all messages are encoded in more than one medium, so the plural **media** is frequently used. In business, the principal media are printed and spoken words. However, messages are presented in many other media, such as images, sounds and even smell!

CHANNEL This refers to the specific route, or technology, used to convey the message to the receiver. The main communication channels include: face-to-face conversation, letter, telephone, fax, e-mail, poster, brochure, video.

'Medium' and 'channel' – confusing terminology?

In this and other communication texts, 'medium' and 'channel' are used to make an important technical distinction between type of coding used (the medium) and the route that a message takes (the channel). Thus, Chapters 3 and 4 of this book focus on the principal media (i.e. words and pictures), whilst the Part II chapters consider how to exploit specific communication channels, such as letters and presentations. However, it is important to bear in mind that these terms are sometimes used interchangeably. For example, when advertising executives talk about alternative 'media', they are generally referring to television, radio, newspapers, poster sites, etc.

MESSAGE Whatever media and channels are used, human communication comprises a vast number of different messages, often transmitted simultaneously. These messages may contain one or more of the following types of material:

- **Facts:** concrete and objective (e.g. that H_2O *is the chemical symbol for water or that Paris is the capital city of France*)
- **Ideas:** abstract and, arguably, objective (e.g. *concepts such as the 'marketing mix' or Adam Smith's theory of the division of labour*)
- **Opinions:** concrete or abstract and subjective (e.g. *'Chelsea will win the match', 'our marketing team is superior to theirs!' or the so-called 'feelgood factor'*)
- **Beliefs:** more strongly held opinions, which are usually linked to an individual's sense of identity and influence their daily behaviour (e.g. *belief in the free market system, vegetarianism or reincarnation*)
- **Emotions:** felt and expressed by the **sender** (e.g. *having feelings of anger, joy, bitterness, passion, weariness, hopefulness*)
- **Motivation:** transmitted 'energy', affecting the **receiver** (e.g. *providing encouragement to achieve sales targets or to feel more positive!*)

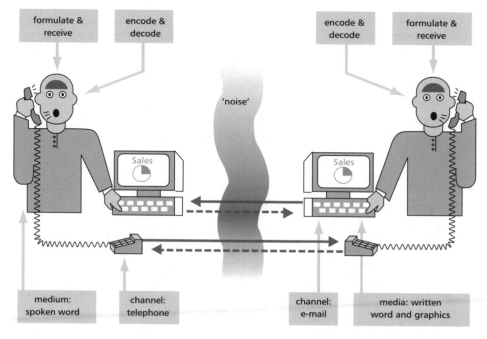

Figure 1.3 Communication model (iii) multi-channel and multi-media.

The terms 'medium', 'channel' and 'message' can now be integrated into the previous diagram, creating a more comprehensive model of the communication process as shown in Figure 1.3.

1.7 ▪▪ Reinforcing the message

All messages are vulnerable to noise and errors in decoding. One of the most effective ways of guarding against costly communication breakdowns is to **reinforce** the message. There are two main types of reinforcement:

- Encode using **multiple media** in one channel (e.g. put words and pictures in a brochure or newspaper article).
- Transmit using **multiple channels** (e.g. give your audience a verbal presentation and provide a written report).

Consider how reinforcement might help the manager in the following exercise:

EXERCISE 1C

Oddjob Engineering – reinforcement pays!

You are a recently appointed sales manager at Oddjob Engineering, and you have a 'hot prospect' on the phone. A party of Italian buyers, on a two-day visit from Milan, are staying at a hotel in Bristol. They have requested urgent directions to your main showrooms in Barnsley. An equipment order worth 120,000 is beckoning but their English is almost as bad as your Italian. How might you go about communicating this vital information?:

1. Begin a lengthy verbal description of the entire route, starting from the Bristol motorway intersection, and pausing while the Italians try to scribble it all down on a hotel napkin.
2. Politely suggest that they buy a national road map in the hotel shop.
3. Describe the route briefly over the phone, but *also* fax them a map, plus a simple written description of the route, noting any obvious landmarks.
4. Any other suggestions?

How 'robust' is the message that you have conveyed in each case? What is likely to get in the way of your message in this situation, and how have you tried to overcome it? What types of reinforcement have you used? Which option would *you* choose?

There are many examples of reinforcement, ranging from the useful but routine procedures to some truly creative communication 'solutions'. Consider the following examples and try to add some of your own:

- *Ensuring a good turn-out* Send out a memo to notify people about a forthcoming meeting, and then phone them with a reminder the day before (i.e. using multiple channels, with written and spoken words).

- *Launching a new product* Produce a television advertisement for a new soft drink, combining striking visual images, music, voice-over and words displayed on screen. Run a linked press advertising and direct mail campaign, plus a 'point of sale' promotion in targeted retail outlets, with free samples to taste (i.e. using multiple channels with a wide range of media in each channel).

Reinforcement must always be **consistent**. If one medium or channel is delivering a different message from the others, your receiver will be confused, and probably annoyed. For example, you might say to a colleague, '*Felicity, I'm really pleased to hear about your promotion*', whilst your unhappy facial expression and tone of voice are busy giving out precisely the opposite message! A common reinforcement error in audio-visual presentations is to talk about topic 'X' whilst the image on the screen relates to topic 'Y'. Unfortunately, that kind of inconsistency is not immediately apparent to you, the sender. Remember that it is the **receiver's** understanding of your messages that determines their success or failure. Keep a constant look-out for feedback.

Case study

First rule – understand the receiver

We are in a hot conference hall in a Central American country. The visiting British tutor is trying to 'break the ice' with a group of formally dressed civil servants attending a short course. 'I would like this to be a relaxed and informal session', she begins with a smile. 'As it is so hot today, I am going to take off my jacket, so please feel free to do so too!' From the assembled group, there is no response whatsoever, just a tense and visibly embarrassed silence. The tutor is understandably bemused and has an uncomfortable time trying to generate some rapport with these apparently 'difficult' tutees.

Later, she discovers why that opening message backfired. The department has a strict rule, forbidding junior staff from removing their jackets without prior approval from their superiors. The senior officers at this tutorial session sat themselves in a prominent position in the front rows. For reasons of their own they then chose to sweat it out, leaving everyone else with an insoluble dilemma.

Source: Linet Arthur

1.8 ■■ Two closing messages

In the following chapters, we explore the main obstacles to communication and consider how to use the available media and channels to the greatest possible effect. Before that, two short messages: firstly, to those who feel they 'know it all already', and, secondly, to anyone thinking they are 'too quiet to be a communicator'.

(a) **Business *IS* different** You may already have fantastic communication skills, but still face problems at work. This is largely due to the greater complexity and formalisation of business organisations. Information flows, culture and politics are going to be quite different from those in your current social circle of family and friends. Complex messages, such as marketing plans, departmental budgets or advertising, have to be formulated by more than one person, and conveyed to larger audiences than you have been used to. Many of your receivers may be unknown to you and their feedback will often be delayed, partial or non-existent. You also have some new skills to learn, such as drafting news releases and giving formal presentations.

(b) **But *ANYONE* can communicate effectively** Many quiet people find communication-based topics intimidating, and simply hate standing up in a tutorial. However, whilst hermits and recluses may not make very effective salespeople, many reticent individuals are very successful in business (Bill Gates, the billionaire founder of the computer software company *Microsoft* springs to mind). In fact, some of the greatest communicators – and most of the effective listeners – have been quiet souls. People communicate in a variety of ways, but the universal requirements for success are to be reasonably open-minded and willing to understand your audience. Ultimately, the outcome depends more on attitude and experience than on simple personality traits.

1.9 ▪▪ Chapter summary

- Business communication is, fundamentally, about our relationships with other people
- To be effective, we need to make some effort to understand both ourselves and those with whom we do business
- The communication process can be modelled, identifying the stages of message formulation, encoding, decoding and receipt. 'Noise' is a widespread obstacle to successful communication
- Messages can be usefully distinguished from the media in which they are encoded (or packaged) and the channels through which they are conveyed
- Use of multiple media and channels can reinforce the message, but any inconsistencies result in confusion
- It is always the receiver's understanding of a message that determines its success or failure. Therefore, communicators need to take the receiver seriously.
- Having good 'social skills' amongst friends is not, in itself, a guarantee of success in an organisation. However, with practice and commitment, anyone can become a successful business communicator

Discussion points

1. Analysing messages

Consider the examples of communication illustrated below. In each case, prepare a brief note and/or discuss in a small group the following questions:

(a) What is being communicated? (nb: try to identify the original messages)
(b) How are they presented or encoded? (i.e. identify the media used)
(c) How were they conveyed? (i.e. identify the channel used)
(d) What messages are *you* receiving: the original messages, or different ones?

2. The Johari Window

Managers often encounter problems dealing with other people. Psychologists, Joseph Luft and Harry Ingram designed a simple matrix, which can be used to consider how we deal with other people, and how relationships of trust develop over time. Practical examples of each type of communication are given overleaf. All relationships begin in the 'Unknown' area. When you first meet another person, they know little or nothing about you. In order to communicate, you begin to disclose things about yourself. They also begin to collect their own impressions, which may include some factors of which you are unaware. The position you have reached in the matrix affects the quality and effectiveness of your communication. You can expand the 'Open' by:

(a) Reducing **'hidden'** areas through **disclosure** (i.e. sending additional messages)
(b) Reducing **'blind'** areas through **feedback** (i.e. receiving additional messages)

In business, there is often a fine balance between disclosure and holding back. Clearly, there are many situations (e.g. the 'tedious client' problem, described

The Johari Window: four types of communication

	I am aware	I am not aware
They are aware	OPEN	BLIND
They are not aware	HIDDEN	UNKNOWN

Type	Practical example
UNKNOWN	You are negotiating with an important new customer, Joanna. Neither of you has realised just how much a problem at home is worrying her. As a result, you misread the situation and see her behaviour as either hostile or apathetic. Unfortunately, the resulting tension in the meeting gives Joanna something else to worry about!
BLIND	You have just presented a budget proposal that involves cost cutting in a vital hospital department. You leave, thinking that your presentation sounded convincing and objective. However, the audience could tell that you were not committed to the proposals; your 'body language' and tone of voice had given the game away without you realising.
HIDDEN	You find an important client's proposals for an advertising campaign very weak and uninspiring. However, you do not want to upset him at this early stage and try very hard to keep your true feelings from him by giving an impression of great enthusiasm for his plan.
OPEN	You and a close colleague are both operating 'on the same wavelength'. Each person knows the other's views and feels free to criticise proposals for a new business venture. You are confident that your colleague will not take the comments personally, and as a result the discussion is very productive.

above) where feelings are better kept to yourself! However, whilst 'Hidden' areas may be necessary, it is *always* useful to minimise communication where you are unaware or 'Blind'. The 'Blind' and 'Unknown' areas are where most communication failure occurs. You can therefore improve communication by seeking and absorbing feedback from others, provided that you have learnt to deal positively with what others may say.

Inter-personal communication exercise In pairs, ideally with someone you do not know well, engage in a five minute discussion on the topic: '*Why did I decide to study here?*' or, alternatively, '*Why did I decide to pursue this career?*' Each person should then sketch a 'Johari Window', noting which issues appeared in the 'Open' and (for your reference only) 'Hidden' areas. Discuss the contents of the 'Open' area with your partner. Try to identify any 'Blind' aspects. Note what you have disclosed during the two stages of the conversation.

Part I

Principles of communication

Chapter two

Barriers to communication

I talk to the trees, but they don't listen to me
I talk to the birds, but they don't understand

Lyric from the musical *Paint your Waggon*,
sung by Clint Eastwood

Objectives

- To highlight the principal reasons behind common communication problems and failures (2.1–2.2)
- To explore some important psychological, social and cultural barriers that have been identified, using selected research findings (2.3–2.4)
- To suggest a broad, three-stage approach to overcoming these barriers (2.5–2.7)

2.1 ▪▪ Introduction

Communication failures are expensive. The 'cost' is not simply the time and resources wasted in *preparing* the message, but also the confusion experienced by someone *receiving* a distorted version, or no message at all. For example, the true cost of a badly executed public relations (PR) campaign is not simply the sum charged by your PR agency; damage inflicted on the image of your organisation may be much more costly in the long run. As communicators, we are almost always *over*-optimistic about our messages, assuming they will survive unscathed, all the way from our own brains to those of our receivers. In fact, all messages are vulnerable to 'noise' (Section 1.3). This chapter shows how insights from physiology, psychology and social sciences can help you overcome noise and get your intended messages across. Though 'noise' was originally the result of **technological** problems (i.e. poor telephone connections), it will become clear that most barriers are due to **human** limitations. By keeping each receiver's strengths and weaknesses in mind, and by using communication channels sensibly, you will be better placed to overcome these barriers to communication.

2.2 ■■ Barriers to communication? – mostly human

In a world of mobile phones, video-conferencing and the *World Wide Web*, it is easy think that our communication problems are over. In fact, technology can only provide us with new **channels**; they may be faster or more portable, but the *quality* of communication flowing through them remains dependent on the human beings at either end. It is always tempting to criticise the technology when a message fails. However, as the old saying goes, '*a bad craftsman always blames his tools*' – the underlying barriers are always human ones.

Some common barriers – human or technological?

Cause	Reason	Practical example
Human	Physiological factors	Blindness, memory loss
	Psychological factors	Selective attention
	Social factors	Conformity
	Cultural	Culture-specific gestures
	Political	Lack of power in organisation
Technological	Technical failure	Fax machine breaks down
	Incorrect technology	Complex message sent by phone
	Incorrect use	Wrongly addressed e-mail

Many communication problems are blamed on technology. With the possible exception of technical failure (when you should have an alternative technology in place as a fallback, such as printed OHP slides as well as a computerised presentation) there are usually human errors lurking behind the technological problem, either choosing an inappropriate channel, or failing to use it effectively.

2.3 ■■ Physical and psychological barriers

People are amazing. Human sensory and information processing capabilities exceed the most advanced computers. However, since we are also organic and self-conscious, these skills are less standardised than those of a machine. The ability of people to communicate with one another is profoundly influenced by three inter-related variables:

- **Alertness & attention:** affecting what messages our senses manage to pick up
- **Perception:** resulting in different interpretations of the same sensory data
- **Memory:** affecting the messages we retain and those we can subsequently recall

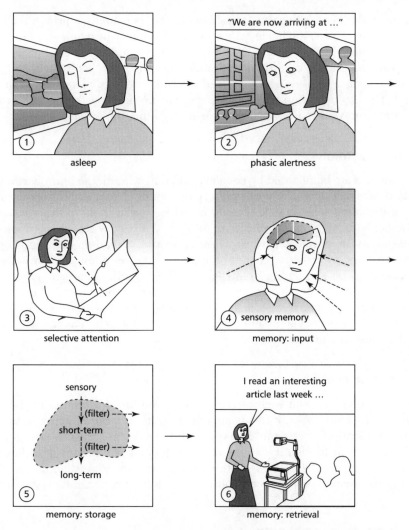

Figure 2.1 From alertness to memory. Imagine that you are on a train journey. Many messages will be sent, but those you actually receive and recall will need to overcome a number of barriers and filters, involving processes of alertness, selective attention and memory.

In each of these areas, there are dramatic differences between individuals. What is more, the *same* individual can demonstrate wide variations at different points in time.

Levels of alertness

Researchers have identified a long-term cycle of alertness, the 25-hour **cicardian rhythm** or 'body clock', and shorter-term variations during the day. A sudden increase in alertness, known as 'phasic alertness', is actually a primeval survival response. You can see it when a cat's ears twitch on hearing a new sound, or when a dozing student is startled into life on hearing his name called out in class. Once a receiver gets used to a particular stimulus (i.e. becomes 'habituated' to it), this survival response is no longer activated, and the message blends into the background. This is one reason why advertisers are constantly searching for novel and more dramatic ways to deliver their messages, so that the impact is maintained.

Selective attention

Since humans are bombarded by so many different stimuli, the brain has to ration out its processing power. We can only 'pay attention' to a small fraction of this mass of incoming sensory data. People have also learnt to jump from one source to another – a common application of this skill is switching between rival conversations in a noisy bar. However, selective attention can work against communicators. In today's 'channel-hopping', satellite television era, **attention spans** seem to be shortening dramatically. Where earlier generations would sit through hour-long church sermons and extended political speeches, modern audiences have become accustomed to multi-media presentations and ten second 'sound bites'. These developments pose a major challenge for anyone with long or complex messages to convey.

Powers of perception

We use information from each of the senses to build up a picture of the world around us. In some cases, humans are able to build a whole picture from a tiny scrap of information. For example, it is possible to recognise a friend's face, glimpsed in a big crowd, or to identify whole objects from close-up photos that show only a small part (Figure 2.2). However, this impressive sensory system has its limits. The optical illusions, reproduced below, show how our perceptions are actually

Figure 2.2 Perception – object recognition. In each case, the whole object (or person) can be identified from very limited information.

(a)

(b)

(c)

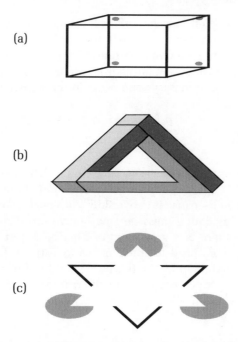

Figure 2.3 Optical illusion – My eyes are playing tricks on me! These simple examples illustrate how the processing of visual stimuli can create in our minds: (a) an ambiguous image – which way is the cube facing?; (b) something physically 'impossible'; and (c) something not present in the printed image – the triangle that is pointing upwards.

based on a hypothesis or 'best guess' from the evidence that our senses have managed to collect. If the evidence is ambiguous, we can misread it and even 'see' things that do not exist (Figure 2.3).

Remembering

In the past, it was witches who got the blame for 'memory-snatching', stealing the contents of people's minds. Today, we are more likely to point to a stressful life, information overload and old age as the main culprits. Whether it is ultimately due to witches or to watches, memory loss is clearly a major problem that the communicator needs to overcome. Psychologists have identified three distinct processes of memory:

• Registration
• Storage
• Retrieval

The brain acts much like a 'left luggage' office. It accepts a message, holds onto it for you, and returns it when you return some time later. Registration of an incoming message is closely related to selective attention (discussed above), but this is not like copying to a computer disk, where the code is held indefinitely in an unchanged state. In the brain, storage of a message can occur at three distinct levels:

- Sensory memory
- Short-term memory
- Long-term memory

Each of these memories appear to have set 'time limits'. The sensory memory is a kind of 'buffer'. Once it is full, any additional information of the same type – such as more words and numbers – cause it to overflow. As a result, some of the original material is lost. Some in-coming messages may move on to the short- and the long-term memory, but there is a great deal of filtering out at each stage. As a communicator, you therefore need to consider two questions: (a) how long does your message need to be retained by the receiver?; and (b) if it is more than a few seconds, how you are going to get through those filters into the longer-term memory? Exercise 2a demonstrates the limits of the sensory memory.

EXERCISE 2A

Testing your sensory memory – listening

How much information can people retain and recall, just a few seconds after first hearing it? Could you, for example, remember four words and two numbers over this short time period? Try the following test on another person or group. The level of recall should vary depending on the type of material conveyed:

Meaningless information, out of context
Read the following extract, or something similar, to a small group. Speak clearly at normal speed – it should take no more than 10 to 12 seconds. Now ask each person to write down as much of the message as he or she remembers. Compare these records with the original.

Field, 5174, Road, Glass, 3052, Kaleidoscope

Meaningful information, in context
Record a radio news report of two to three minutes duration. Replay it once, then ask a series of ten pre-prepared factual questions on *specific details* from the report. How many items are either forgotten or recalled incorrectly?

Information in narrative ('story') form
Read a short (two to three minutes duration) narrative, including lots of visual imagery, as in *'they crossed a rickety wooden bridge over a cool mountain stream . . .'* and so on: children's stories are ideal. Ask ten factual questions. Is recall any better than before?
How do you account for any differences in recall between these three examples?

2.4 ■■ Social and cultural barriers

In business, we rarely communicate with other people in isolation, senders and receivers are both individuals and members of some kind of organisation. In this section, we review two of the more significant factors affecting communication within and between groups of people – conformity and cultural difference:

- **Conformity:** is the process by which individuals in a group tend to follow the norms, values or behaviours of the group itself, of a charismatic leader.
- **Cultural difference:** is where one group or individual may have different norms, values or behaviour to others.

Both conformity and cultural difference are an inevitable, and very desirable, fact of life. Without some conformity, there would be even more war crime and anarchy; without cultural difference, the world would be even more dull, standardised and reactionary. It is clear, however, that *excessive* conformity and *unbridged* cultural differences are each bound to result in communication failure.

Conformity

In the shadow of the Nazi Holocaust, researchers tried to discover why individuals in a group are willing to do things that they would never do on their own. In the 1970s, a North American researcher, Janis, used the term '**groupthink**' to explain an extreme type of conformity occurring within close-knit groups. Using real life case studies, he argued that the following management failures can result from groupthink:

1. Incomplete survey of alternatives
2. Incomplete survey of objectives
3. Failure to examine risks of preferred choice
4. Poor information search
5. Selective bias in processing available information
6. Failure to re-appraise alternatives
7. Failure to work out contingency plans

Groupthink occurs in highly cohesive groups which are insulated from others, have single-minded leaders, and are under stress with no clear-cut solution to their problems. Unfortunately, these are *precisely* the conditions found in many company boardrooms, and government offices. In the late 1980s, the final years of Lady Thatcher's premiership displayed a number of Janis's symptoms of groupthink:

1. Illusion of invulnerability
2. Collective rationalisation of the problem
3. Belief in the inherent morality of the group
4. Sterotyping of 'out-groups'
5. Direct pressure on dissenters
6. Self-censorship by group members
7. Illusion of unanimity created, masking any divisions
8. Self-appointed 'mind-guards' ensure that all conform

These symptoms can be seen in many organisations. Each one represents an obstacle to effective communication, but in combination they can be fatal.

| Case study |

Pearl Harbor – a case of groupthink?

It is December 1941. Admiral Kimmel, Commander-in-Chief of the US Navy's Pacific Fleet, knows that war with Japan is imminent. He is clearly under considerable pressure, but has a detailed strategy in place. Unfortunately, this strategy does not incorporate the possibility that his home base, Pearl Harbor on the island of Hawaii, will be attacked. During the autumn, military intelligence have been suggesting that such an attack *is* a distinct possibility. Japanese embassy staff in Hawaii are known to be burning their files. Incoming information is being discussed by Kimmel and his staff, but they appear consistently to put an incorrect interpretation on it. In particular, they filter out facts that do not fit their existing position and emphasise anything that supports it. Five hours before the attack, on 7 December 1941, two US minesweepers spot a submerged submarine just outside Pearl Harbor, *but do not report it to their superiors*. The subsequent three-hour-long attack is the worst disaster in US naval history; some 2,340 people are killed and 19 vessels are destroyed.

Source: Janis (1972): adapted

Cultural differences

Cultures shape the way we think and behave. However, it is only when we experience *other* cultures at close hand that the power of a culture is apparent. Nations, occupations, companies, colleges and social groups each have a tendency to develop their own distinctive culture. This variety is clearly valuable. However, when people from dissimilar cultures get together, obstacles to communication can arise. These 'culture clashes' are sometimes amusing, but the consequences can be disastrous for the individuals and organisations involved.

Figure 2.4 Cultural convergence? Global soft drink brands are now distributed in China. Western fast food is sold alongside traditional street traders. Is this convergence, or are the changes only skin deep?

A Dutch researcher, Geert Hofstede, set out to test the 'convergence thesis', the view that we are all becoming more alike, with cultural difference squeezed out by global products such as *Coca-Cola* and *MTV*. His conclusion was that important variations do persist, despite these pressures. Furthermore, cultural factors do need to be taken into consideration when communicating internationally.

Case study

Geert Hofstede – testing cultural difference

Hofstede carried out extensive questionnaire-based research, based on staff of a major multinational computer firm. The respondents had similar occupations, but came from company subsidiaries in 40 different countries. Using a statistical clustering technique, he distinguished four key dimensions that appear to characterise particular cultures. Please note that it is possible to include only brief, and therefore fairly crude, summaries of each dimension here:

- **Individualism/collectivism:** This is reflected in the ways that managers communicate. In collectivist cultures, there is a stronger emphasis on reaching consensus but may be less room for individual initiative. Individualist cultures appear more argumentative but, arguably, may be more likely to generate creative solutions.

- **Power distance:** This relates to inequalities between senior managers and subordinates. Power distance and status affects the way that information flows up and down the hierarchy, and the levels at which decisions are made.

- **Uncertainty avoidance:** There are differences in how willing managers are to tolerate unstructured, unclear situations. Managers from 'high' uncertainty avoidance cultures tend to plan activities in more detail, which can be associated with rigid, inflexible procedures. Those from 'low' uncertainty avoidance cultures tend to 'muddle through'.

- **Masculinity/femininity:** This factor affects the core values of businesses from that culture and the ways that they operate. Those in so-called 'Masculine' cultures tend to emphasise material gain and aggressive competition, rather than on creativity and mutual support.

Hofstede has described cultural difference as '*the collective programming of the mind, which distinguishes one human group from another*'. His subsequent work, and that of other researchers in this field, has further refined and broadly supported these findings, posing a strong challenge to the convergence thesis.

Source: Hofstede (1984); Hickson (1997)

For international businesses, culture clash is a key issue. Even close neighbours have problems. Management writer Charles Handy describes the problems that arose when a collaborative group of French and British engineers were drawing up the contract for a major project. The French team wanted each part of the contract signed before moving on to the next one. The British interpreted this as a lack of trust on the part of the French and resisted their request. However, the French team saw reluctance to sign the documentation as displaying a lack of commitment on the part of the British ! Fortunately, someone eventually spotted the cultural obstacle and defused the situation. Otherwise, the negotiation could have broken up, resulting in a costly delay (Handy, 1996).

Understanding other people: the blind men and the elephant

It is human nature to generalise from our own experience of the world, but since everyone has a unique set of experiences, different perspectives are created. In the classical Indian story, some blind men encounter an elephant for the first time. One grabs its tail and says, '*so an elephant is thin, like a rope*'. Another man touches its hide and says, 'You are wrong, an elephant is rough and flat like a wall'. A third feels for its leg and says, 'Not at all, it is tall and round like a tree ...' The men are unable to agree on what an elephant *is*. Each is aware of only one part of the animal so each goes away with a different perception of the whole. The lesson for professional communicators is simple: recognise that each person's view of the world is incomplete, including your own; try to deal with other people in terms of their own experience.

2.5 ■■ Overcoming the barriers – a three-part solution

Having reviewed some of the main barriers to communication, it is time to develop constructive proposals for overcoming them. In very broad terms, these can be summarised as: (a) consider the receiver; (b) think clearly; and (c) deliver skilfully. Each is considered in turn:

(a) Consider the receiver

There are a number of things that the **sender** can do to minimise the risk of communication failure. Firstly, you can take responsibility for delivery and not simply for sending your messages. As management writer Peter Drucker has pointed out, the outcome of any communication is ultimately dependent on the **receiver**. When framing a message you therefore need to consider the receiver's:

- **Attitudes**
- **Expectations**
- **Involvement**

This could involve some background **research**. For example, you may need to discover what the receiver already knows about the *subject* of your message and also how they feel about it. In particular, does it interest, frighten, annoy or bore them? It may also be relevant to find out what they know and feel about *you*. Do you and your organisation have the credibility required to re-inforce the message?

EXERCISE 2B

Understanding the receiver's needs

Read through the following, all-too-common, remarks made by a receiver. In each case try to suggest:

(a) The likely reason for communication failure
(b) How it might have been avoided

Remember that the reasons for non-communication are sometimes more complex than they might at first appear.

1. *'That snooty young lady from the Hamburg office is talking utter nonsense. I've been in the computer software industry 25 years and I've never heard such rubbish . . .'*
2. *'Well, I thought she said first right and then take the second turning on the left after the traffic lights, then left at the third mini-roundabout . . . but we seem to have ended up on a building site!'*
3. *'Did she say sales were up by 25 per cent in the last 12 months? I thought it said 20 per cent on the OHP slide, but I can't be sure. Bernard? Not having a post-prandial doze, are we?'*
4. *'Apparently they had a big splash for the product launch . . . TV campaign and direct mail. That kids' programme presenter did the voice-over and the soundtrack was by some teenagers' band . . . but I certainly don't remember it!'*

(b) Think clearly

In other words, look before you leap! Young children have a refreshingly honest tendency to blurt out the first thing that comes into their minds (e.g. the child on a bus who asks, '*Mummy, why has that man got a funny leg?*'). Adults tend to be more careful, but their casual everyday conversations are not prepared in advance.

However, in **business**, many messages *do* need to be thought out carefully before being delivered. This preparation may be necessary for a variety of reasons; perhaps most commonly, it is because there are complex or contentious facts and ideas to convey.

One of the most useful techniques for generating and organising your thoughts, before attempting to communicate them, is to use **diagrams**. The idea behind this is that it is often easier to express, share and structure ideas if they are presented graphically. By using large sheets of paper or a whiteboard, a whole group of people can become involved, working through the problem together. Diagrams can also be used to work out a logical order in which to present the material to an audience.

EXERCISE 2C

Using diagrams to generate and structure a talk

Simple sketch (or 'spider') diagrams can help you to take notes, or to analyse a problem. Our minds appear to work by association, and the diagram provides a visual link between different words and ideas. Firstly, to generate ideas: instead of simply listing points down a page, write your main subject word in the centre of a blank sheet of paper. Begin to draw a series of lines from it, labelled with linked ideas. The simple example below is based on the topic, 'Holidays':

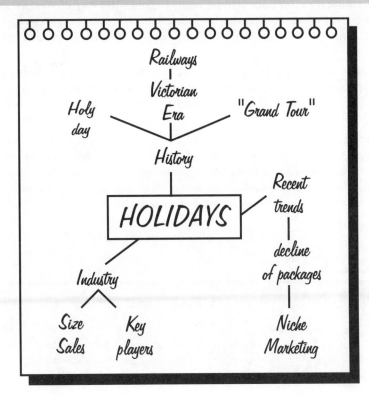

Now, to structure those ideas into a report or presentation, consider the logical links between them. You can order the material in various ways, including: importance, urgency, simple to complex and chronological order. This is always a matter of judgement, based on the material you need to communicate and the needs of your audience (see Chapter 9 for practical examples).

For this exercise, imagine that you have been asked to give a talk, with five minutes notice, on a topic about which you know virtually nothing ('Archaeology', for example). Experiment with diagramming to generate related ideas on the topic, and use a second diagram to order these ideas. Give the talk based on what you have prepared. Did the diagrams help in this task? Were you suprised at how much was stored away in your mind?

(c) Deliver skilfully

There are three *general* rules for effective delivery of any message, whatever media and channels are used:

- **Forget yourself** Self-consciousness tends to get in the way of your message, and can lead you to misinterpret any feedback that you receive. Try to forget yourself – your feelings, interests, priorities, concerns – and focus instead on those of your receiver.

- **Go 'multi-media'** If the receiver is likely to find your message difficult to absorb, use more than one medium and more than one channel to reinforce your message. Select the media and channels carefully and be sure to avoid inconsistent messages.

- **Get feedback** Check for any responses from your receiver and, if necessary, revise and repeat the process. If you do get 'negative feedback', try not to take the criticism personally. For example, if someone says to you: *That was an awful meeting, and the presentation was completely useless!*, avoid the temptation to return an insult. Find out exactly what caused this negative reaction.

EXERCISE 2D

Mnemonics – making memorable messages!

Mnemonics are memory aids. Everyone has their own favourite ways of memorising information, but certain techniques have proven to be particularly effective. You can use them in two ways: firstly, to help you memorise a message you are sending, and, secondly, to help your receivers remember the message you have sent:

- **Anagrams and key words** To construct an anagram, simply take the initial letter of the words you want to remember, and turn them into another (preferably memorable!) word. For example, *SWOT* refers to the analysis of a business's strengths, weaknesses, opportunities and threats. Key words operate on a similar principle, one word being used to trigger recall of a related piece of information. With key words you can compress a presentation on to a few small 'cue cards'. They can also be used as 'bullet points' on a presentation slide or poster display.

- **Rhyming words and melody** Patterns in a rhyme or a song help people to remember the component words. Hence, the words of an old song can be recalled by 'singing' it aloud or in your head. 'Metre', the rhythm in a poem, has a similar effect. In business, the main application is advertising, where some classic slogans have been created (e.g. *'Beanz meanz Heinz'* and *'A Mars a day helps you work, rest and play'*).

- **Using other senses** There is evidence that by linking more than one sense together, storage in LTM and subsequent recall is improved. Managers, lecturers and others who have many names to remember, often try to associate a name with a distinctive visual feature, voice pattern, etc. (e.g. Freida – tall, red hair; James – London accent, large ears).

Record on a flip chart or whiteboard the different techniques used by each person to memorise information. Which have been successful and which have failed? (n.b. If studying individually, ask colleagues and friends for their views on the value on mnemonics). Where else could mnemonics be used in business?

Even with thorough preparation, there are bound to be some communication failures. However, the important thing is not to make the same mistake again! A bad communication habit, like bad driving technique, is very difficult to un-learn, Hence, the best practitioners are never satisfied with their most recent effort. Instead, they are self-confident *and* self-aware enough to accept and make use of constructive criticism. Like the leading Japanese companies, they strive for *'kai-zen'*, or continuous improvement.

2.6 ▇▇ Chapter summary

- It is important to understand something of the psychology and culture of the people with whom you are communicating; it is here where the causes of most failed messages can be found.

- There are a number of simple techniques, such as diagramming, that can help people to overcome communication barriers.

- Consider all messages from the *receiver's* point of view, be clear about the contents and take time to practice the method of delivery.

Discussion points

1. The importance of listening

Writing in the *Harvard Business Review* back in 1952, F.J. Roethlisberger suggested that:

> **The biggest block to personal communication is man's inability to listen** intelligently, understandingly *and* skilfully *to another person.* *(emphasis added)*

(a) Do you agree with Roethlisberger's assessment? Give examples to support your argument.
(b) What do you see as the main skills of a good 'listener'? Draw up a list and compare with those prepared by colleagues.

2. Avoiding the question – analysing interviews

There are some situations where the receiver puts up obstacles to communication (e.g. as a defensive shield against unwelcome questions). Today's 'professional' politicians, are often skilled at avoiding the question. Extensive media training, often provided by former journalists, helps them to replace a meaningful answer to the interviewer's question with their own, often anodyne, 'sound bite'. These 'non-answers' can sound very convincing, and you have to be very alert to spot them!

Analysing interview technique Record an interview on radio and/or television. Make a note of the tactics used by the interviewees and the ways that interviewers try to obtain answers. How successful are they? Identify those occasions where a 'non-answer' is accepted, and others where the interviewer does get a meaningful reply.

Chapter three

Words: using language

Prose is words in their best order;
poetry is the best words in the best order

Samuel Taylor Coleridge, poet

Objectives

- To consider the key role of written and spoken words in business (3.1)

- To introduce the KISS principle of using clear and simple language (3.2)

- To identify the main pit-falls that lead to an ineffective use of words, and how these can be avoided (3.3)

- To show how meaning can be altered without a change of words, through differences in emphasis, grammar and punctuation (3.4–3.5)

- To develop a more self-aware and flexible use of words, adapting styles to meet the needs of different business situations (3.6)

3.1 ▪▪ Introduction

This chapter focuses on the ways that words are used, and frequently abused, in business communication. It shows how to use fewer words to better effect, ensuring that the words you *do* use are strong and meaningful. Getting more of the right words in the right order is not going to transform you into the twenty-first century's answer to Shakespeare, Jane Austen or W.B. Yeats. However, it should increase the chances that your messages will hit their targets.

3.2 ▪▪ The *KISS* principle

Perhaps the most important lesson to learn in business communication is the *KISS* principle, usually defined as '*Keep it short and simple*' (or, alternatively, '*Keep it simple, stupid*'). *KISS* is a fundamental requirement for almost all written and spoken communication in business. Managers simply do not have time to wade through 'waffle'; they want the key points and nothing more. *KISS* also saves secretarial time and even has an environmental benefit. Imagine the paper and ink cartridges that would be saved if all of the world's business letters were 5 per cent shorter! *KISS* is a plea that you are sure to hear from increasingly pressured, prematurely grey bosses everywhere. Once you have generated your message, and structured it in a logical sequence (Section 2.6), the *KISS* principle can be reduced to three basic rules:

(a) **Shorter words**
(b) **Fewer words**
(c) **Pictures if possible**

In isolation, these rules may seem obvious, but achieving *KISS* across a wide range of media and channels requires practice and commitment. At first, time taken to redraft and refine text might seem wasted. However, the streamlined results are sure to repay that effort many times over.

(a) Shorter words

Replace long words with shorter alternatives! English is a particularly rich language. Its older words, with Anglo-Saxon and Nordic roots, have more elaborate counterparts from the 'Romance' languages, derived from Latin, including Norman French. In general, the older words are shorter and more direct. Note the difference in **length** and also **tone** in this example:

Romance   ***The introductory oration was protracted, pedestrian and vacuous ...***

Anglo/Nordic ***The first speech was long, dull and empty ...***

If the shorter word lacks a subtle meaning that you need to convey, use a longer alternative. However, to make your point clearly and concisely, shorter words must be the general rule.

EXERCISE 3A

Drafting simple instructions

(a) Prepare a draft set of written instructions for someone carrying out one of the following tasks for the *first* time:

Prepare, cook and serve a cheese and mushroom omelette
Withdraw £50 from a 'cash-point' machine
Deal with a punctured cycle or car tyre

(b) Ask someone to test your instructions, and to point out any faults or ambiguities.
(c) Re-draft the instructions to make them clearer and more concise. Use a red pen to mark the changes on the old draft, then write out your revised version on a separate sheet. Compare your final draft with the original.

Figure 3.1 A world of words. There may be as many as 5,000 languages worldwide, but fewer distinct written forms. The major languages, based on the number of native speakers, are: Chinese (1 billion), English (350 million), Spanish (250 million), Hindi (200 million) and Russian (150 million).

(b) Fewer words

It is easy for an unnecessary word to slip into a sentence. Like any intruder, it will do its best to hide, so writers need to be vigilant. How can text be condensed without losing the essential messages? Consider the following extract:

Chief Executive's annual address to shareholders of 'Wordco plc': first draft

Of course, it is indeed extremely heartening and reassuring to be in a position where Wordco shareholders' attention can be drawn to the absence of any seriously negative repercussions, affecting active corporate-wide operations, that have arisen as a direct consequence of a not inconsiderable diminution in the principal influential macro-economic indicators over the preceding annual financial reporting period. Moreover, during the course of the period in question, a significant enhancement in the company's sales turnover performance and financial profitability measures in the markets of southern continental Europe has been achieved, with a particularly significant and notable improvement in the countries of the Iberian peninsular region. A relatively optimistic trend extrapolation can be forecasted at this stage, suggesting a realisation or modest transcendence of prior-year forecast projections for the indigenous market in those non-alcoholic beverages destined for domestic consumption. A pro-active commitment to the development of the corporate human resources is seen as a necessary and vital pre-requisite for the continued upward elevation of the company's fortunes.

This paragraph contains about 170 words. See how far you can shorten the word count without losing the essence. A shortened version is included below, but make your own attempt at sub-editing before reading on.

There are three main ways of shortening an existing draft:

- **Remove non-essential words** Sentence openers, such as, '*Of course ...*' or '*Clearly...*' are pure padding. They can be omitted without affecting the message. Some adjectives and adverbs, such as, '*quite*', '*fairly*' and '*comparatively*' are meaningless without a reference point. What, for instance, is meant by, '*a relatively optimistic trend ...*'? You should also delete cosmetic and redundant words, such as, '*a pro-active commitment ...*' and '*an upward elevation ...*'.

- **Replace long-winded expressions** These are often a sign of insecurity. People try to compensate for their lack of confidence in the message content by expressing it in grandiose terms (e.g. '*... a not inconsiderable diminution in the principal influential economic indicators over the preceding annual financial reporting period ...*' means simply, '*the recession last year*').

- **Switch from passive to active** The 'Wordco' address is written in the 'passive' voice (object-verb-subject), rather than the 'active' (subject-verb-object). The passive is normal practice for scientific reports. It sounds objective and is useful if you need to distance yourself from the action. For example, '*Granny was thrown off the roof, by myself ...*' appears less incriminating than, '*I threw*

Granny off the roof ...' However, the passive uses more words and is less interesting to read.

***

Here is one way of condensing the extract, using the techniques described above. It is reduced by more than 50 per cent, to about 75 words without any loss of meaning and with some useful details added. As a bonus, the text has a livelier, more direct tone. Try to build *KISS* principles into all your work, so that written and spoken English is 'concise first time'.

Chief Executive's annual address to Wordco plc shareholders: shorter version

I am pleased to report that the company is thriving, despite the recession last year. Sales in southern Europe are up 20 per cent from 1996, with margins improving to 15 per cent. Spain and Portugal are even stronger, with a 25 per cent increase in turnover and margins of over 17 per cent. We forecast even higher 1998 sales of £14 million in the UK retail soft drinks market. At Wordco plc, we believe that investing in people is the key to future success.

(c) Use pictures if possible

A picture paints a thousand words. In many cases it really is more efficient and effective to substitute images for spoken or written words. The term 'picture' can be interpreted very loosely, including, for instance:

- a bar chart
- a route map
- a product photograph

In Chapter 4 we consider how pictures can be used as a powerful communication tool.

3.3 ■■ Meaningful words?

Language is a living thing. New words and expressions are created all the time, whilst others become redundant, lose meaning and fade away. It is essential to use words that are meaningful to the receiver. Otherwise, you run the risk of being misunderstood. Try to avoid the following:

- **Clichés** This includes the old favourites (e.g. '*do not cry over spilt milk*', or '*we are rallying the troops*') and some fashionable clichés, slipped into a sentence for cosmetic effect (e.g. '*we have **taken it on board** ...*', '*it is a **ball park figure** ...*', or '*Jane is **interfacing** with Leeds tomorrow ...*'). A politician recently described greedy company directors as '*having their snouts in the gravy train*', thereby managing to combine two old clichés in a bizarre 'mixed metaphor'.

- **Euphemisms** A euphemism is a 'nice' word disguising an unpleasant reality. Hence, instead of dying, we '*pass away*'; rather than bomb cities and kill babies, we engage in '*surgical strikes*' resulting in some '*collateral damage*'. Euphemisms are commonly found in persuasive communication (Chapter 5), but if your main objective is **clarity**, they are best avoided.

- **Jargon** Specialist groups, from train-spotters to brain surgeons, each develop their own vocabulary. Jargon is a useful shorthand for terms the group uses regularly. However, it can be a serious obstacle to communication with a non-specialist audience. People stop listening, and their attention switches to unscrambling the jargon. Either explain the jargon at the beginning, or use language that non-specialists understand.

EXERCISE 3B

Jargon-busting

Prepare a list of the 'Top Ten' worst examples of jargon in one of the following fields, or in your own specialist area, presenting them in a poster format:

Accountancy, Business/Management, Computing, Economics, Engineering, Finance, Marketing, Personnel, Purchasing, Sales.

For each jargon word or expression, suggest a sensible alternative that can be understood by a non-specialist. Did you find any jargon words that do not have any 'layperson's' equivalent?

3.4 ▪▪ Meaning and emphasis

It is essential to make your meaning crystal clear. In a notorious 1950s court case, Derek Bentley was charged with the murder of a policeman. He did not fire the fatal shot, but was heard shouting to an armed accomplice, '*let him have it!*'. Did this mean: '*shoot him!*' or alternatively, '*give him the gun!*'? The words were ambiguous, but the hapless Bentley did not get the benefit of the doubt. He was found guilty and hanged. Similar errors, albeit with less tragic results, occur in business every day. With a more thoughtful use of words, these errors can be avoided.

The meaning of a sentence can be altered radically by **inflection**, using your voice to change the emphasis on particular words. Receivers are able to detect the tiniest variation in tone. Consider the simple sentence, 'We don't want your money.' How would inflections change the message when it is spoken aloud?:

(a) **We** don't want your money ...
(b) We **don't** want your money ...
(c) We don't **want** your money ...
(d) We don't want **your** money ...
(e) We don't want your **money** ...

In each case, the statement is 'qualified'. The listener is being led to expect a pause, followed by, '*but* . . .'. Watch out for this type of misinterpretation of your intended message in presentations and 'one-to-one' conversations.

3.5 ■■ Spelling, grammar and punctuation – so what?

Some people argue that correction of spelling, grammar and punctuation is just tedious and unnecessary, the '*who cares, so long as they understand me?*' school of thought. Unfortunately, many errors in punctuation and grammar *do* cause misunderstanding, wasting valuable time. For anyone who remains sceptical, here are some examples where errors make a message ambiguous or difficult to read:

- **Confused 'dependent' clause**
  Welsh Rugby Union chiefs gave their full backing to a judge after he jailed a violent player who stamped on an opponent's head for six months.

- **Too many conjunctions, not enough punctuation**
  We sell a range of products to the wholesale market because it is profitable to do so and also since there is the prospect of growth with signs of improvement in the Northern area and some opportunities in the West though we only have one sales representative located there at present whilst the warehousing issue is being resolved and we are rushed off our feet therefore I really do hope that you will be able to bear with us in the meantime because for some reason or other we seem to barely have time to take a breather!

- **Faulty grammar and punctuation**
  Our company were very pleased, to have done the presentation for your office, yesterday. As you would have clearly seen the best features of, our service is above all their very top qualified technicians. Each one of them have been awarded, full industry certification, commitment to the job and with an extensive two years training programmes. I hope we can therefore look forward, to hear from you in due course.

You may want to proof read and correct these errors. Readers who have either by-passed or forgotten their school grammar can refer to Appendix 1.

Helvetica bold 18pt

Times bold italic 18pt

OCRa 24pt

Handel Gothic l5pt

ENGRAVERS GOTHIC 20PT

Bodoni Poster 14pt

Bedrock 21pt

New Century Schoolbook 14pt

Englische Schreibschrift 21pt

american uncial 15 pt

BREMEN BOLD 14PT

Marydale 21pt

Figure 3.2 Choosing a suitable font. You can change the visual impact of a printed document by selecting a different 'font' or typeface. To ensure that the text remains readable, avoid both 'upper case' (i.e. all capital letters) and the more 'flowery' fonts; these may be effective for titles, but never use them for extended sections of text. It is also important not to mix too many different fonts or point sizes in one document.

For a clear and professional-looking business report, use a *sans serif* font, such as 'Helvetica' or 'Arial' for your subject headings, and a serif font, such as 'Times' or 'Arrus', for your body text. The reason for this is that the *serifs* (the little lines at the ends of each letter) help lead your eye along a line of text increasing your reading speed. To see the difference that the choice of font can make, retype this paragraph of text and make three copies on separate sheets. Format the first as upper-case text, the second as bold Helvetica, and the third as Times Roman, or similar. Print out and re-read each version.

Case study

Bad language at the supermarket – '12 items or less'

Most supermarket checkouts have an 'express' lane. A few years ago, in response to a customer campaign, signs reading '*12 items or less*' were replaced with '*12 items or fewer'*. Protesters argued, correctly, that the adjective *'less'* relates to a **single** item (e.g. *'I have **less mashed potato** than you'*), whilst *'fewer'* describes a **number** of items (e.g. *'I have **fewer chips** than you'*). Hence, for the checkout signs, 'fewer' was the correct word to use. Was this an unnecessary protest? Is it important to guard the way words are used in order to retain these differences in meaning?

3.6 ■■ Language – it is a matter of style

Written and spoken style can be seen as a combination of all the areas discussed so far. It relates to choice of vocabulary, intonation, sentence structure and to the rules of grammar and punctuation. The style most commonly used in business writing is sometimes described as 'plain English'. In essence, it is based on the *KISS* principles from Section 3.2. However, there is no one 'right' way to communicate with words. It is important to develop flexibility, adapting your language style to the requirements of specific messages and readers.

EXERCISE 3C

Use synonyms for variety!

The *KISS* principle is essential in keeping messages **concise**. However, this is no reason to make them **dull**! The English language is shaped by centuries of invasion, conquest and trade. As a result, it is uniquely rich in 'synonyms', alternative words of similar meaning. You can liven up your prose style quickly and painlessly, through regular use of a decent **thesaurus** and **dictionary** in book form (nb: though most word processing packages include a thesaurus function, it can be rather limited). Try the following exercise.

Take the following six words, commonly used in the business world – **income, educate, mechanism, challenge, salary, manager**:

(a) Using a dictionary, find out their origins and any alternative meanings that have developed from those origins.
(b) Using a thesaurus, identify as many synonyms as possible for each word, noting differences in meaning or emphasis in the words selected. For example, each of the synonyms, 'audience', 'spectators' and 'crowd' has its own flavour.
(c) Draft a sentence using all six of the original words, then write a second version using a selection of the synonyms. Has the underlying meaning of your message changed?

EXERCISE 3D

Exprimenting with style

In the popular television show, *Whose line is it anyway?*, comedians improvise a piece of dialogue 'in the style of' (say) a Hollywood epic or a party political broadcast. In this exercise, write a brief description of your university, college or business as it might appear in each of the following contexts:

- In a purely factual publication (e.g. a year book or trade directory)
- As part of a lurid tabloid news story
- In an official promotional statement by a senior academic or manager
- During an informal conversation between two friends in a pub

Compare the four pieces of text that you have prepared. How does the vocabulary, tone, sentence length and overall structure vary between these different communication channels?

3.7 ▪▪ Chapter summary

- Business people demand clear, simple and unambiguous language.
- The *KISS* principles are: fewer words, shorter words and 'pictures if possible'.
- Summarising is a key management skill. It involves the removal of redundant words, replacing of long-winded expressions and writing in the 'active' form.
- If your objective is clarity, avoid using any words that have lost their meaning and any jargon that is not readily understood by a particular audience.
- Correct use of grammar, spelling and punctuation is important. It avoids misunderstanding and speeds up communication.
- Use this rich language creatively. By selecting synonyms and considering the effect of alternative words, messages can become more attractive and interesting, whilst remaining clear and concise.

Discussion points

1. Language in decline?

Read this short extract from an article by the writer and journalist, George Orwell:

> Most people who bother with the matter at all would admit that the English language is in a bad way, but it is generally assumed that we cannot by conscious action do anything about it. Our civilisation is decadent and our language – so the

argument runs – must inevitably share in the general collapse. It follows that any struggle against the abuse of language is a sentimental archaism, like preferring candles to electric light or hansom cabs to aeroplanes. Underneath this lies the half-conscious belief that language is a natural growth and not an instrument which we shape for our own purposes.

Now, it is clear that the decline of a language must ultimately have political and economic causes: it is not due simply to the bad influence of this or that individual writer. But an effect can become a cause, reinforcing the original cause and producing the same effect in an intensified form, and so on indefinitely. A man may take to drink because he feels himself a failure, and then fail all the more because he drinks. It is rather the same thing that is happening to the English language. It becomes ugly and inaccurate because our thoughts are foolish, but the slovenliness of our language makes it easier for us to have foolish thoughts. The point is that the process is reversible. Modern English, especially written English, is full of bad habits which spread by imitation and which can be avoided if one is willing to take the necessary trouble. If one gets rid of these habits one can think more clearly, and to think more clearly is a necessary first step towards political regeneration.

Extracted from: Politics and the English language (1946).

Summarise Orwell's main arguments in 'bullet point' format. Do you agree with his proposition that there is a link between the state of the language and the quality of decisions made by politicians or other key figures? Give practical examples to support your argument.

2. Using words metaphorically

Words are not always used literally; metaphors and figurative expressions can give a message greater impact. We know, for example that references to a 'stony silence' or an 'uphill struggle' have nothing to do with *real* stones or hills. The image of gold is often used metaphorically to describe how people are paid: encouraging them to join a company ('golden handshakes'), allowing them to leave a troubled company painlessly ('golden parachutes'), or forcing them to stay on ('golden handcuffs' and 'gilded cages'). Metaphors are also used to make abstract ideas more concrete. Winston Churchill famously depicted the post-1945 division of Europe as 'The Iron Curtain', and referred to his own clinical depression as the 'Black Dog'.

The 'glass ceiling'

The 'glass ceiling' is a vivid metaphor from North America, where most of the major corporations are housed in 20- or 30-storey skyscrapers. The top floors of these buildings are commonly reserved for the spacious offices of the chief executives and other senior staff. Hence, the 'glass ceiling' captures the idea that women, in particular, face an unyielding but invisible barrier, blocking their promotion from middle management positions.

Imagine that you have to give a talk about the glass ceiling to an audience with no experience of skyscrapers. Can you suggest any alternative metaphors that would convey a similar meaning?

'Pigs will fly?'

Powerful effects can be achieved by adapting or embellishing an existing figurative expression. Once, whilst attacking the policies of his opponents, the British politician Kenneth Clarke suggested that: '*It is not just a matter of pigs flying. It is a whole farmyard on a mission deep into space.*' Another politician, Dennis Healey applied animal imagery to an opponent when he likened Geoffrey Howe's parliamentary performance to being, '*. . . savaged by a dead sheep.*'

Try to find at least five examples of figurative language from recent television, radio or newspaper coverage. In each case, prepare a brief comment on the effectiveness of the image used. If possible, try to suggest your own alternative version.

Chapter four

Pictures: using images

'What is the use of a book', thought Alice,
'without pictures or conversations?'

Lewis Caroll, *Alice in Wonderland*

Objectives

- To consider how visual images can be used in different areas of business communication, ranging from gestures to graphs (4.1–4.2)
- To evaluate the main benefits of visual media (4.3)
- To identify potential pitfalls when using images and how they can be overcome (4.4)
- To review the uses and abuses of business graphs and charts (4.5)
- To consider the visual aspects of corporate identity (4.6)

4.1 ▪▪ Introduction

A wide range of visual images are used in business. These 'pictures' range, from body language and gesture (e.g. the thumbs up/thumbs down sign), to diagrams, photographs and video. They can have a powerful effect. For example, a well-designed reception room, with smartly dressed staff is bound to influence a prospective customer's overall impression of the company and its products. By considering this potpourri of images together, it is possible to reach some useful general conclusions about non-verbal communication. Having explored the advantages of visual media, the chapter concludes with a review of the most common problem areas, identifying the ways that they can be avoided or overcome. This is linked to a short section on the special problems of creating and maintaining a visual identity for your organisation.

4.2 ▪▪ Using 'pictures' at work

In some situations, visual images can replace words entirely. Commodities market traders and racetrack bookies overcome the twin problems of noise and distance by using elaborate hand signals to communicate. International businesses have

Figure 4.1 Some international signs and icons.

overcome language barriers using pictures. At major airports, the 'restaurant', 'no smoking' and 'exit' signs are now internationally recognised, conveying their message without words. Standardised 'icons' have been adopted in computer software programs, allowing them to be used worldwide.

The other main function of visual images in business is to reinforce written or spoken words. This occurs in many different ways, for example:

- A skilled conference speaker uses an outstretched arms gesture to make the audience feel more directly involved (see Figure 4.2).
- A finance manager giving a presentation to City analysts uses bar graphs and pie charts to display the raw data from a complex profit forecast in a clearer and more attractive way.
- A brochure-designer searches photo libraries to find just the right image to support the central messages that appear in the text.

4.3 ▦▦▦ Potential benefits of visual media

Images can be quickly assimilated and may help to simplify an otherwise complex message. They can also attract the attention of an audience, motivate them to act, and help them to retain a message, once the original stimulus has gone:

Figure 4.2 Using gesture to emphasise a point.

(a) Making messages quick to absorb

People are all very adept at 'speed reading' visual messages. If you ask someone a question, for example, their face (e.g. a smile, raised eyebrows or a grimace) can communicate the answer long before their spoken reply. In addition to *human* facial expressions and gestures, we use all sorts of *manufactured* signs to convey information quickly and easily.

EXERCISE 4A

Designing icons, symbols & signs

The meaning behind the images reproduced in Figure 4.1 can be absorbed 'at a glance', avoiding the need for a verbal explanation. The images are also designed to be understood instantly by people from a wide variety of cultures and language groups. With these requirements in mind, design your own images for the following purposes:

(a) A 'button bar' computer icon for getting access to a home shopping service.
(b) A sign to identify the police station at an international airport.
(c) 'No overtaking' and 'cycle workshop ahead' signs for use on a national cycle route.
(d) An international symbol to show that products are environmentally sustainable.

(b) Simplifying 'difficult' messages

Most senior managers want incoming information simplified. By taking your key findings and displaying them in graphical form, as bar charts, pie charts, cluster plots, etc., you enable your audience to *visualise* the information, making it much easier for them to comprehend (see Section 4.5 below). Graphics can also be used to explain relationships and actions that would be difficult to convey concisely in words. Examples of this include: an organisational structure chart for a large government department, a flow diagram outlining the manufacturing process in a workshop or the instructions for assembling a chair.

Case study

IKEA beat the language barrier

The dynamic Swedish furniture retailer, IKEA, has more than 125 stores in 26 countries and receives about 120 million visitors a year. The IKEA Group entered the UK market in 1987 and its franchisees now operate six stores around the country. The organisation has many years' experience in designing multi-language instruction leaflets for its 'flat pack', home assembly products. IKEA leaflets are based on simple line drawings in a numbered sequence. The easily understood instructions, combined with good basic product design and manufacture, ensure that the same instructions can be readily understood by the company's customers, whether they are French, Czech, Italian or British.

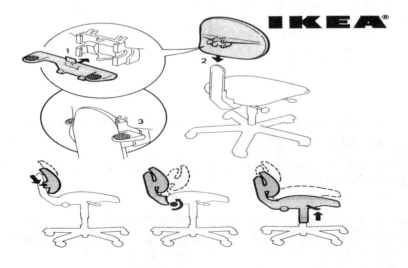

Source: Inter Ikea Systems BV

(c) Securing audience attention

A striking image can make us stop and look, exploiting 'phasic alertness' (see Section 2.3). For example, the unusual photograph below was (hopefully!) the first thing you noticed on turning this page. Dramatic or unexpected images can be used in many situations, including newspapers, advertisements, brochures, presentations and exhibition stands. How, for example, could advertisers convey (to a twenty-something audience) the unpalatable message that, '*though you are young now, it really is time to start thinking about a pension*'. In a recent television campaign, they created a storyline involving an elderly man who dresses up like a young teenager in a very belated attempt to enrol on a pension plan. The image is a powerful one, combining a 'humorous' jibe at ageing trendies with a sobering reminder to its intended audience that they too must start to face the realities of financing their retirement.

Figure 4.3 Dramatic image. In a world that is increasingly saturated with strong visual images, the ones that you use have to work even harder to secure the attention of an audience. Your organisation's photographers and graphic artists need to be aware of this important lesson.

(d) Persuading and motivating

Images can persuade an audience, and even motivate them into action. For instance, the bank manager is sure to give your business plan a more sympathetic hearing if you arrive smartly dressed, rather than in a scruffy jumper and torn jeans. In the same way, an attractively packaged product or service can encourage repeat purchase, especially if it has an image which is consistent with the prospective buyer's own values and self-image. Of course, negative images, such as a pile of rubbish outside an expensive restaurant, will have the opposite effect. The use of images as persuaders is considered in Chapter 5.

(e) Making messages memorable

Lastly, visual images can help to get your message into a receiver's short- or long- term memory (Section 2.3). For example, advertisers make extensive use of 'visual hooks', to establish and build brand awareness. Repeated exposure to an image, such as a company logo or the face of a spokesperson, increases the likelihood that any message linked to it will be retained by the target audience.

EXERCISE 4B

Using more complex images

Based on the discussion and illustrations in Section 4.3, sketch a suitable visual image to meet each of the following requirements:

(a) A wordless diagram which explains exactly how to carry out one of the tasks described in Exercise 3a:
   Prepare, cook and serve a cheese and mushroom omelette
   Withdraw £50 from a 'cash-point' machine
   Deal with a punctured cycle or car tyre
(b) A visual brand identity for a new range of 'green' consumer products, either household detergents or clothes. The manufacturer needs to build a distinctive and memorable image in the domestic retail market.

What did you find most difficult in preparing each image? How should your rough drafts be improved, when re-drawn by a professional artist, to make them more effective?

| Case study |

The CBSO – orchestrating a positive image

The City of Birmingham Symphony Orchestra (CBSO) is one of the country's most distinguished and well-known orchestras. The CBSO reaches an audience of over 100,000 from its base at Birmingham's Symphony Hall, and it also tours internationally. The orchestra is financed through ticket sales, corporate sponsorship, recordings and grant income. Competition is fierce in each of these areas. The critical success factors for an orchestra are the quality of its professional musicians, and their ability to work together in performance. Though the end product is music, a strong visual identity also plays an important part. This identity has many elements. In the CBSO's case, these include its distinctive logo, its long association with a charismatic Music Director, Sir Simon Rattle, and its location in a prestigious and brilliantly designed concert hall.

Source: CBSO (photo credits: Steve Wragg – rehearsal in Symphony Hall; Alan Wood – Sir Simon Rattle)

4.4 ▦ Potential problems with visual media

Chapter 3 showed how language can be mis-used in business. The aim of this section is to consider why particular images might be inappropriate, either for the **message** to be sent or the **audience** that you are trying to reach. Managers often spend too long on the words and numbers in a message, and forget the visual element. As a result, their 'pictures' may be obsolete, inconsistent or distorted:

(a) Obsolete and clichéd images

Over-used 'pictures' fail to attract attention. However, they might also send an unintended message. For example, an annual report full of 'standard' pictures of factory sites and smiling workers might suggest that a company was old-fashioned and uncreative. Similarly, most charities and campaign groups have stopped using images that portray disabled people and those from less-developed countries in a stereotyped way.

(b) Inconsistent and misleading images

There are two main types of inconsistency. Firstly, between the image and other media, and, secondly, between the image and the 'real world'. Both of these can undermine your central message, confusing and probably alienating the receiver:

* *Between image and other media* For example, during a company presentation, highlighting recent improvements in health and safety, you inadvertently include old photographs showing scrap materials blocking a factory gangway or workers not wearing protective clothing. Someone in the audience is bound to spot your error.
* *Between image and reality* Your audience may not believe the photographs or other images that you use. In the past, holiday brochures were notorious for using misleading photography. Holiday-makers are now wary of these 'glossy' images. Charts, maps and diagrams can also be misleading. The scale may be distorted, or the type of graphic may not be suitable for the information being communicated.

4.5 ▦ Business graphics – their uses and abuses

Graphs and charts can be very effective communication media, but it is easy to confuse an audience by selecting the wrong type for your data, or by constructing it incorrectly. This brief guide suggests how some of the more common types of graphs and charts can be used and abused.

Classic Sound Music plc
1997 first quarter sales by region

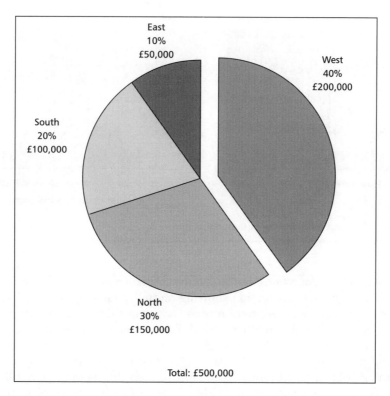

Figure 4.4 Pie chart.

1. Pie charts

Pies are used to show the relative size of different items making up a total. The largest segment is usually shown running clockwise from the 'top' of the pie. Each segment should be labelled, including a value and a percentage share. The overall total should also be stated at the 'bottom' of the pie. If you wish to emphasise a particular segment, it can be 'exploded' (as shown in Figure 4.4). Component bar charts offer an alternative method of displaying this kind of data.

2. Bar charts and histograms

Also used to compare the values of different items, they can be presented vertically or horizontally. Their major advantage over pie charts is that values can be easily read off against the scale (which should always be inserted on the appropriate axis).

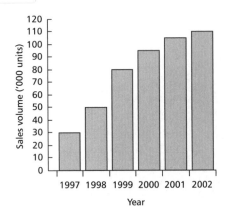

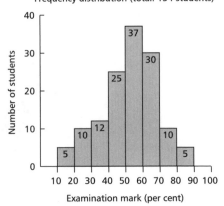

Figure 4.5 Bar chart (left) and histogram (right).

Bar charts and histograms must not be confused. Histograms are used for **continuous** data (e.g. a frequency distribution showing mortality rates by age of population) whereas a bar chart is for **discrete** or **non-continuous** data (e.g. showing average mortality rates in five different countries). Histograms should be drawn with the bars touching. If there are large intervals in the data with low values, these can be combined to create some bars that are wider than others. The overall trend of a histogram can be shown by linking the tops of each bar with a curved line. Bar charts are best drawn with separated bars. These should always be of the same width and, because they represent discrete items, must never be linked together with a line. More complex data can be presented using either multiple or component bar charts. In both cases, it is important to avoid distorting the data by introducing a 'false zero'. Your scale should ideally run from zero. If it is essential to insert a break in the scale, this must be clearly marked with two 'zig-zag' lines through the axis.

3. Line graphs

These are used to present continuous data, including all sorts of time series and trends (e.g. inflation or unemployment rates over the last 30 years). For most business applications, two or more lines are plotted on the same graph, so that comparisons can be made between two variables. In this case, it is important to select suitable scales, line types and labelling so that each line can be distinguished. It is also possible to combine line graphs with histograms or even bar charts. Different data values (e.g. sales volume in units and trading profit in sterling) can also be combined on the same graph by using two scales on either side of the graph. However, it is

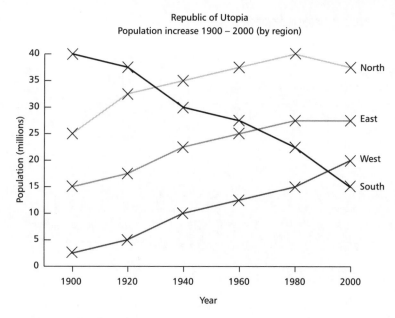

Figure 4.6 Multiple line graph.

essential to avoid overloading the graph with information; the better option is usually to break it down into a number of simpler graphs.

4. Pictograms and maps

Pictograms are based on the idea that data may be more appealing and informative if it is turned into a representative image (e.g. number of employees is shown using a picture of 'matchstick' people). The classic problem with pictograms is the misrepresentation of quantities because the scaling is unclear. Imagine that you want to show that house prices doubled between 1980 and 1990 by drawing two houses, one twice the height of the other. Visually, your pictogram will suggest that prices quadrupled, because the area of the 1990 house will be four times that of the 1980 one. Maps can be a useful way of presenting regional data (e.g. crime rates or average household income). However, they can also be misleading, since the *size* of the areas shaded is usually unrelated to the data that are being displayed.

The illustrations in this section have been in a straightforward two-dimensional format. Computer packages now offer a range of so-called 'three-dimensional' graphs and charts which may appear to make data look more attractive. However, these are simply 'blocked-out' versions of the traditional two-dimensional formats (e.g. line graphs are transformed into a series of ribbons). The cosmetic benefits of blocked-out graphs and charts are usually outweighed by the problems of readability; 'three-dimensional' lines and bars cannot be lined up against the relevant scale, so data values are difficult to determine.

Classical Sound Music plc. Employee numbers by department

Key: = 5 employees

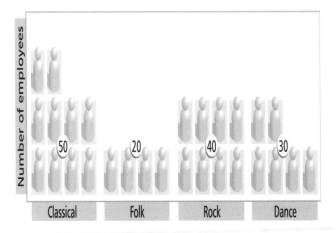

Classical Sound Music plc.

First quarter sales by region

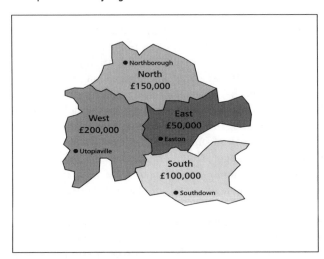

Figure 4.7 Pictogram and map, two effective ways to present data graphically.

EXERCISE 4C

'Lies, damned lies and statistics'

What is misleading about the business graphics illustrated below? List the faults and prepare your own alternative versions, removing these distortions.

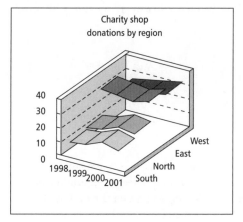

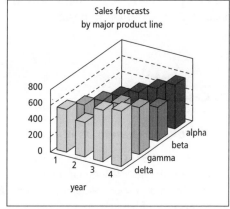

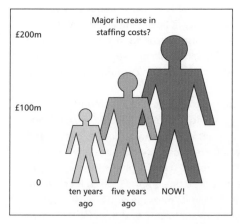

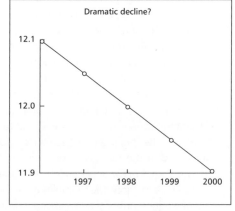

4.6 ■■ Corporate identity: the visual aspects

The image of a 'start-up' or one person business is closely associated with the individual who runs it. However, larger organisations inevitably become more impersonal and their identity has to be actively managed. Recent developments in the UK's largest company, BT, show how important the visual aspects of identity have become. In the late 1970s, BT was portrayed using a cartoon bird (called *Buzby*), and in the 1980s the comic actress Maureen Lipman (as the doting mother, *Beattie*) provided the company with a friendly face. However, by the 1990s, BT needed a more radical re-design:

Case study

Why did BT change its image?

In 1911, the Post Office took control of the telephone business, and it remained in the public sector until 1984. At this stage, the newly privatised British Telecommunications plc, was known by a shortened trading name, *British Telecom*, and a simple logo based on the initial 'T' outlined by a circle. By the late 1980s the name and logo were still working well in the UK, but problems arose when using them abroad. The symbol was almost identical to those used in other countries (e.g. Telefonica in Spain), meaning that it could not be registered as a trade mark. The name was also perceived in some markets as 'conservative and unexciting, reliable but not forward-looking', suggesting that the company was national, rather than international in scope. Design consultants were asked to review the overall corporate identity.

The subsequent re-design was more than 'cosmetic'. It followed a six month research study, geared to the company's vision of becoming the most successful worldwide telecommunications group. It was linked to changes in company structure, culture and operations. The 'piper' figure seen on the new logo represents two figures, the 'listener' (who is red in the full colour versions) and the 'teller' (who is blue). This symbolises two-way communication, enabling customers to talk to one another, which is central to BT's business mission. The symbol is universal, conveys its message across most cultures. A human figure, rather than an abstract design, is meant to convey the personal element in the company's activities.

On the practical side, the logo had to be suitable for a wide range of applications, from payphone kiosks to stationery. It had to be reproducible in monochrome and in a four-colour format, and it had to look equally effective displayed on a computer screen or moulded into a plastic product. Other aspects of the re-design included improved typefaces and documentation. The company now trades under the 'BT' banner, whilst the full corporate name is only used in formal documents, such as contracts and share certificates.

Source: British Telecommunications plc.

4.7 ▪▪ Chapter summary

- A wide range of visual images, or 'pictures', are used in business, but managers are often unaware of how useful they can be.

- There are many potential advantages of visual media: messages are quickly assimilated, complex content can be simplified, the attention of an audience can be caught, and messages are made more memorable. In addition, images are often powerful persuaders and motivators.

- The most common problems arise when 'pictures' are used carelessly and the images are either obsolete or inconsistent or misleading. Take care to ensure that images cannot be mis-interpreted by the viewer.

- Graphs and charts can be used to present data in more informative and appealing ways. However, it is important to use the most appropriate type and format, ensuring that you communicate a clear and undistorted impression of the underlying figures.

- To be effective, changes in the visual identity if an organisation should always be well thought-out and linked to its real values and activities. Managing the identity of a large business involves a complex mixture of strategic and practical issues.

Discussion points

1. Using pictures creatively

Study the two images reproduced below. How might you make use of these images in a business situation? Suggest at least three alternative messages that might be conveyed using each image. Add words to the images, if you think this is appropriate.

2. Unacceptable images?

Images can be powerful communicators. At one extreme, horrific war photography has forced national governments and the United Nations to change their policies, whilst, at the other, beautiful landscapes have been used to promote everything from tourism to shampoo. Of course, any powerful technique can be abused. In one notorious example, a 1930s Nazi propaganda film based its anti-Semitic message on close-up images of rats scurrying through the contents of a house. What limits, if any, would *you* place on the use of images in business? Imagine that your objective was one of the following:

To warn drivers of the serious dangers of speeding
To persuade young people not to start smoking
To persuade smokers to continue purchasing your brand
To inform schoolchildren about drugs or contraception

List examples of the kinds of images you would consider acceptable, and those (if any) that should not be used to reinforce the message. In each case, give reasons for your choice. If working in a group, discuss any differences of opinion between individuals. Were your decisions based mainly on moral/ethical grounds, or on practical ones?

Chapter five

Powers of persuasion: changing minds

There's a sucker born every minute

Phineas T. Barnum: publicist and circus promoter

Objectives

- To identify and investigate the role of persuasion in various business situations and the problems that occur when persuasive messages fail (5.1–5.2)

- To highlight the key factors to consider when preparing a persuasive message (5.3)

- To introduce various insights into to human motivation and then to explore reasons that people change their minds (5.4)

- To outline a process of persuasion, noting how words and images can be used to secure attention, develop an argument and reach agreement (5.5)

- To consider other, less obvious media to support persuasive messages, including sound, smell and direct action (5.6)

- To introduce ethical aspects of persuasion in business (5.7)

5.1 ▦ Introduction

Everyone is involved in persuasion. Sometimes we seek to persuade others, but more frequently, we are on the receiving end of someone else's attempts to affect, convert, convince, exhort, induce, influence, prompt, sway, urge or otherwise win us over. Persuasive messages are being transmitted all around us, and many of them are now highly sophisticated. Yet even the 'professional' communicators find it difficult to guarantee a successful result. Television advertisers and tabloid journalists are sometimes accused of 'brain-washing' their audiences. In reality, the starting point for persuasive communication is that the receiver has some **freedom** to choose. If there was no freedom, there would be no need to persuade; in our relatively free society, audiences can opt to accept or reject the messages they are sent.

All kinds of messages contain an element of persuasion, however simple or discreet it might appear. For example, the eager applicant's choice of clothing for a job interview is not simply a personal preference, it is designed to influence the

Figure 5.1   The speed camera sign – informing or persuading?

interview panel's decision. Similarly, a 'speed camera' sign beside a busy road is not placed there for information, it is a calculated attempt to alter the behaviour of drivers. In this chapter, we review the many kinds of persuasion you are likely to use at work. Taking practical examples from business life, we explore ways that words, pictures and other media can help in communicating more persuasively.

5.2 ▮▮ Persuasion in business

Persuasive communication is used in all areas of business, though some occasions are particularly 'persuasion-rich'. Persuasion is most obvious in face-to-face situations, such as Board meetings and interviews. However, similar principles can be applied to less direct channels of communication, such as advertisements, reports and even business letters. Further practical examples are given below. Each channel gets more detailed coverage in Part II of this book.

- **Business meetings and negotiations:** In committee meetings and project team briefings, you will sometimes have to work hard, persuading others to accept your ideas and proposals. There are also those occasions when you want to deliver an effective counter-argument against another individual or group.

- **Advertising:** Persuasive techniques are used to the secure attention of a target audience and to increase their subsequent recall of the message. Contrary to popular opinion, many adverts are concerned with ideas, such as building brand 'identity' and 'values', rather than action in the form of an immediate purchase decision.

- **Public relations (PR) and lobbying:** Public relations practitioners are often ridiculed as 'hooray Henries' swilling gin and tonic, or cynical manipulators oiling the wheels of power. Neither stereotype is entirely accurate. Public relations is mainly concerned with managing the links between an organisation and the people outside, including customers, local communities and journalists. Lobbying means presenting an organisation's case to the key decision makers. Today, this is mostly done using briefing documents, lunchtime meetings and other PR tools; though the traditional meetings in the lobbies (i.e. hallways) of parliament do still occur. These specialised forms of persuasion are used by all types of organisation, including companies, trades unions, single issue campaigners and charities.

Case study

Perrier versus British beef – handling a reputation crisis

For many years, mineral water has been a boom sector in the UK's food and drink retailing sector. In the early *1990s* Perrier, the undisputed brand leader, survived a 'worst case scenario' when contamination was discovered in its water source. In Perrier's favour was an established reputation with the public, plus the fact that no-one's health had suffered as a consequence of the problem. Even so, in a fiercely competitive industry the potential damage to its credibility might have destroyed the brand. How did Perrier go about persuading its customers, both retailers and end-consumers, to stay with the product? Above all, the company acted quickly and decisively. They succeeded in recovering the entire retail stock, comprising some 40 million bottles in the UK market alone. They also set up a telephone helpline for the general public and kept the media and their retailer customers well briefed on the company's strenuous efforts to eliminate the contaminant. In due course, the product was re-launched.

Perrier's communications strategy combined a good long-term reputation with an open approach, positive action to deal with the fault and a free flow of information. Together, these factors contributed to a prompt sales recovery, with no lasting damage to the brand.

This successful operation contrasts sharply with the succession of communications crises that have arisen through the 1990s as the British government attempted to deal with the – admittedly more complex and emotive – issues arising from Bovine Spongiform Encephalopathy (BSE) in cattle. The government's persuasive messages produced mixed results. British consumers continued to buy beef, but the Vegetarian Society saw an unprecedented increase in membership. At the same time overseas audiences remained largely unconvinced. The UK's Beef and dairy farmers mounted repeated attacks on the Minister of Agriculture as the country's European Union partners refused to lift a ban on exports of British beef. Over a period of many months, the reports of independent scientific advisors, the culling and incineration of tens of thousands of disease-free cattle, professional lobbying in Brussels and an extensive public relations exercise failed to persuade this key overseas audience.

Perrier's reputation was quickly restored, whilst the British beef industry has suffered long-term damage. What are the lessons for communicators?

5.3 ▮▮ The task of persuasion: scale and objectives

As the case study illustrates, persuasive communication can be very difficult to manage successfully. It is useful to assess the scale of the problem before any message is sent. There are three main factors to consider, the people with whom you are communicating, the message itself, and the general circumstances:

(i)   **The receivers** What is their previous experience of you or your organisation? What do they already know and feel about the subject matter of your message? What is their current state of mind? What kind of personalities do they have? Are you trying to persuade a single individual or a group of people? Are they acting independently, or as representatives or agents of an organisation? What factors might be persuading them in the opposite direction?

(ii) **The message** What kind of message are you trying to convey? Does it comprise facts, ideas, opinions or a mixture? Is your message simple or complex? Is it likely to be surprising, unwelcome or threatening to the receiver? Pay special attention to the non-rational aspects of the message, since these can have a decisive effect on the outcome. For example, are you likely to be threatening the receiver's sense of identity or drawing on basic emotions such as charity, greed or national pride.

(iii) **The context** In what kind of situation is your message being communicated? Is it *within* a business (e.g. encouraging employees to improve product quality or rival departments to work together)? Is it in the *outside* world (e.g. tempting customers to try a new product, or lobbying the Government to increase its spending on sports or the arts)? Are you under pressure to obtain a quick result? Are other parties competing for the 'hearts and minds' of your audience?

While you are reviewing these issues, it is also worth considering the underlying **objectives** of your persuasive message. More specifically, are you aiming to stimulate changes in what the receiver knows, something that they believe or in the way that they behave?

(a) Changing facts and ideas

If the relevant facts are clear, non-contentious and supported by factual evidence, this basic form of persuasion is easy, as the following dialogue makes clear:

EMILY: So, are you coming to the team briefing?
IFOR: Don't be stupid. It's not even 9am yet!
EMILY: Jay re-scheduled yesterday.
IFOR: You can't be serious, it's always at 11. I'm sure he would have told me.
EMILY: Yes, it's definite. I checked with his PA, and there's an e-mail to confirm it.
IFOR: OK, you win. Well, let's get a move on then or we'll be late!

However, it can be far more difficult to persuade people to accept novel, complex and controversial facts and ideas. The pioneering scientist Galileo faced stiff opposition when he tried to persuade religious leaders that the Earth revolved around the Sun. His books were banned, and he was forced to spend the rest of his life under house arrest. Many people today are equally unwilling to tolerate evidence that suggests their world has changed.

If your audience is having problems absorbing a new concept, the task of persuasion is bound to be much more difficult. The best strategy in this situation is to express the new material in terms that the receiver can already understand and accept. For example, imagine that a manager is trying to explain a new way of working to long-serving warehouse staff, based on a competitive internal market of the kind adopted in the National Health Service:

MANAGER: OK, so you've all heard about this 'internal market'? What it really means is that those of us working in the warehouse need to start treating the factory staff as though they were our most important customers.
QUESTIONER: But how can they be 'customers' if we work for the same company?
MANAGER: Because we'll be offering them a service, like your local pub for instance. The good news is that, if we do a decent job, we can attract

more customers, including some from outside the company. But there is a down side. If we do things badly, our 'customers' in the factory are free to use outside suppliers.

QUESTIONER: So what you're saying is ... they can buy their 'pint' wherever they like?

MANAGER: Exactly.

(b) Changing beliefs and values

Whilst they *contain* facts and ideas, a person's beliefs and values are bolstered by other powerful factors, including: self-image, cultural background and peer group pressure. Therefore, if you are seeking to influence an individual's beliefs and values, it is essential to consider more than the basic information content of your message. For example, the following message from the Regional Manager seems unlikely to convince a 55-year-old supermarket manager to change his long-established approach to the job:

> Listen, Ron. Our retail strategy has changed. We don't 'pile it high and sell it cheap' any more. Now, I know what you're thinking, 'Why now, after I've done 40 years in the business?'. Well, because it's necessary, Ron. We need you to start making customer satisfaction your number one priority.

If you are dealing with entrenched beliefs, successful persuasion may take some time. The communication involved is also likely to have an inter-personal and emotional dimension. A dramatic example of this process was recorded in a television documentary; a former member of a white supremacist group had 'switched sides' and joined an anti-racist campaign. For this individual, the catalyst for change was the friendship he had developed with a work colleague who happened to be black. It required a personal relationship, rather than logical argument, to provide the energy needed to drive such a radical change.

(c) Changing actions and behaviour

Influencing another person's actions can be very straightforward. For example, asking a colleague to send you a copy of her report or asking someone to speak at a meeting does not normally require much persuasive effort. Full-scale persuasion only arises where the receiver has an in-built resistance towards the action or change in behaviour:

Dr SMITH: Listen, Joanna, you really do need to start cutting down on the cigarettes, whisky and amphetamines.

Dr BROWN: What is the problem, exactly?

Dr SMITH: Well, it doesn't set a very good example to our patients, Joanna!

Like changes in beliefs, these more fundamental behavioural changes require more than just polite and rational discussion. For example, countless public health

Figure 5.2 Anti-drink-driving poster. In this poster, a powerful visual image is combined with a simple slogan to emphasise the consequences of drink driving. The poster supports a national television and radio campaign aimed at young male drivers (Source: Department of Transport).

campaigns have tried to discourage smoking, drug abuse and 'unsafe' sex. Posters, leaflets and other channels are full of clear-cut information on the related risks. Can this type of communication compete effectively with peer group pressure and slick commercialisation? Direct contact with people who have experienced the consequences may be more persuasive. However, there is a particular persuasion problem among certain audiences. Teenagers, for instance, have been known to confuse 'being young' with discovering the secret of immortality.

EXERCISE 5A

Are you convinced?

We have all experienced being persuaded to do something, to change an opinion or alter our behaviour. Much of this persuasion relates to fairly trivial issues, but occasionally we are persuaded to make a more significant change. Spend a few minutes thinking back on an occasion when you were persuaded to change your mind:

(a) What type of change was involved? Was it concerned with facts, concepts, beliefs, behaviour - or a mixture of these?
(b) What persuasive techniques were used on you?
(c) How did you respond to this persuasive effort?
(d) Ultimately, what do you think was *decisive* in making you make the change?

If you are working in a **group**, compare your answers with others. Does the type of persuasion appear to vary, depending on the subject matter? Can you reach any conclusions about the most effective persuaders?

Figure 5.3 Persuasion and human rights? Campaigning organisations, such as Amnesty International, are involved in persuasive communication at a number of different levels, ranging from street-based events to advertising and lobbying.

5.4 ■■ Motivation theories: what makes us tick?

If you are in the business of persuading people, it is helpful to know what *motivates* them. Unfortunately, this is not easy to discover. Hence, despite considerable efforts, social science has made little progress in explaining why one person is law-abiding whilst another is not. Similarly, extensive market research studies may never untangle the reasons why consumers prefer to buy '*Clean-a-Dent*' toothpaste rather than '*Dent-a-Clean*'. A variety of motivation theories has appeared over the last century, each attempting to reveal the underlying factors. This research does not begin to offer a comprehensive explanation of how human beings tick. At best, it suggests a few relevant issues to consider when creating a persuasive message:

- Everyone shares some basic motivations in common (e.g. food, security, love).
- It seems that once these motivations are satisfied, people seek 'higher level' goals.
- Levels of motivation vary enormously, both between individuals and over time.
- Avoiding dissatisfaction is not the same as creating satisfaction.
- People frequently conceal and deny their underlying motivations.
- Above all, people may often be totally unaware of what really motivates them.

Four approaches to motivation

This is a brief outline of four influential research perspectives on human motivation. More detailed references are given under Further Reading:

- **Drive theories** These suggest that we are driven by a combination of physiological needs (primarily, thirst, hunger and sex) plus a range of others, such as the need to play, to complete tasks competently and to be in control of our lives. The relative and absolute strength of these drives appears to vary between individuals. However, anyone who has given a presentation just before lunchtime will be aware that an audience's primeval demand for food invariably outweighs their intellectual interest in the topic. This phenomenon provides a link with Maslow's work on the 'hierarchy of needs' and Herzberg's work on job satisfaction.

- **Maslow's hierarchy of needs** Abraham Maslow emphasised that 'self-actualisation' is a distinctive human trait. The main argument behind Maslow's often quoted hierarchy of needs is that so-called lower-level needs (food, drink, rest, etc.) have to be satisfied *before* an individual can focus on the higher-level ones (self-esteem, knowledge, aesthetics). At the lower end, actions are directed towards removing perceived deficiencies. For example, thirst is a deficiency that makes us search for a drink. By contrast, higher-level needs are pursued for their own intrinsic satisfaction.

- **Herzberg's motivators and hygiene factors** This research explored the main sources of satisfaction and dissatisfaction at work. A key finding was that only certain factors, relating mainly to job content, could actually generate job satisfaction. These included a sense of achievement, recognition, responsibility and prospects for advancement. These were labelled 'motivators'. By contrast, many other factors relating to the context of the job (company policy, supervision, work conditions, etc.) tended to be sources of dissatisfaction. Critically, these 'hygiene' factors could not, in themselves generate satisfaction - they could only prevent dissatisfaction. Whilst the general argument appears to reflect anecdotal evidence, some critics have questioned whether 'satisfaction' is quantifiable and whether it really correlates with the quality and quantity of work produced.

- **Freudian theories** Sigmund Freud proposed that our personalities comprise three conflicting elements: the biological, pleasure-seeking *id*, the moralising *superego* and, somewhere between them, the *ego*. It is the *ego* which has the difficult task of negotiating between these competing elements and the 'real world' outside. Freud also identified different levels of consciousness. He suggested that only a small fraction of our thoughts, those in the *conscious* mind, are immediately accessible to us. The *unconscious* mind plays an unseen but decisive role in human behaviour. It is sometimes glimpsed, through half-remembered dreams, or when people make a 'Freudian slip', inserting an incorrect word in a sentence that betrays the real thoughts that they are trying to hide.

Paying attention: a cost–benefit equation?

People are basically selfish. This most useful lesson in human motivation is also the most contentious. However saintly we appear, day-to-day decisions are mostly based on a simple calculation: 'which option seems most beneficial to me?' Think, for example, of the many occasions that you have sat through a lecture or business presentation. Have you ever found that little voice in your head asking, 'why on earth am I bothering to listen to this?' Have you subsequently chosen to do something else, such as reading, doodling on a notepad, talking to your neighbour or gazing out of the window? Were these options somehow more rewarding than paying attention to the person at the front?

Now imagine that you *are* the person at the front. Armed with the amazing insight that all audiences are basically self-interested, you can stop complaining about them, or feeling horribly insecure if someone decides to yawn. Instead, ensure that you are providing enough of the benefits that a 'selfish' audience is looking for. Listening to a speaker for an extended period of time is hard work, after all. Do the benefits that you have to offer outweigh the 'cost' of paying attention? Provide the essential counter-balance in your communications by including one or more of the following elements:

- **Something useful** Receivers need to be convinced at the outset that messages are going to contain a 'pearl', something which could be of value to them. This is the cost–benefit equation in its crudest and most rational form. The key point here is that the *receiver's* perception of value is the only one that counts. Be sure that your messages include something that they are looking for.

- **Something entertaining** Everyone is attracted to forms of entertainment, including: novelty, excitement, distraction and – above all – humour. Entertainment is an important benefit to offer the receiver. Even when your main objective is more serious, it can act as the 'sugar on the pill'. The greatest danger, of course, is that people will enjoy the entertainment but forget the underlying message.

- **Something satisfying** There are other, less tangible factors that persuade an audience to pay attention. Everything can hinge on whether they like the style of delivery, identify with the person presenting, or feel personally involved and valued. The opposite argument is also true. Audiences simply 'switch off' if the delivery is poor or if the presenter is considered unappealing. The greatest obstacles appear when people feel uncomfortable, excluded or patronised.

The writer and broadcaster, Sonya Hamlyn, provides a neat summary for this section, pointing out how an effective communicator is able to recognise and exploit the inevitable self-interest of an audience:

> *When what you have to say clearly intersects with what the other person wants or needs or cares about, you have given [them] a primary, compelling reason for listening. You're not actually demanding that he/she give up self-involvement. You're just piggy-backing on some part of the listener's own momentum . . . you're defining your message as another facet of his or her ongoing life concerns.*
>
> *(Hamlyn 1989, p. 38)*

EXERCISE 5B

Motivation theory and the television advert

Record and replay an advertisement for a branded food or drink product.

(a) What approaches to motivation (if any) do you think the advertiser is applying?
(b) Did you find the advert persuasive? If so, why?
(c) In general, what factors motivate *you* to choose a particular brand of food or drink?

If you are working in a **group**, compare your answers with others and try to identify any common ground. You might also repeat the exercise with a different product area, such as luxury cars or private health insurance. Is there a different approach to motivation for these products?

Barry and Bitsa demonstrate the effectiveness of TV advertising.

5.5 ■■ The process of persuasion

To persuade an audience, we need to select and exploit media and channels of communication in ways that secure the attention of receivers so that a strong, coherent argument can be presented:

(a) Securing audience attention

As we have seen, it is essential that your audience is paying attention. Depending on the circumstances, one or more of the following stimuli may help you to obtain a positive response:

- *Address people by name* This is a good way to secure the attention which can be used with individuals or groups. You have probably had the experience of 'hearing your name mentioned' at a noisy party, even though you were talking to someone else at the time. The use of names exploits your receivers' capacity for selective perception, it increases alertness *and* it makes them feel involved. Reference to a specific group in your audience, such as 'the team from our Cardiff office', has a similar effect. Direct **eye contact** is another powerful attention-grabber in face-to-face meetings and seminars.

- *Pose a question* As problem-solving animals, people find it difficult to resist a challenging question. If you are giving a talk, simply turn your opening statement into a question, such as '*Thank you for coming along this afternoon. Now, how do you think we can double our retail sales in the next six months?*'. Visual puzzles are another form of question that can attract people's attention in some channels, including posters and television adverts.

- *Be provocative* You can alert and shock people with a statement, an action or a question. For example, a marketing consultancy once used the banner headline, '*Are you bloody brilliant?*' to attract attention to a job advertisement. Images can also be provocative. In the early 1990s, the Italian fashion company Beneton ran a highly controversial poster and magazine campaign using photographic images, including an AIDS patient, a newly born baby and the bloodstained uniform of a Bosnian soldier.

(b) Developing a strong and coherent argument

The heart of persuasion is building an argument, with credible evidence to support it. You also need to be prompt and effective in responding to counter-arguments. The classic error, repeated by many individuals and organisations, is trying to argue from *your own* position rather than that of the other party. To be successful, it is essential to appreciate – and to work from – the receiver's point of view. As Section 5.3 suggests, you also need to consider both rational/logical and non-rational/emotional aspects of the argument in order to be convincing. Exercise 5c highlights the need to take the other person's perspective seriously.

EXERCISE 5C

Persuasion problems for 'AOK Chemicals'

The environmental campaigners, '*Green Earth*' allege that AOK Chemicals plc are polluting a waterway and harming wildlife, including the 'Bay Gull', an endangered sea bird. The senior management of AOK are mostly former scientists. They are justifiably proud of their technical innovation record. The company is internationally recognised as a centre of excellence in all the technical issues relating to the supposed pollutant. It has independent scientific evidence that (a) AOK plc's outflows have no measurable effect on local concentrations of the chemical concerned, and (b) the birds are indeed being harmed, but the culprit is a *different* chemical, which is produced by a number of other companies in the area.

The managing director of AOK, Dr Keith Kleen, opts for a direct approach. He issues a terse press release, dismissing the campaigners' evidence as 'amateurish' and 'subversive'. Attached to the press release is a 15-page technical survey of the AOK plant, incorporating the evidence of independent researchers. Confident that the company is in the clear, Dr Kleen and his family leave for a relaxing weekend at a country house hotel.

And the result? The *Sunday Inquisitor* publishes a front-page colour picture of space-suited figures, taking samples of a bright orange liquid pouring from AOK's outfall pipe. Their headline blazes: *'Is it AOK to Poison a Bay?'*. The article continues on page 2, illustrated with a photograph of dead Bay Gull chicks in a nest. The television cameras catch up with a tired and emotional Dr Kleen in the early hours of Sunday morning, following a dinner-dance at the hotel. The public's perception, based on edited highlights from this interview, is that Dr Kleen is complacent, incompetent, secretive and uncaring. The independent technical report is completely forgotten. AOK's share price collapses and trading is temporarily suspended. Two day's later, a trespassing tabloid journalist is pursued by an AOK security guard. In the ensuing confusion, he is accidentally savaged to death by Raymond, a guard dog. The entire Board of AOK is forced to resign. Three years later, the pollution continues unabated, the Bay Gull is extinct and AOK Chemicals plc continues to get the blame.

It seems that AOK's management could have been rather more persuasive in this situation, to the benefit of the Bay Gull, and everyone concerned.

(a) Identify what you consider to be AOK's key communication errors.
(b) Which messages had the greatest persuasive power:
    for the AOK management team?
    for the media?
    for the general public?
(c) With the benefit of hindsight, devise an alternative communication strategy for AOK. Suggest how the company should have responded at each stage, noting the likely media reactions.

5.6 ▇▇ Other persuaders? – using less obvious media

Words and pictures may be the 'easiest' and most accessible media for the average business person. However, some other powerful persuasive 'weapons' are available. With a little practice and imagination, communicators can also make effective use of sound, smell, taste and direct action:

- **Sounds and music** Music is sometimes described as 'organised sound'. Throughout history, sounds of all kinds have been used in persuasion communication. Songs have always been used to attract prospective lovers, whilst drums were beaten in order to terrify the enemy and lead reluctant soldiers into war. Because it is based on regular patterns, melody is readily absorbed and remembered. As a result, music provides a kind of mental 'hook' on to which other messages can be tagged. Adverts are often reinforced with extracts from rock or classical music. Ceremonial music at public events such as the Olympic Games plays a similar motivational role.
- **Smell and taste** Though our sense of smell is less developed than that of other animals, it remains an influential stimulant. As the smell of cooking emerges

from a restaurant, passers-by begin to feel hungry and may decide to stop for a meal. The multi-million pound perfume industry prospers on the belief that its well-packaged aromas have a persuasive effect on users and those they want to attract. Smells can seduce, stimulate, warn and repel. The related sense of taste shares these attributes, though there are obvious practical limitations on its use in business!

Sound, music, smell and taste have a particularly strong persuasive impact because they are able to by-pass the receiver's intellect, going straight for the emotions and instincts. Hence, these media offer a useful reinforcement for verbal messages.

- **Direct action** People are often persuaded by actions rather than rational arguments. Direct action is usually associated with political protest movements, but it can also be effective in a business environment. A research scientist wanted to convince the materials company '3M' that his invention had real market potential. Instead of using the conventional persuasion methods of formal presentations and feasibility studies, he produced a trial batch of his *entirely new* stationery product, distributing it to the secretaries of 3M's senior executives. The product proved very popular and supplies soon ran out. The secretaries, who were unable to obtain more stock, told their bosses just how useful the product was. Thanks to this direct action, the development project was approved and the '*Post-it note*' became a highly successful product worldwide.

EXERCISE 5D

The ultimate persuasion challenge?

(a) Divide into groups and spend 15 minutes devising the most difficult persuasive communication task you can imagine. It can be for a commercial business, a voluntary organisation or a public sector body. Write out the task on a large sheet of paper, specifying the message to be communicated, the sender, the receiver(s) and the general context. The following sample task can also be used by those studying independently:

Sender: Brokesville City Council
Receivers: Brokesville council tax payers
Message: Please agree to increase local taxes by 25 per cent next year, the funds are needed for essential economic development work.
Context: High regional unemployment, particularly amongst the 'under 25' and 'over 50' age groups. Essential to encourage inward investment.

(b) Exchange your task with another group, and spend 30 minutes developing a communication proposal, designed to overcome the problem that you have been set. Try to be as creative and convincing as possible, whilst trying to base all your arguments on the perceptions of the *receivers*. If time allows, present your solutions and discuss how effectively you have made use of all available media and techniques.

5.7 ▨▨ The ethics of persuasion

This chapter began with PT Barnum's cynical maxim, '*There's a sucker born every minute*'. Hopefully, the chapter has demonstrated that effective persuasion has very little to do with misleading or deceiving an audience. In most business situations, this 'win–lose' approach is not particularly useful, since your long-term reputation suffers. The techniques of persuasive communication that have been discussed are only effective if receivers are taken seriously. However, there are other reasons for behaving honestly. During the 1990s, many organisations have begun to take business ethics more seriously. Under pressure from consumers, shareholders, journalists and public agencies, businesses are developing 'codes of conduct' to regulate their behaviour. Persuasive communication raises a number of ethical issues. The most obvious of these is the use of lies and deception. In many cases, this is likely to be illegal as well as unethical. The other important ethical issues relating to persuasion can be divided into three broad areas, the purpose, content and delivery of a message. To highlight a few of these issues, brief illustrations are taken from the advertising industry:

- **Purpose of message** The objectives behind certain messages may be unacceptable, but geographic and cultural variations complicate the picture. For example, UK television advertising targeted at children is closely regulated, but in some countries *all* such advertising is banned. Similarly, it is illegal to advertise political parties on UK television, though this is permitted in the United States.

- **Content of message** Beneton's controversial advertising campaign (Section 5.5), based on such serious issues as war and disease, was criticised on the grounds that it exploited its sources in order to promote an unrelated consumer product. There have been frequent arguments over nudity in advertisements, their portrayal of women and the comic stereotyping of other nationalities. These concerns also tend to be culture-specific.

- **Media and channels used** Some techniques of persuasion may be unethical. For example, 'subliminal' techniques fool the senses by projecting images for very short periods or broadcasting messages that are not readily apparent to the conscious mind. These forms of advertising have been outlawed for many years. However, new technologies are likely to present further challenges to the limits of acceptability. More widespread are the 'hard sales' techniques, as perfected by the more unscrupulous dealers in double-glazing, time-share property and religion. Though their activities are supposed to be regulated, cases of undue pressure and misrepresentation seem to be all-too-common.

5.8 ▨▨ Chapter summary

- Persuasion is an essential element in business communication, and is communicated through all kinds of media and channels. We are frequently involved in persuasion, either sending messages or responding to them.

- The scale of the persuasive task depends on the nature of the message, the receiver and the context in which it is being communicated.
- Persuasive communication attempts to change the knowledge, ideas, beliefs and behaviour of the receiver.
- There is no definitive approach to human motivation, but senders should recognise that most receivers' actions are geared to meeting their 'self-interested' needs.
- The process of persuasion involves securing attention and developing a strong, coherent argument. It must always address the receiver's perceptions and feelings.
- Words and images can act as powerful persuaders, as can music, smell and direct action. Effective persuasion requires creative use of all the media available; words alone may not be enough.
- Persuasion is not the same as deception. However, there are important ethical issues to consider. These relate to the purpose and content of persuasive messages, and to the ways that they are conveyed.

Discussion points

1. Ethiopia 1984 – 'Feed the world'

The 1980s are now characterised as a period of pure greed, based around stock market speculation and a property market boom. However, in the middle of that decade, a televised human tragedy and an unprecedented charity event combined to influence a global audience.

A fatal mixture of war and sustained drought had driven over 10,000 refugees into 'feeding centres' at Korem and Makele, deep within Ethiopia. Their exodus attracted very little media coverage. Aid agencies operating in the country lacked the logistical support necessary to feed so many starving people. In October 1984, the BBC's Michael Buerk reported on the desperate plight of these refugees. His sombre words and obvious emotion were themselves a powerful influence on viewers, but the decisive factor appeared to be the accompanying images of the starving women and children, a seemingly endless expanse of people waiting quietly to die. Public reaction to the televised report helped to galvanise western politicians into a major emergency aid programme. At the same time, Bob Geldof and Midge Ure persuaded a group of musicians (known collectively as 'Band Aid') to record the single '*Do they know it's Christmas?*'. The £8 million proceeds of this chart-topping recording were used for emergency food and medical supplies. In the summer of 1985, the 'Live Aid' rock concerts were broadcast to a television audience of 1.5 billion people worldwide, raising around £70 million.

Live Aid had a major short-term impact, both financially and in raising public awareness. However, the problems of acute and chronic poverty are still with us. Commentators are now suggesting that continued exposure to traumatic images in news and documentary programmes creates 'compassion fatigue' and a reluctance to respond to future requests for support from aid agencies. Images of starvation also give a false picture of developing nations as chaotic and dependent. The UK's National Lottery, which was launched in the mid-1990s, is also seen by charity fundraisers as serious competition.

(a) Draw up a new fundraising campaign, using visual and verbal media. Your client can be a charity of your choice, but assume that they are faced with compassion fatigue.
(b) What messages and persuasive techniques have you used in your campaign, and why?

2. The speechwriter's art: 'We shall fight on the beaches ...'

It was early in 1940, and for the first time since 1066 Britain was on the brink of invasion. There was a real possibility that, with the USA still neutral, the war would be lost. In the circumstances, Churchill and his speechwriters realised that something resonant and motivational was needed, as the following extract shows:

> *We shall defend our island, whatever the cost may be, we shall fight on the beaches, we shall fight on the landing grounds, we shall fight in the fields and in the streets, we shall fight in the hills; we shall never surrender.*

> *Winston Churchill, Speech in the House of Commons, 13 May 1940*

What makes this such a dynamic sentence, and more powerful still if spoken aloud? The **information** content of the message could be reduced to a concise, but unmoving, *'We must continue fighting'*. The **persuasive** effect is created by a combination of:

- **Audience identification** Churchill is talking directly to his audience; the language is 'inclusive', with the repeated use of *'we'*, and of *'our island'* (an unusual way of describing Britain, but one that cleverly evokes both isolation and unity – standing alone and standing together).
- **Visual imagery** The references to familiar scenes, fields, beaches, streets encourage listeners to *visualise* the struggle for the survival of their own local surroundings, where fundamental loyalties are based.
- **Repetition** The key phrases *'we shall ...'* are repeated, building up a rhythm or 'metre', like that of a song or poem. This literally 'hammers home' the message.

- **A dramatic pause** A well-timed silence can add enormously to the impact of the words that follow it. Note the semi-colon, suggesting a pause for dramatic effect, before the last clause. Stand-up comics also rely on this technique.

Do you think Churchill's 'tricks of the trade' would still be effective in the age of television and the Internet? Try to see a variety of different speakers in action, on television, at college or in public meetings, in order to test your views.

Chapter six

The organisational dimension

Man is not the enemy of man, but through the medium of a false system of government

Thomas Paine, *Rights of Man* (1792)

Objectives

- To identify some important links between organisation theory and communication (6.1–6.2)

- To highlight recent changes in the ways that businesses are organised (6.2)

- To explore the main barriers to communication that occur within and between organisations (6.3–6.4)

- To consider the special problems of a growing business and the isolated Chief Executive (6.5)

- To propose practical solutions to those communication problems arising from the ways that business is organised (6.6)

6.1 ▪▪▪ Introduction

Even in the private sector of a free enterprise economy, business is essentially a *collective* activity. All of the individuals in an organisation have to collaborate with other people, even though they might prefer to soldier on alone. The success or failure of an organisation depends on how well its various individuals and groups interact. Previous chapters have focused on some of the key barriers to inter-personal communication. Here, we consider the *additional* problems that arise when people try to communicate within and between organisations. Their frustrations are invariably personalised. However, it is pointless blaming a **symptom**, which may be a difficult individual or clique, when the underlying **cause** of the problem is a structural fault. When your over-heated boss starts attacking '*that dozy, incompetent waste of space in Engineering department*', it may be unwise, or suicidal, to suggest that he is missing the point. However, taking the occasional step back from day-to-day management pressures can be very revealing. If the symptoms are put in context and linked to some of the more useful insights from organisation theory, it is possible to make real improvements in communication and create a healthier business.

6.2 ▪▪ Organisation structure: always a compromise

All organisations need a certain amount of structure and procedure. Structure is necessary for a number of reasons. It helps managers to allocate tasks and responsibilities (e.g. marketing, finance, production, etc.) and it establishes a chain of command. There are many alternative structures available. Factors influencing your choice include:

- Size of organisation
- Type of activity and technology in use
- Goals or objectives
- Competitive environment

The guiding principle, which emerged from 'contingency' approaches to management, is that an organisation's structure should 'fit' the **functions** it carries out and

Figure 6.1 Typical functional structure (above) and product structure (below).

the **environment** in which it operates. This leads to two basic ways of structuring a business, based on its functions (i.e. internal operations) or its products (i.e. the external environment) as shown in Figure 6.1

Functional structures tend to be more **efficient** ways of organising 'production' but are less flexible in responding to changes in the market. By contrast, product-based structures can be more **effective** in meeting customer needs but are less well co-ordinated internally. As a result, the structure chosen is inevitably a compromise. Managers attempt to get the best of both worlds, using '**hybrid**' structures, such as the typical regional office structure, illustrated below. Each region has its own set of functions, with 'dotted line' links to head office, as shown in Figure 6.2.

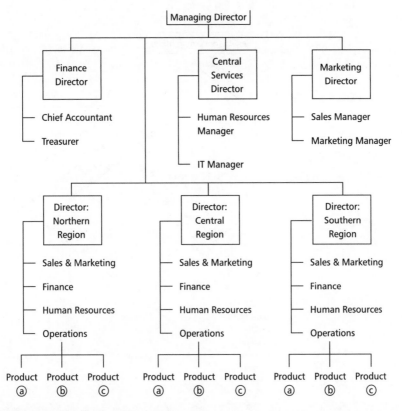

Figure 6.2 Regional offices – a 'hybrid' structure.

Structure and communication

Each of these structures results in a distinct pattern of communication, both inside the organisation and between it and the outside world. To illustrate this, consider the following exercise which looks at the communication problems of another popular hybrid, known as a '**matrix**' structure.

EXERCISE 6A

Communicating across a matrix?

Matrix structures are an attempt to combine the benefits of product-based and functional structures by operating both *simultaneously* and with equal weight being given to each 'arm' of the matrix. Some universities, for example, have experimented with this type of structure; the 'products' are the courses and the 'functions' are the academic departments and other services. A typical matrix structure chart for a university is shown in Exercise 6A.

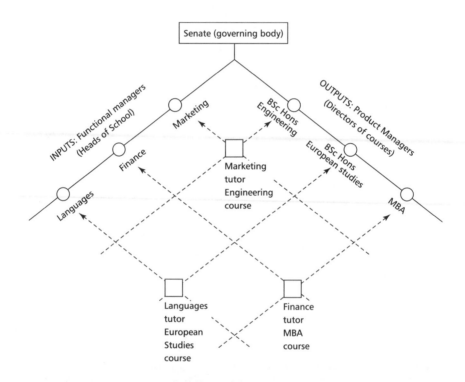

(a) What do you think the benefits of this structure might be?
(b) What **communication** problems would you envisage?
(c) How might these be resolved?

If possible, make contact with a manager who has experience of operating a matrix-type structure. See how far your assumptions prove to be correct in practice.

6.3 ■■ Blurring the boundaries: business in the 1990s

In the late 1990s the borders of organisations are becoming increasingly blurred. Management writers of previous decades discussed companies such as Ford or ICI as if each was a discrete and well-defined entity. More recently, four major 'drivers' of change, TQM, alliances, out-sourcing and relationship marketing, have made things less clear cut:

- **Total Quality Management** The 'TQM' revolution of the 1980s introduced the concept of '*quality chains*', whereby a company's suppliers were built into the quality assurance process. Instead of shopping around for components at the cheapest price, companies entered into much closer, long-term relationships with suppliers, sharing their financial, stock control and marketing data.

- **Alliances** The need to obtain specialist skills and the rising cost of research & development have encouraged companies to collaborate through consortia (e.g. the European *Airbus* project), joint ventures and strategic alliances. These are often a more attractive option than mergers and acquisitions, or trying to operate alone.

- **Out-sourcing** Also known as '*contracting-out*' or '*market-testing*', this is where a company brings in external suppliers to run '*non-core*' parts of the business. Hence, local government services such as waste collection and maintenance are now operated by private sector contractors. Information technology (IT) services are a growth area for out-sourcing. Corporations and even government departments are hiving off their entire IT functions to specialist providers, such as EDS (a subsidiary of General Motors) on long-term service contracts. Another result of out-sourcing is that many of the people working for an organisation are no longer employees. In their place are various types of consultant and short-term contract staff who may be working for a number of other businesses simultaneously.

- **Relationship marketing** In mature markets, companies are seeking to *retain* existing customers rather than focusing on *winning* new ones. They build customer loyalty by keeping in closer touch with purchasers, long after the initial sale. Through a range of communication techniques, they obtain feedback on their products, discuss new developments and provide various add-on services.

Each of these changes affects the ways that organisations communicate. In the past, there was a clear dividing line between 'internal' and 'external' communication, and some writers continue to emphasise this outmoded distinction. Today's business managers need to think in much broader terms. Any meaningful communication strategy must take full account of an organisation's on-going links with suppliers, collaborative partners, consultants, contracted-out personnel and customers.

6.4 ■■ The problems of organisation

As we have seen, organisations always represent a compromise between differing requirements and objectives. As a result, a certain amount of tension is inevitable. In fact, organisations actually *need* a degree of tension in order to work effectively. If completely freed of stress, they are likely collapse into a kind of directionless jelly! However, when stress levels become *excessive*, everyone connected with the organisation begins to suffer and to under-perform. The main causes of communication blockages and destructive stress levels are hierarchy, cultural difference, constant change and the grapevine:

(a) Hierarchy and distance

The distances between people in organisations can be vertical, horizontal or geographic. Vertical distance is a measure of the degree of 'hierarchy', the number of levels in an organisational structure. Since the 1980s, large businesses have been cutting out levels of management ('delayering') in order to reduce costs and improve information flow. However, overly aggressive cuts can lead to problems where essential knowledge and skills are lost, or certain managers become over-burdened. Horizontal (or lateral) distance relates to the number of groupings at a particular level in the hierarchy. Together, these create the overall shape of the organisation. The UK Civil Service, for example, is a fairly 'tall' structure, whereas the Roman Catholic church is surprisingly 'flat', with only a few levels separating the Pope and the parish priest. Geographic distance can be a problem, even where departments are only located on the opposite sides of a road. New technologies promise to eliminate the obstacles of geography, though other factors – such as cultural differences may intervene.

(b) Cultural differences

Any human grouping, is bound to develop its own culture, with initiation rites, myths, symbolism and so on. Hence, the 'IBM culture' is different in almost every way from that of other computer firms, like Dell or Compaq. Cultures are also self-perpetuating, since like-minded people tend to be recruited whilst 'deviants' soon choose to quit. For communicators, the real problem is how to manage the 'interface' between cultures. People can very quickly begin to identify with a group, particularly when they have shared experiences, interests and goals. If the organisation has a culture, its various departments are likely to display their own distinctive sub-cultures. The term 'sub-culture' is usually associated with juvenile delinquents and football hooligans, but as Exercise 6b suggests, nobody is immune from the lure of the 'tribe'.

EXERCISE 6B

The sub-culture clash – Accountants versus the Sales Team

It is all-out war at 'Warmley Heating plc'. The accounts clerks are refusing to process invoices, customers are cancelling orders and the Sales Director is engaged in a 24-hour shouting match with the Finance Director in the main corridor. What has led to this crisis?

The Accountants are responsible for producing accurate and reliable performance figures for all areas of the company. They follow their profession's 'conservatism' principle, always understating profits if the figures are uncertain. The accountants are scrupulous, methodical and insist on following procedure. Financial control is their top priority. They think that Warmley's salespeople are flashy, disorganised loud-mouths. They spend all their time in the office and have a suspicion that the overseas expense claims are being fiddled.

The Sales Team are responsible for securing orders and achieving ambitious sales targets. They are natural optimists and extroverts, able to take the 'knocks' when a big order falls through. They are flexible and energetic, always on the move in the UK and abroad. They hate paperwork. Creating business is their top priority, especially since the MD launched the company's new attack on the European market. The Sales Team think that Warmley's accountants are sad, boring bureaucratic nit-pickers.

Sales figures were down in the previous quarter, and the Sales Team are under pressure to perform. In the rush to record details of new orders, salespeople are not filling in all the necessary details on the forms. As a result, Accounts Department have been sending out incorrect invoices, and are having to handle subsequent customer complaints. Accounts clerks keep calling the sales office in order to check these forms, but the people they need are never around. The Chief Accountant has started sending warning memos to members of the sales team, but these have only exacerbated the problem: 'Who does that . . . bean counter think he is?' complained one irate Sales Manager. 'He really should get out more', added a colleague, as they marched briskly into the bar of the Budapest Hilton.

***

You are the Managing Director of Warmley Heating plc. How would you deal with this – all-too-common – communication breakdown? Explain how your solution would help to overcome the organisational problems that are identified in this case.

(c) Continuous motion

Today, most businesses seem to be in a constant state of flux. Staff turnover is high as people are recruited, relocated, made redundant, or take up job offers elsewhere. As Section 6.3 suggested, companies are also making increased use of consultants and short-term contract staff in order to retain flexibility in an uncertain market.

Mergers, acquisitions and periodic reviews of public sector bodies can also lead to large-scale restructuring. These changes are generally preceded by a period of *uncertainty*, and followed by a process of *adaptation*, as people settle into the new arrangements.

(d) Informal networks: 'I heard it on the grapevine'

Company grapevines are rather like the *Internet*, consisting of overlapping, informal networks of friends and colleagues who circulate information around an organisation. Grapevines can be very effective communication channels. They are considerably *faster* than conventional routes, more likely to gain the *attention* of receivers, and they are effectively *cost-free*! For these reasons, managers occasionally make use of grapevines to release their official messages, with well-placed rumours preparing the ground for a subsequent formal announcement. However, grapevines can become counter-productive. In a time of uncertainty, such as restructuring or redundancy, harmless gossip is often replaced by misinformation. In these conditions, grapevines tend to distort and exaggerate messages as they are passed around. The best antidote is for managers to act quickly and decisively, not punishing an individual gossip (i.e. a symptom), but dealing with the underlying cause.

6.5 ▇▇ Implications for managers

We have seen that communication problems can be both a **symptom** of underlying organisational ill health, and a **contributory factor**, perpetuating and even worsening the problem. Unless the root cause of the problem is tackled, a communication-based 'solution' will be correctly perceived as purely cosmetic, and hence discredited. Many senior managers fail to recognise that 'technological fixes', like the introduction of e-mail, are not sufficient to tackle deep-seated cultural clashes or political strife. Increased contact between the parties may even exacerbate the conflict, due to 'noise', incorrect decoding and distorted feedback (Chapter 1). Ironically, as Exercise 6c highlights, it is often top managers who find themselves most isolated from the rest of their organisation.

EXERCISE 6C

The Chief Executive's padded cell

The one person who really *should* be in touch with the entire organisation is the chief executive. However, many factors conspire to block communication between the leader and his or her troops. Paradoxically, this insulation from reality leaves them dangerously isolated and exposed. Some bosses are remarkably approachable, but the more domineering personalities tend to attract an inner circle of sycophants or 'yes men', whose main talents (in the worthy tradition of Rowan Atkinson's character in the television comedy series *Blackadder*) are internal politics rather than business strategy. Because of the complexity of a large organisation, the chief executive has to depend on others for information of company performance. Due to time pressures, this is generally provided in a very summarised form. As a result, there is considerable scope for 'special pleading' by particular divisional heads, using partial information to make a case for their own operation, or to attack the performance of another. When the boss *does* try to communicate downwards, it is usually via senior and middle managers, opening up further risks of distortion. For the same reasons, it is difficult for the boss to check whether the message has got through to the 'grass roots'.

Individually, or in small groups, discuss the issues raised in the paragraph above. Develop a 'five-point plan' to improve the communication flows to and from the Chief Executive of either: (a) a multinational company, or (b) a large NHS Trust hospital.

Can communication really help?

Effective two-way communication channels should provide advance warning of excess stress in an organisation, and subsequently help in its reduction. To illustrate how communication can assist in overcoming structural problems, consider the following imaginary case. How could the managers of a major High Street retailer, '*Goodfoods*' deal with the inevitable difficulties arising when they integrate a recently acquired company, '*Cheapsave*', so that it can trade under their brand:

(i) **Recognise potential problems and take them seriously** Before an acquisition, companies make 'due diligence' checks on their target business to check on the 'hard' issues of financial security and legal status. These should be expanded to include so-called 'soft' issues of culture clash and informal communication.

(ii) **Develop a communication strategy** This should run alongside other aspects of the acquisition, addressing the practical problems of integrating two distinct operations with their own histories, cultures and procedures. An essential part of this is ensuring that concerns of staff in both companies are aired and dealt with.

(iii) **Ensure that official statements match the 'realities'** Avoid giving a guarantee of no redundancies at '*Cheapsave*' unless you mean it. And do not let the '*Goodfoods*' Chief Executive make glib remarks about 'our commitment to employees' and 'emphasis on teamworking' if the new employees still perceive their company as miserly and over-centralised.

(iv) **Take action to address specific communication weaknesses** Consider a range of practical techniques, such as team briefing, quality circles and customer satisfaction workshops. Use integrated project teams to bring the managers in both companies together (see Further Reading).

(v) **Monitor carefully and adjust as required** A communication strategy needs to be flexible in order to respond to change. Organisations sometimes conduct a 'communication audit', involving questionnaire surveys of staff, suppliers and customers, in order to ensure that their current approach is working satisfactorily.

6.6 ▮▮ Chapter summary

- Organisation structures and procedures are essential, but they are always a compromise between efficiency and effectiveness.

- The main structural types are functional, product-based and hybrids (including the matrix form). These represent different balances between internal and external factors.

- In the 1990s, the borders of organisations have become much less clearly defined. This is due to a number of developments, including: total quality management systems, strategic alliances, out-sourcing and relationship marketing.

- Four features of organisations are especially likely to cause communication problems. These are: hierarchy, cultural clashes, continuous change and (in some circumstances) the grapevine.

- Communication failures can be both a symptom of, and a contributor to, organisational problems. It is always essential to get to the root cause, rather than relying on cosmetic solutions or technical fixes.

- With senior management awareness and commitment, plus a flexible communication strategy, many of the most common structural tensions can be overcome.

Discussion points

1. Power, influence and information

Consider the following extreme descriptions of the ways that businesses might operate, as wholly 'rational' or as 'political' organisations:

(a) **Wholly rational** Organisations always pursue their objectives in a logical, orderly manner. There is a full and objective review of information. Companies make efficient and effective progress towards clearly defined goals.

(b) **Wholly political** Organisations run through pure 'power' politics. There is a continuous technicolour drama, full of conflict and uncertainty, with subjective and partial information used by loose coalitions to bargain their way towards a private agenda.

Based on your own experience, or research, which description is closest to the truth. Try to develop your own categories to describe the kinds of organisations that you have found. In each case, suggest the likely implications for a communicator who is trying to operate in that situation.

2. Marriages made in heaven?

Find a recent corporate merger or acquisition story from *The Financial Times* or other sources. Based on the information that you have obtained about the companies involved, prepare a list of communications tasks that you would undertake to ensure that the 'marriage' is a successful one. The kind of background issues you might investigate include:

- History of each company – how did it grow?
- Cultural origins of each company – still tied to 'home' country?
- Technologies used – degree of automation?
- Types of employee – mostly professional, manual, researchers, craft skills?
- Products and services – innovative or traditional?
- Markets and customers – types and locations?

Part II

Communication in practice

Chapter seven

Information capture: forms and questionnaires

*Half of the money I spend on advertising is wasted;
the trouble is, I don't know which half*

William Hesketh Lever

Objectives

- To identify the functions and essential requirements of successful forms and survey questionnaires (7.1–7.2)
- To outline the main types of questionnaire, their appropriate uses, advantages and disadvantages (7.3)
- To highlight four important considerations when framing survey questions (7.4)
- To consider how information captured on forms and in questionnaires is analysed and reported (7.5)

7.1 ■■ Introduction

It is said that we live in 'the information age' – the tag that provides a sub-title for this book. The reality is that, at home and at work, we are bombarded with an increasing variety and volume of facts, figures and opinions. Indeed, many people are complaining of 'information overload'. So why should anyone in their right mind spend money searching for yet more data? The answer is summed up in the phrase '*quality, not quantity*'. Obtaining high quality data and turning it into meaningful information can help you to create competitive advantage or to achieve your organisation's aims. In this chapter we look how business information is collected, focusing on the use of pre-printed forms and questionnaires. There is practical advice on structuring a document, appropriate wording and overall design. This is backed up by examples of the most commonly used formats. Millions of pounds are wasted each year on poorly thought-out research and data collection. The following case study illustrates a common problem in business – adopting an unthinking approach to 'form-filling'.

Case study

'Carry on, Constable' – the dangers of form-filling

Something peculiar was happening at 'Hill Street' police station. Each week, the duty officer disappeared into a back-room cupboard, armed with a small book. A newly appointed Superintendant decided to find out what was going on. It turned out that the book was used to record the latest reading on the station's electricity meter. 'Hang on', said the Superintendant, 'why are we recording this meter reading every week?' There was an embarrassed silence, and a constable was ordered to investigate. In due course, the awful truth was unearthed. Hill Street had been taking part in a competition, involving other police stations in the area, to see who could save the most electricity each week. A worthy effort, you might think, except that the competition took place during World War Two ! Many years later, the diligent officers at Hill Street had continued to collect this redundant information.

Is 'Hill Street' the only organisation making that kind of mistake? How can businesses ensure that their information collection is relevant and up to date?

Source: Derek George (personal correspondence with author)

7.2 ■■ Using forms in business

The primary purpose of a form is to collect routine information in a logical and standardised way. Forms range in complexity from the simple 'tear off' coupons found in newspapers and magazines to multi-page documents, such as:

- Job application forms
- Employment records (pay, promotion, sick leave, etc.)
- Tax returns
- Grant applications

There are two people who need to be considered by anyone designing a form. Firstly, the person **completing** the form, and, secondly the person whose task is **processing** the information provided. The time that you invest in preparing a 'user-friendly' document is more than justified, since it minimises the errors and avoids hours of frustration that can otherwise occur when the form is used for real.

7.3 ■■ Preparing forms and questionnaires

Whether you are working on a form or a questionnaire (Section 7.4 below), the following four questions need to be answered at the outset:

Personnel Record

Form: 103
Issue Date: 12/01/96

Name: _____ Staff No: _____ Commence: _____

Name: _____

Address: _____ Tel: _____

Address: _____ Tel: _____

Address: _____ Tel: _____

Emergency tel no: _____

Progress chart:

Date	Position	Reporting to	Salary

Date

Contract signed   _____

Benefits: **Details attached (✓)**

Company car   _____
Car allowance   _____
Sales commission   _____
PRBS   _____
Company pension contributions   _____
Share purchase option   _____

_____   _____
_____   _____

Date of termination of contract:

Form 103 Page 1 of 1

Figure 7.1 Business forms enable you to collect essential information in a logical and standardised way.

(i) **What do I really need to know?** There is always a fine balance between asking too little and too much. You do not want to collect information needlessly, and an over-long form is likely to alienate the person who has to complete it. On the other hand, missing out a key question can have disastrous results. For example, forgetting to ask for a contact telephone number when you had planned to make follow-up calls.

(ii) **Are the questions clear, concise and acceptable?** Questions and instructions must be unambiguous and readily understood by anyone who might need to complete the form. Campaigners have fought a long battle with government agencies and businesses for the use of plain English in social security forms, tax returns, etc. It is also important to avoid questions that might upset the respondent, leading to a non-response or a complaint. For example, 'ethnic monitoring' questions that are now included in most job applications need to be worded carefully, normally with an assurance that they play no part in the selection process.

(iii) **Is the structure logical?** Again, you need to focus on the person completing the form. If you are jumping between unrelated questions, they will become confused and are unlikely to respond correctly.

(iv) **Am I encouraging a positive response?** Taking care over the previous three points should help to increase the response rate and ensure that useful information is obtained. You can also motivate those who have to spend time completing the document with attractive design and incentives for completion:

Attractive design With desktop publishing (DTP) and wordprocessing software anyone can produce professional-looking material. Unfortunately, DTP has also raised the expectations of the form-fillers. A dull, typewritten form will no longer suffice, especially when you are trying to present a professional image.

Incentives Some forms have their own 'built-in' incentives for completion. For example, a job application form holds out the prospect of employment, whilst a tax return comes with a threat of legal action if it is not sent back within 30 days. In some cases, you may need to provide additional incentives, such as free product samples, prize draws, competitions and contributions to charity (e.g. £1 donated for every completed form or questionnaire). In your covering letter, you may also be able to exploit some 'intangible' incentives, such as the respondent's personal satisfaction in 'having their say' on a topical issue, or in helping with a 'good cause'.

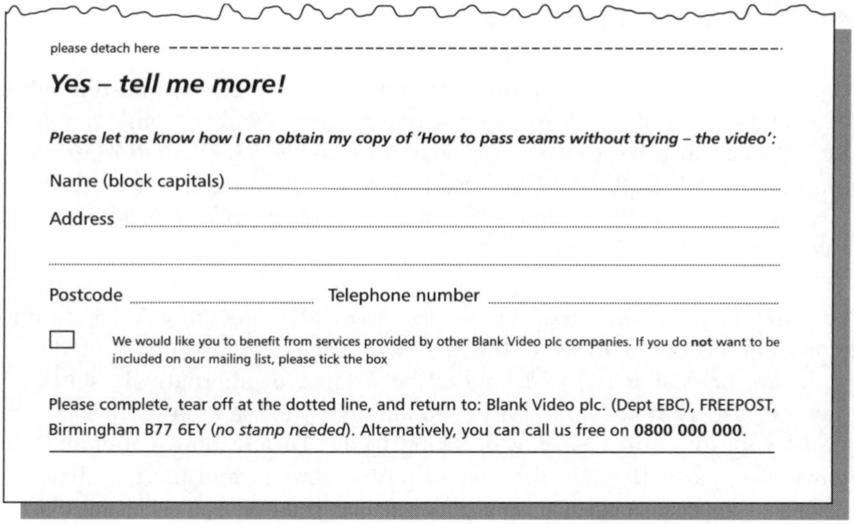

---

please detach here --

Yes – tell me more!

Please let me know how I can obtain my copy of 'How to pass exams without trying – the video':

Name (block capitals) ....

Address ....

....

Postcode .... Telephone number ....

☐ We would like you to benefit from services provided by other Blank Video plc companies. If you do **not** want to be included on our mailing list, please tick the box

Please complete, tear off at the dotted line, and return to: Blank Video plc. (Dept EBC), FREEPOST, Birmingham B77 6EY (*no stamp needed*). Alternatively, you can call us free on **0800 000 000**.

Figure 7.2 A simple 'tear off' reply form.

EXERCISE 7A

'Sun, Sea and Sand' – designing an application form

You are the recruitment manager at 'Sun, Sea & Sand' holiday villages, with sites in Spain, Portugal, Greece and Morocco. You need to recruit 20 summer staff, primarily to run the wide range of watersports, the restaurant-bar and childrens' daytime activities. Recruitment advertising is targeted at UK-based students.

(a) Prepare an application form, suitable for this purpose. What questions do you need to ask? What factors do you need to consider in designing the layout?

(b) Make a photocopy of your form and ask another person to complete it with either their own or fictional details (nb: copying your form onto an A3 size sheet will give you a useful 4 × A4 document).

(c) Review the completed form. Did *the other person* find it clear and unambiguous? Did *you* get the information you expected and required? Consider any ways in which the form could be improved.

sun, sea and sand

7.4 ■■ Questionnaire-based research

Most people have, at one time or another, been asked to complete a questionnaire. These are used for marketing research, government surveys and academic research. Questionnaires can also be used within organisations, in job evaluation or communication auditing (Chapter 5). The broad term 'questionnaire' is used here to cover a variety of research methods. Some of the most widely used types of questionnaire are outlined below:

- **Self-completion questionnaires** These are preprinted documents containing questions and full instructions for the respondent. They may be distributed (e.g. to employees or customers) and handed back later, or alternatively sent and returned by post. They are commonly used for large-scale sample surveys, where their relatively low unit cost is a deciding factor. Disadvantages include low response rates, particularly in the case of postal surveys, and the fact that you are unable to 'converse' with the respondent (i.e. the researcher cannot clarify any uncertainties or probe for underlying thoughts).

- **Telephone questionnaires** This method requires a team of trained interviewers who call people and read out a prepared 'schedule' of questions. Telephone interviewers often work from home, reducing overhead costs. However, the greater staff and call costs make telephone surveys more expensive than their postal counterpart. Their main advantages are speed and the opportunity to help the respondent with any points they find unclear. Computer assisted telephone interviewing (CATI) software makes surveying even more efficient; questions are displayed on the interviewer's computer screen, and the responses can be keyed in directly, cutting out the 'data input' stage. Disadvantages include the potential under-representation of some groups (i.e. those who either do not have access to a 'phone, or are too busy to respond via this channel) and an inability to use visual prompts (e.g. showing the respondent a new product or packaging idea and asking them what they think of it).

- **Street and 'door-to-door' questionnaires** Sometimes mocked as 'the middle-aged, middle-class woman with a clip-board', these are similar to telephone-based questionnaires, except that the interviewer and respondent are 'face to face'. This method can also be streamlined with personal interviewing software (CAPI), running on portable computers. Surveys are often targeted at social groups that are of particular interest to the researcher. Interviewers may be asked to call on specific residential areas, or to sample people leaving a supermarket or a football stadium. Whatever sampling method is adopted, the principal advantages of face-to-face interviewing are the opportunity to develop a dialogue and to use visual prompts. However, it is a labour-intensive technique, and is therefore considered too costly for most large-scale commercial surveys.

- **Depth interview checklists** Research is sometimes based on longer 'depth' (or 'in-depth') interviews which are generally pre-booked and at the respondent's own home or workplace. In this case, the highly structured questionnaire is replaced by a semi-structured 'checklist' (or 'schedule') of questions which the interviewer reads aloud. Checklists are more flexible than a questionnaire, allowing the interviewer to spend more time on one question or to skip another, depending on the responses of the particular interviewee. Depth interviews are normally tape recorded, freeing the interviewer from note-taking. Once the series of interviews is completed, the tapes are replayed and the responses are summarised under relevant section headings. Representative quotations are often added in order to give a better 'flavour' of the discussions that have taken place. The main advantage of depth interviews is the opportunity to probe for deeper meanings and subtle distinctions that can be missed by 'tick box' questioning techniques. Against this, researchers need to assess the cost and time required to compile meaningful results.

- **Group discussions checklists** Group discussions extend the depth interview method by allowing a number of respondents to interact. The discussion leader may provide some direction, raising questions from the checklist, but then allowing the group to discuss their responses. The 'focus group', popular with marketing researchers, is an informal variant on this, which is often held in someone's home. Typically, the focus group leader will pass around samples of a new product, or advertising material, allowing the group to express their feelings, with a minimum of intervention. These discussions may be recorded on audio or video for subsequent analysis by the researchers. Groups can provide very rich material, though do they have limitations. Some topics, such as sexual behaviour or the financing of businesses may prove too sensitive to discuss on a group basis.

Figure 7.3 Collecting information using a street interview questionnaire.

What do farmers think? Example of a postal questionnaire, designed to be distributed with covering letter:

DAIRY FARMER SATISFACTION SURVEY

Section A – About Your Farm

1. How many dairy cows do you have? _____ cows

2. What area does your farm cover? Grassland: _____ acres Arable: _____ acres

3. What form of tenure do you have on your farm? (tick one)

   Owner occupier [ ]   Tenant [ ]
   Owner and tenant [ ]   Landlord [ ]
   Manager/agent [ ]   Share farmer [ ]

4. What is the legal form of your farm? (tick one)

   Sole trader [ ]   Partnership [ ]   Limited Company [ ]

5. Which of the following best describes your dairy cow feeding system? (tick as many as apply)

   Self-feed silage [ ]   Concentrate in parlour [ ]
   Trough-fed silage [ ]   Concentrate out-of-parlour [ ]
   Complete diet feeding [ ]   Other _____ (please specify)

Section B – About Your Dairy Cow Feed Suppliers

1. Which company supplies most of your dairy cow feed? _____

2. How many years have you been with this supplier? _____ years

3. Do you have a contract with this supplier?   Yes [ ]   No [ ]

   If 'Yes', how long is the contract? 3 months [ ] 6 months [ ] 9 months [ ] other _____ [ ]

4. How important are the following factors when deciding from which company to buy dairy cow feed? (circle one number per factor)

Factor	Fairly Important			Very Important	No Opinion
Price	1	2	3	4	5	6
Physical product quality	1	2	3	4	5	6
Nutritional product quality	1	2	3	4	5	6
Advice and services	1	2	3	4	5	6
Committed to customers	1	2	3	4	5	6
Prompt delivery	1	2	3	4	5	6
Wide product range	1	2	3	4	5	6
Well trained representatives	1	2	3	4	5	6
Reputation	1	2	3	4	5	6
Other _____	1	2	3	4	5	6

Section D – About Yourself

1. Are you a first time farmer?   Yes [ ]   No [ ]

2. Have you inherited your farm?   Yes [ ]   No [ ]

3. What is your current position in the farm business? (tick one)

   Farmer [ ]   Farmer's wife [ ]
   Farmer's son [ ]   Farmer's daughter [ ]
   Partner [ ]   Manager [ ]
              Other [ ]

4. Who else is active in managing the farm? (tick as many as apply)

   Husband [ ]   Wife [ ]
   Son [ ]   Daughter [ ]
   Manager [ ]   Partner [ ]
              Other [ ]

5. Do you have a son or daughter who will continue the business?

   Yes [ ]   No [ ]   Don't know [ ]

6. What is your age? (tick one)

   Up to 34 [ ]   35 to 49 [ ]
   50 to 64 [ ]   65 or over [ ]

7. What qualifications do you hold?

   GCSE / O-level [ ]   A-level [ ]   Lifetime
   ND or similar [ ]   HND / degree [ ]   experience [ ]

8. How good is the farming advice given by the following?
   (1=Very good; 2=Good; 3=Average; 4=Poor; 5=Very poor; 6=No opinion)

   Feed supplier _____   Other farmers _____
   ADAS _____   Independent consultants _____
   Genus _____   Farming press _____
   Banks _____   (Farmers weekly etc) _____
   Other _____

9. Can you suggest what, in a few words, you think it takes for a dairy feed supplier to create a satisfied customer?

_____

Thank you for completing this questionnaire. Please return it in the **FREEPOST** envelope provided. A £1 donation will be made to **Children In Need** for each questionnaire returned completed.

7.5 ■■ Questions and questioning

We have already noted that each question must be clear and unambiguous. Other considerations include, whether to use 'open' or 'closed' questions and avoidance of 'leading' questions, which suggest to the respondent the answer that you expect (nb: leading questions are discussed further in Section 13.4, in relation to interviewing technique). There are four further practical issues to be covered when preparing a questionnaire or interview schedule:

(i) **Pre-code the questions if possible** Coding is used to convert responses into numerical form, so that they can be counted and analysed. It is suprising how complex the coding can become. For example, the seemingly clear-cut question *'Does your office computer have a modem link?'* requires five codes: 'yes' = 1, 'no' = 2, 'don't know' = 3, 'not applicable' = 4, 'no response' = 5

Closed questions like this should be **pre-coded**, as has been done in the sample postal questionnaire. Pre-coding saves a lot of time at the data input stage. If code numbers are included on a self-completion questionnaire, they need to be printed in a small type, to avoid distracting the respondent.

(ii) **Make any 'filters' clear** Respondents need to feel that every question is relevant to them. However, you may want to ask some questions (e.g. *'How often do you use your portable computer?'*) that do not apply to *all* of the respondents. Use a filter to guide respondents past the non-relevant questions. For example:

(6) Do you have access to a portable computer?   ☐ yes   ☐ no

If YES, please go to question (7)
If NO, please go to question (8)

(iii) **Use 'open' questions selectively** Use open questions if the issues are complex and the full range of likely responses cannot be predicted in advance. Because you are providing no pre-determined categories, analysis of open questions is more difficult and time consuming. Imagine, for instance, the mixture of answers you might obtain from this open question:

(9) What benefits do you get from owning a portable computer?

The best way to minimise this problem to adopt a **two-stage research plan**. Begin your research with a limited number of 'exploratory' depth interviews, asking open questions and generating a list of typical responses. These responses can then be converted into a series of 'options', within a pre-coded closed question. Say, for instance, that your depth interviews have revealed five broad types of answer to the portable computer question. These can be re-used in a self-completion questionnaire, of the following form:

(9) I get the following benefits from owning a portable computer:
     (Please tick as many items as apply)

Saves time preparing paperwork ☐
More flexible working hours ☐
Reduced storage requirements ☐
Easier to prepare my accounts ☐
Status symbol ☐

Other (please specify): _____

(iv) **Simple questions first, sensitive ones last** Whatever method you are using, try to begin with simple, uncontentious questions. Once the respondent is 'committed' to completing the questionnaire, it may be possible to ask more personal or probing questions. However, avoid leaving any *essential* questions until the end (i.e. after a ten-minute session, a street interviewer reaches her most vital question, only to be told, '*Sorry love, I've got a train to catch!*').

EXERCISE 7B

Library Users Survey – designing a questionnaire

You have been asked by senior management to research the views of people using your organisation's library and learning resources centre.

(a) Develop a series of questions that might be of interest to management (you may want to use 'brainstorming' techniques), relating to the quality of service, patterns of usage, user needs, etc.
(b) Convert these questions into the following questionnaire formats:
    A self-completion questionnaire
    A 'face-to-face' interview schedule
    A depth interview 'checklist'
(c) With the help of a fellow student or work colleague, carry out a 'pilot' test of each format. Are the questions readily understood? Have you made full use of pre-coding and filtering? Is the order logical, from the *respondent's* point of view?

7.6 ■■ Analysing and reporting

Depth interviews and small-scale surveys can be analysed manually. However, most large quantitative surveys are conducted using statistical software, such as *SPSS* or *Statgraphics*. There is also software capable of handling qualitative data, such as the text of an interview. Examples include *NUD.IST* and *The Ethnograph*. The latest software packages have powerful data manipulation facilities and produce high quality graphics. However, despite the advanced technology, data analysis is still a minefield for the inexperienced. It is now extremely easy to present findings that are both visually stunning and utterly meaningless! See Further Reading for recommended texts on research methods. Report-writing and presentation skills are discussed in Chapters 9 and 13.

7.7 ■■ Chapter summary

- Successful information capture is vital to business success.
- Careful preparation is essential in order to obtain high quality information cost effectively.
- Forms are a useful method of collecting routine information
- Four key questions for a form or questionnaire designer are:
    What do I need to know?
    Are my questions clear?
    Is my structure logical?
    Am I encouraging a positive response?
- The main methods of questionnaire-based research are:
    Self-completion
    Telephone
    Street and door-to-door
    Depth interviews and group discussions make use of a more flexible version of the questionnaire, called an interview 'checklist' or 'schedule'.
- When drafting questions, it is important to pre-code if possible, make any filters clear and use open questions selectively. A two-stage research plan can help to minimise coding problems.
- Software packages can assist in the process of analysis and reporting. However, there are many pitfalls in the use of statistical techniques, and thorough preparation is necessary.

Practical exercises

1. Form design

Design a form suitable for collecting information in one of the following situations. Create your own background information and draft an appropriate covering letter:

(a) Application form for a new 'National Sports Fellowship Fund', sponsoring selected students through university, based on their sporting prowess, potential, motivation, involvement in community activities and academic ability.
(b) Booking form for a three-day international business conference, to be held at a major hotel complex in Houston, Texas. The bookings should cover both the conference sessions, social events and accommodation.

Photocopy your form and use it to prepare a 'completed' version, as it would be filled in by the imaginary applicant/conference delegate, 'Sam Smith'.

2. Questionnaire design

You have been commissioned to research attitudes or behaviour in one of the following areas:

- Traffic congestion, road building, public transport and the environment.
- Alcohol and tobacco consumption patterns in different age groups.
- Changes in reading habits, including newspapers, books and magazines.
- Comparison of internal communication systems within different organisations.
- Another research topic of your own choice.

Prepare a more specific brief, stating which questions your research is attempting to answer, and outline your proposed approach. Select ONE suitable research method, such as a telephone survey or depth interview. (nb: As the chapter suggests, fieldwork often involves a number of complementary methods). Prepare a draft questionnaire or interview checklist.

Chapter eight

Business letters and direct mail

*I had letters, I am persecuted with letters, I hate letters;
nobody knows how to write letters*

William Congreve, *The Way of the World* (1700)

Objectives

- To establish the advantages and disadvantages of the letter as a channel of communication, compared with the alternatives now available (8.1–8.2)

- To review business letter format, including page layout and open punctuation (8.2)

- To develop skills in formulating business letters, including overall structure, content and writing style (8.3–8.4)

- To introduce direct mail techniques and terminology (8.5)

- To review legal, practical and promotional aspects of letterhead design (8.6)

8.1 ▪▪ Introduction

For centuries, letters were the only practical form of long-distance communication short of dispatching an 'envoy' or travelling there yourself. Today, there are many faster and sometimes more reliable technologies, ranging from telephones to fax and e-mail. Given these alternatives, why do we continue to send so many letters, including around 650 million items of direct mail each year? (Royal Mail/DMIS 1996). This chapter looks at the key elements of the business letter, assessing its inherent advantages and disadvantages. Illustrations and exercises show how to use business letters to maximum effect in a variety of situations. However, Exercise 8a begins with a warning of how *not* to do it.

EXERCISE 8A

Knott-Underfoot – making the wrong impression?

What is your initial impression of the following *promotional* letter from Knott-Underfoot Carpeting? What are the intentional and unintentional messages, and how are these conveyed?
Assume that the person reading this letter has no other knowledge of the company.

KNOTT-UNDERFOOT
Carpeting Contractors
of Distinction
45a Gasworks Street
Rummidge RU46 7QP

Dear sir/Madam

   Please let me take this opportunity to introduce ourselves, we
are a new Company who are trying to build an excellent reputation
for ourselves in these hard times. We have beeen in the Carpeting
Trade approx 15 years, sub contracting for other Companys
through the years we have seen a lot of Companies fold, some say
this was due to the recession, some were due to Companies building a bad
reputation through a lot of <u>HARD SELLING</u>, <u>BAD FITTING</u>, and
none existant <u>AFTER SALES</u>.

   Our main priority of the Company is AFTER SALES (if any)
this is where we strongly believe most companies fail we
believe the main way of building an excellent reputation is from
recommendation thats what we want all our customers to do
(we only use high quality materiels).

   All the <u>FITTING</u> is done by professionel craftsmen which will
carry a 2 year guarantee.
Please don't hesitate to contact us for a free no obligation
quotation, there will be no <u>HARD SELLING</u> as we do not employ
salesmen.

For and on behalf of KnottUnderfoot Carpet Contractors

<u>Wayne Knott</u>
Sales manager

8.2 ■■ Principal uses and channel characteristics

The following table summarises some common types of business letter by recipient,
noting some of their varied message objectives.

Various types of business letter

Receiver	Type of letter	Typical communication objectives
Customer	Promotional	Increase brand awareness, stimulate sales
	Sales documents	Establish clearly defined contract terms
	Credit control	Speed up customer payments – politely
	Adjustment/complaints	Keep customer loyalty by prompt action
	Information gathering	Obtain data on attitudes and behaviour
Supplier	Purchases contract	Establish clearly defined contract terms
	Credit control	Avoid conflict over firm's late payment
	Adjustment/complaints	Obtain refund or replacement supplies
Employee	Recruitment	Inform and attract potential applicants
	Pay and conditions	Provide clear and accurate information
	Posting, promotion	Provide factual detail and encouragement
	Disciplinary	Inform and encourage behaviour change
	Redundancy	Provide factual detail and offer support

Despite the arrival of fax and e-mail, letters continue to serve a variety of functions. This long-established channel of communication has three main characteristics:

- **It is 'one-way' and non-interruptible:** In contrast to a telephone conversation, for example, receivers cannot, in the short term, request clarification or additional information. Your written message must therefore be well thought out, clear and comprehensive. Try to predict likely questions and explain anything that receivers are unlikely to understand.

- **It involves a time delay between sending and receipt:** Letters are clearly unsuitable for *urgent* (as distinct from *important*) messages since they take at least a day to arrive. As a sender, you do not know whether the recipient has read your letter. One advantage of e-mail is its ability to confirm when a message is read. When a rapid response is essential, consider a combination of phone plus either fax or e-mail.

- **It provides a permanent record of the message:** Letters can be retained by the receiver and reviewed at their leisure. This makes them more suitable than the telephone or face-to face conversation for long and complex messages. However, there is a down-side, since any rash promises or 'spur of the moment' criticisms that you make in a letter cannot easily be retracted. Incidentally, this is also a feature of e-mail, where it is even easier to send out a hasty remark that you may later regret!

The mysteries of page layout

There has been a radical simplification of page layout in recent years, based on so-called '**fully blocked**' page layouts and '**open**' **punctuation**. Fully blocked layout simply means that all text, including dates, recipient's address and subject heading, is aligned with the left-hand margin. Traditionalists regard this layout as unbalanced, but it is quick and easy for anyone to reproduce, especially when using a wordprocessing package. Open punctuation means that all of the commas and full stops are omitted in the address section, greeting and complimentary close of your letter. In a modern type font, open punctuation looks crisp and concise. It also saves on the keystrokes required (there are 25 fewer in the 'open' version of the address below), saving time and reducing the risk of typing errors.

Traditional (indented) layout with 'closed' punctuation

Our Ref. FAH/AJR

3rd. February, 1967

Mrs. E. A. Gaskell, M.A., B.Sc.(Econ.), F.R.S.A.,
  Cranford Cottage,
    12, Church Row,
      Little Gidding,
        Gloucestershire,
          GL31 7KP

Dear Mrs. Gaskell,

HERBERT HERBS CATALOGUE

      Thank you for your letter regarding our recent advertisement in The Little Gidding Times, and for your complimentary remarks about our products.

      I am pleased to enclose a copy of our new 1967 catalogue and look forward to dealing with your order.

Yours sincerely,

For : <u>HERBERT HERB GARDENS LIMITED</u>,

George Herbert, Chairman & M.D.

Modern fully blocked layout with 'open' punctuation

Our Ref FAH/AJR

3 February 1998

Mrs E A Gaskell MA BSc (Econ) FRSA
Cranford Cottage
12 Church Row
Little Gidding
Gloucestershire
GL31 7KP

Dear Ms Gaskell

HERBERT HERBS CATALOGUE

Thank you for your letter regarding our recent advertisement in The Little Gidding Times, and for your complimentary remarks about our products. I am pleased to enclose a copy of our new 1998/99 catalogue and look forward to dealing with your order.

Yours sincerely

Patricia Anderson
Marketing Manager

EXERCISE 8B

Layout and letter-writing practice

Draft a short letter, using fully blocked layout, to the Sales Manager of Knott-Underfoot Carpeting Contractors (Exercise 8a), requesting a quotation for an office carpet. Invent a suitable business name, address and any other incidental details.

8.3 ▬▬ Structuring a business letter

The basic framework for a business letter is logical and straightforward. However, it is worth considering in more detail the three main functions of its central paragraphs: establishing the context, delivering main messages and stating any action required.

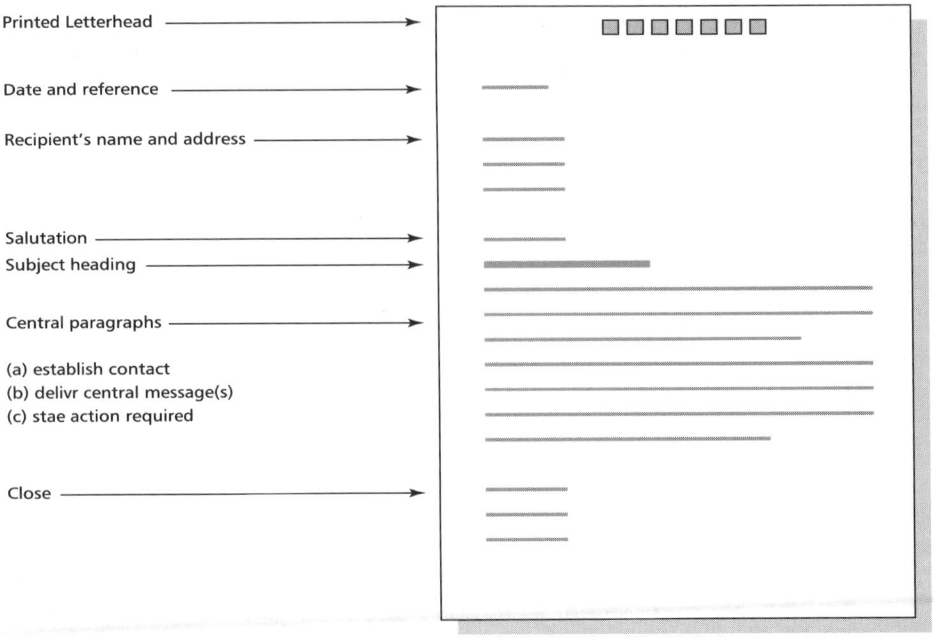

Figure 8.1 Structure of a business letter.

(a) Establishing the context

It is always tempting to jump straight in with your main messages. Resist that temptation. Imagine your letter arriving on the recipient's desk. It may be half-way down in a pile of other urgent correspondence. Three telephones are ringing and her marketing assistant has just poured a cup of coffee into his computer keyboard. How can you help this hard-pressed receiver find her way into your letter in the simplest and most painless way?:

- **Provide a reference** If you have previous correspondence from her, copy that reference onto your letter as 'Your ref'. Most reference numbers today refer to computer filenames, sometimes incorporating the initials of either originator or typist, such as 'SAL72/LJH'.

- **Include a short heading** This should be in bold text or underlined, identifying the purpose of the letter as concisely as possible. For example: 'LASER PRINTER MODEL EXL345A – PAPER TRAY FAULT'

- **Provide a link** Use your opening lines to refer to the most recent contact with the recipient regarding this topic. Typical openers include: '*Further to your letter of 14th January . . .*' , '*Thank you for your fax dated 5th March . . .*' and '*I am writing regarding yesterday's meeting . . .*'

- **Explain your reasons** Assist the receiver by telling her why you are writing the letter! By providing a sound rationale, you can help to establish the importance or the urgency of your subsequent main messages.

(b) Delivering the main messages

Business-related messages typically consist of a number of inter-related points. These need to be strung together in a logical order, with any significant changes of subject area identified by inserting a new paragraph (see Chapters 1–3 for further advice on structuring messages).

(c) Stating any action required

Most business letters are written to achieve some kind of practical response from the receiver. However, letter writers frequently under-emphasise or forget to include this essential section. The results of this are all too predictable:

- Action not carried out at all
- Action carried out late, after numerous reminders
- Action carried out incorrectly, or in a different way to that envisaged

In a hectic business world, your request for action must be clearly stated if it is to stand any chance of it being acted upon. You should also:

- Give a brief **explanation** of why the action is important and/or urgent.
- Include clear and realistic **deadlines**.
- Check that the receiver has the **authority** and **capacity** to act as required.
- But in all cases, even when chasing an unpaid bill, remain **polite**.

8.4 ▪▪ The style and content of a letter

The previous section provides us with a skeleton which we now need to flesh out in words. In doing so, it is useful to bear in mind the special characteristics of the letter. Recipients cannot easily question you about anything that they find ambiguous or unclear. They have to interpret your message based on the words used and what they already know about you and your organisation. The style of a letter is the product of a number of factors, including: vocabulary, grammar, overall length and appearance (see Chapter 4 and Appendix 1). Ideally, the style should be adapted to suit both the receiver and the purpose of your message. However, since recipients are not visible and may often be unknown, writers are in danger of 'speaking' to them inappropriately. This can result in anger, confusion and less credible messages. An example of this occurs when 'Midburg Bank' sends out its standard letter to Mr Wilson, a current account customer who has an overdraft.

14th January 1998

Major JK Wilson
Dumnarchin
12 Castle Street
Dimbury
Wiltshire SN87 PDQ

Dear Major Wilson

CURRENT ACCOUNT NUMBER: 7868686 – OVERDRAFT

It has come to our attention that this account is at present overdrawn by a sum of £254.46. This overdraft has not been authorised. Please note that in accordance with the regulations governing this account, an administration charge of 25.50 has been debited. Please take immediate action to correct this situation. If you have any difficulty in making the necessary payment, you should contact Midburg's Financial Helpline as soon as possible.

Yours sincerely

IM Younger
Credit control assistant

Mr Wilson is a retired soldier and respected magistrate whose overdraft was caused when Midburg Bank made an incorrect standing order payment. He is outraged at the tone of this letter, which 'totally ignores my unblemished record of loyalty and prompt payment'. After 38 years with the same bank, Mr Wilson moves his account and starts a one-man campaign to reveal Midburg Bank's incompetence and bad manners to the wider world. How might the bank have avoided this upset, and the subsequent bad publicity? The following guide highlights some of the more common pitfalls for the business letter-writer.

The good letter-writing guide

- **Structure**
  Is the structure clear and logical?

- **Tone**
  Who is the recipient (long-standing customer, boss, supplier, tax office)?
  Does my tone sound appropriate for them? (unsure? – try reading it out aloud!)
  What am I doing? . . . informing, persuading, criticising, apologising . . . ?
  Do I sound rude, tactless, uninterested, over-familiar?
  If the roles were reversed, how would I react to the letter?

- **Length**
  Does the letter contain any unnecessary information?
  And does it also include everything that is essential?
  Is every sentence as concise as possible?
  Is there any repetition (other than intentional repetition for impact)?

- **Jargon, cliches and colloquialisms**
  Will the recipient understand any technical, specialist terms or abbreviations?
  If not, have I explained them simply, or replaced them with an 'everyday' alternative?
  Have I used 'corny' or clichéd expressions (e.g. *'light at the end of the tunnel'*)?
  Have I used over-informal or slang phrases (e.g. *'productivity's gone down the tubes'*)?

- **Errors**
  Have I checked the spelling, punctuation and grammar?
  Am I relying on the wordprocessor's spellchecker (nb: they are *not* infallible!)?
  Have I checked for factual errors (e.g. incorrect dates, prices, contract terms)?
  Have I definitely printed out the *final* version, not an earlier draft on disk?

- **Qualifications and other titles**
  Like the pigs in George Orwell's *Animal Farm*, *'we are all equal, but some are more equal than others'*. History has given us many conventions, such as using the first name for a Knight ('Dear Sir John') but the surname for a Lord. The proper abbreviation of recipients' qualifications and professional memberships is a perennial problem. The normal order of precedence is as follows:

	Qualification or award	Examples
1.	Civil and military decorations & orders	OBE CBE MBE VC DSO
2.	Higher degrees	PhD DPhil MPhil MSc MA MBA
3.	Bachelor's degrees	BA BSc BEng
4.	Diplomas and similar	Cert Ed Dip M
5.	Professional memberships	MCIM ACA MIStructE

The following distinguished individuals illustrate how this works in practice:

Helena J Swinburne CBE PhD BA Cert ED FIPM
Kenneth T Peary-Sykes DSM DPhil MA FRSA

More detailed advice can be found in larger dictionaries and specialist reference books such as *Burke's Peerage* and *Black's Titles* (see: Further Reading).

EXERCISE 8C

Erskine Food Stores Limited

Consider the following exchange of correspondence between a customer and retailer. This is an example of a letter of complaint, followed up with a letter of 'adjustment' (i.e. seeking to resolve the complaint or dispute). First, consider the customer's letter.

(a) What do you detect from the style and tone of his letter?
(b) What do you think he expects the company to do?

Now, note how the reply is structured, its general layout, use of language, tone, etc.

(c) How would you feel on receiving the retailer's letter?
(d) What messages do you think Mrs Kelly has managed to communicate?
(e) What changes would you make to improve its effectiveness?

                                                    37 Wilson Street
                                                    Ickleston
                                                    Middlesex
                                                    UB22 8TX

12th December 1996

Customer Services Department
H ERSKINE FOOD STORES
545 Wroxeter Boulevard
Watlington
Herefordshire HE5 8WX

Dear Sir/Madam

HELPFUL 'QUICKIE' SOUP: CHICKEN AND VEGETABLE WITH CROUTONS

I am extremely happy with our new Erskines branch in Ickleston, with its friendly staff and (generally) good products. However, the enclosed soup sachet comes as a big disappointment. Try it!

Having added your boiling water, see how rich and substantial it looks, a real improvement on the competition. Now sense the disillusion when you actually taste it. Regrettably, as I am sure you will agree, any initial flavour is overwhelmed by an excessive, lingering SALTINESS. On gastronomic and health grounds, your soup under-performs and does Erskine's a dis-service.

Do I have a duff batch, or do Erskines have a duff Buyer?

Yours faithfully

Ronald Quincy-Smith

enc
cc Mr Bill Badger, 'Consumer Watch' (XBC Television)

ERSKINES FOOD STORES
545 Wroxeter Boulevard, Watlington
Herefordshire HE5 8WX

Tel: 01999 876543   Fax: 01999 876321   email: custser@erskines.co.uk

11 January 1997

Mr R Quincy-Smith
37 Wilson Street
Ickleston
Middlesex
UB22 8TX

Dear Mr Quincy-Smith

We thank you for your letter and your kind comments about the staff and general standards at our Ickleston branch.

However, we were sorry to learn of the problem you experienced with the Quick soup and apologise for the inconvenience caused when the product was found to be too salty.

We examined the sample you kindly returned and it was tasted by our Buyer who agreed that it did have an excess of salt and was not according to the specification. As we were not sure if this was an isolated instance or a more general problem, it was necessary to obtain further samples from stock for checking and we regret the delay this caused when responding to your letter.

Although the salt level in the stock packs was not as high as the one you purchased, there was more than the specified amount and therefore the supply was removed from sale pending further enquiries with our suppliers.

Meanwhile, we were concerned that this could happen and escape detection during the strict quality control procedures and we are continuing to monitor the situation closely to ensure there is no further lapse in standards.

May we say again how sorry we are that you had reason to complain in this way. Occasionally, in spite of all the care taken, things can go wrong and we are grateful to be alerted so that we can take any action necessary to correct any shortcomings.

We hope you will continue to shop with us without further disappointment and you will accept our apologies together with the enclosed voucher towards the out of pocket expenses you have incurred.

Yours sincerely

B V Kelly (Mrs)
Customer Services

Enclosed Voucher: 70987 £5.00

KW Erskine Food Stores Limited
Registered in England 6789101112
Registered Office 34 Victoria Avenue, Farebury, Wiltshire SN67 2JK

8.5 ▇▇ Direct mail and 'mailmerge' techniques

Many letters contain similar or identical information that needs to be reproduced for different receivers, including the routine letters sent out by banks, tax offices and education departments. Rather than re-draft these each time, organisations used to generate 'standard' letters, constructed from a series of model paragraphs. Inevitably, these letters sounded rather impersonal. As the 'Midburg Bank' example suggests (Section 8.4), there are some obvious dangers in using standardised text which ignore individual differences. However, by linking wordprocessing software and databases imaginatively, personalised letters can now be generated in large quantities. These **mailmerge** techniques are used in many types of business correspondence, but the most common application is communicating with current and prospective customers.

Mailmerge is one of the basic techniques of **direct marketing**, whereby databases are used to target products and services on particular individuals rather than broad market segments. For example, imagine that you are a food manufacturer, specialising in tinned baby ready-meals. How might you encourage new parents to trial '*Goolux*', your up-market brand? You *could* run an extended series of adverts on breakfast TV, but this 'shotgun' approach would be largely wasted, since many viewers do not have babies. Alternatively, you could purchase a list of prospects, the data set being captured from a wedding dress or mothers-to-be competition, run in a specialist magazine. This data would be used to generate perhaps 500,000 personalised letters with samples or money-off vouchers enclosed. Given a high quality data set, the 'direct' approach can be very closely targeted. Letters are the ideal direct marketing channel. As in the '*Goolux*' example, their promotional messages can be re-inforced with product samples and related offers. Voluntary organisations are also making increasing use of direct marketing techniques for fund-raising and member recruitment.

Direct mail terminology

Mailmerge This facility is offered by most wordprocessing packages (e.g. *Word*, *Wordperfect*, *Word Pro*) allowing you to link a database file containing names, addresses and other information, to a wordprocessor file containing a standard letter. Name, address and other data are drawn ('merged') into the standard letter in the appropriate locations which are marked by keying in a code letter. The mailmerge is activated as the letters are printed out.

Database A flexible electronic filing cabinet, comprising an often vast number of discrete pieces of data. Data can be sorted, filtered and extracted in ways that would be time-consuming and impractical using paper-based files. Popular software packages include *Paradox*, *dBase*, **Approach** and *Access*, though spreadsheets and wordprocessing packages now incorporate some useful database functions.

Data set The raw data loaded into a database for subsequent manipulation. Data sets may also consist of statistical data, analysed using specialist statistics and market research packages such as *SPSS*, *Statgraphics* and *SNAP*. The data set may be a list of customer addresses, or the results of a questionnaire survey.

Record Within a data set, a block of information relating to an individual person or organisation. This is the electronic equivalent of a file placed inside a filing cabinet.

Figure 8.2 Junk mail makes excellent bedding for Bill's favourite animals.

Field	Within a particular record, a single item of information, such as one line of an address, a surname, date of birth or nationality. In the case of survey data, a field may also contain the response to a question.
List	Term used by marketing people for data sets. These contain names and addresses, along with lifestyle and purchasing behaviour. Lists are created from market research surveys, competitions, returned product guarantee cards, etc. Depending on your company's product or service, you may purchase a list of, for example, 725,000 paraglider pilots, or 543,000 knitting machine owners.

Direct mail can be a powerful communication technique, but many people dismiss it as 'junk mail'. In fact, industry-sponsored research suggests that up to 83 per cent of direct mail is opened (Royal Mail/DMIS 1996). However, you can reduce the wastage rate further by asking yourself the following questions:

- Have I targeted the recipients as closely as possible? (e.g. filtering out existing customers when promoting introductory offers)
- Is the style and content appropriate to all recipients? You may need to produce variants for different segments.
- Have I considered using reply slips to help assess quality of the list?
- Is the data set 'clean' and up to date? Avoid the hurt and embarrassment of trying to sell life insurance to the deceased; be wary of cheap or undated mailing lists.

Ensure, above all, that your data fields are in the correct sequence and that all of them are from the same record. When an organisation gets its 'name' fields and 'address' fields out of sequence, absolutely everyone – perhaps many thousands of customers – receives a letter with someone else's name on it!

EXERCISE 8D

Create a direct mail letter

Prepare your own direct mail letter, using one of the scenarios below. Prepare two versions. In the first version, highlight each point in the letter where information would be merged from a database file. This will obviously include the recipient's name and address, but should also involve the main body of your letter. Try to be as creative as possible. Specify precisely the contents of each record and field. The second version of your letter should be addressed to a specific recipient, showing how a finished letter would look. Prepare a note to accompany the sample letter, suggest how you might capture the data that has been used.

(a) You are an insurance company, wanting to promote a new financial services product, *'Golden Oldies'*, a pre-retirement savings plan for 45–65-year-olds in regular employment. You want to reach both new and existing customers.

(b) You are a high street retailer, moving into catalogue sales of your *'Sandale'* range of women's fashion shoes. You need to reach 20–35-year-old women in socio-economic categories ABC1.

(c) Your company manufactures *'Gripit'* original and replacement disc brakes for the motor industry. You need covering letters to accompany a product brochure, for distribution to all the major manufacturers and spare parts retailers.

8.6 ▓▓ Business stationery and letterhead design

Picture yourself opening a letter. What do you notice first? Before you read a word, you are likely to notice the quality of the **paper** and the design of the **letterhead**. Business stationery transmits important first impressions and gives you an opportunity to convey a positive, consistent image. There are promotional, practical and legal issues to consider.

(a) Promotional and practical aspects

The letterhead contains factual information, including: company name, business address, telephone, fax and e-mail numbers. However, recipients can also be influenced by design aspects, such as: the organisation's logo, use of colour, typeface and overall layout (see Chapter 4). When preparing or selecting a letterhead design, managers should not lose sight of some basic practical points:

- Is adequate space left for the letter?
- Are the address details still legible if a letter is photocopied or faxed?
- Is the design consistent with the organisation's other stationery and signage?
- Will the design look out-dated in five years' time?
- Are we likely to be changing address, telephone, fax or e-mail numbers soon?

It is essential to consider printing costs. The key factors here are the number of colours used, size of print run and choice of paper (see Appendix 3). Small print runs remain prohibitively expensive, despite advances in print technology. Against this, there is the danger of writing off store rooms full of unused stationery when your address details change. Some large, multi-site organisations print only the corporate logo on their stationery, with all the other details being added when the letters are printed out. In some cases, this is a more flexible and cost-effective solution.

(b) Statutory requirements

Most of the relevant UK legislation can be found in the Business Names Act, 1985 and the Companies Act, 1985. The law covers business signs, letterheads and other formal documentation, including written orders, invoices, receipts and demands for payment. The law is concerned with two main issues:

(i) Those business names that cannot be used
(ii) Disclosure of information on business ownership

These controls are designed to protect those who deal with a business from being misled or obstructed should they need to take subsequent legal action. For example, certain words cannot normally be used in the name of a business. These include: 'Royal', 'National' and 'University'. There are various disclosure requirements for business stationery and signs, depending on its legal structure:

- **Sole traders and Partnerships** If you trade under your own name, the Business Names Act, does not apply. If using a different business name, your own name(s) and address must be included on all documentation. Large partnerships, with more than 20 partners, are allowed to omit names of partners from their stationery, so long as a full list is available for inspection. You cannot list some but not all of the partners.

- **Companies** The Companies Act, 1985 requires that the following are disclosed on the letterhead:
  Full corporate name (indicating if it is a public or private limited company)
  Country or countries of registration
  Company registration number (issued by Companies House)
  Registered office address

Directors are not usually listed on the letterhead. If this is done then, as for partnerships, all must be included. In practice, these details are normally printed, in a small font size, at the bottom of the letterhead page. The registered office address is often different from the business address. It may be the corporate headquarters or, in the case of a smaller business, the office of its solicitor.

Statutory disclosure requirements: examples

Sole trader   **Red Revolution Records** (proprietor: F Smith)
34 High Street
Northtown
Northshire MI4 3QG

Partnership   **Lewis, Singh & Jones (Dental Surgeons)**
(*Partners: P Lewis, J Singh and KE Jones*)
654 Market Street
Northtown
Northshire MI3 8YP

Limited company **Molto Bene Pasta Houses**
Molto Bene House
56 New Lane Expressway
Northtown
Northshire M24 9LZ
... and in small type at the bottom of the page:
Molto Bene Pasta Houses Limited
Registered in England and Wales
Registration Number: 1234567
Registered Office: 45 Lion Terrace, London SE44 2XY

8.7 ■■ Chapter summary

- Business letters remain an important communication channel for a variety of purposes, though they do face competition from alternatives such as fax and e-mail.

- When selecting and using letters for your messages, it is important to bear in mind three features of this channel:
  It is 'one-way' and non-interruptible
  It involves a time delay between sending and receipt
  It provides a permanent record of the message

- Modern 'fully blocked' page layout and 'open' punctuation' makes it easy for anyone to produce professional-looking letters.

- Letters should be carefully structured, covering three areas: (a) establishing the context; (b) delivering your main message(s); (c) stating any action required.

- The style and content of any letter should aim to take account of the receiver and the purpose of your message. However, this is particularly difficult in the case of standard letters, such as notification of an overdraft. A polite but businesslike approach is usually appropriate.

- Direct mail offers the opportunity to create fairly customised letters in large quantities by combining wordprocessing and database techniques. However, without careful targeting and appropriate contents, it can become wasteful 'junk mail'.

- The design of business stationery can convey a positive image of your organisation. To achieve this, it is important to consider promotional, practical and legal aspects of the design. Since errors in these areas can be costly to correct, it is worth investing time in getting letterheads and other stationery right

Practical exercises

1. Knott-Underfoot – The sequel

(a) Re-read the promotional letter (Exercise 8a in Section 8.1), and highlight any errors in spelling, grammar, punctuation and layout.
(b) Re-draft the letter, correcting the errors identified in question (a).
(c) Draft a new letter, drawing on the lessons learnt in this chapter, as a more effective promotional vehicle for the company. You may wish to invent some incidental details.
(d) Produce another new letter, suitable for use as direct mail. Label all database fields clearly and attach examples to illustrate the field contents that would be used.

2. Stationery and letterhead design

Your boss, at a small manufacturing company or voluntary organisation, has asked you to re-design the office stationery. Invent a business name and all necessary details, including your address. Prepare a design to meet the promotional, practical and legal requirements discussed in this chapter. Draft a memo to your boss, requesting approval of the design and dealing with any production issues, such as the cost of printing and paper to be used.

Chapter nine

Reports, memos and briefings

*They have committed false report; moreover, they have
spoken untruths; secondarily, they are slanders; sixthly and
lastly, they have belied a lady; thirdly they have verified
unjust things; and to conclude, they are lying knaves*

Shakespeare's idea of a badly presented report, from *Much Ado About Nothing* (1598)

Objectives

- To discuss the uses of memoranda and e-mail, and identify the features of an effective message using these channels (9.1–9.2)

- To consider the different types of reports used in business and to introduce the requirements of a successful written report (9.3)

- To provide practical advice and experience in the three stages of report-writing: preparation, drafting and completion (9.4–9.6)

- To emphasise the importance of summarising skills, and provide practice in preparing executive summaries and briefings (9.7)

9.1 ▪▪ Introduction

This chapter considers the main forms of written communication used *within* an organisation: memos, reports and briefing papers. As with business letters (Chapter 8), care and practice is needed to structure the material logically. It is also important to refine your writing style in order to suit a particular audience and task. The following section deals with key elements of memos and e-mail messages. The focus then switches to report-writing techniques, including suggestions for improving the structure and content of your business reports. The chapter concludes with practical exercises and advice on the preparation of executive summaries and briefings – a vital management task.

9.2 ▪▪ Memos and e-mail messages: short and sweet

The memorandum or 'memo' is commonly used for short messages within an organisation. It has a wide variety of applications, and may be used to send messages between individuals or groups. 'Official' memos from company or departmental heads are used for internal announcements on issues such as pay, health and safety or security; this type of memo is often placed on the staff noticeboard for future reference. A memo format, with appropriate headings and sub-headings, is also used for some short business reports.

In many organisations, memos are being replaced by e-mail messages sent over the internal network or 'intranet'. Of course, e-mail is also widely used for external communication (Chapter 14). However, in this chapter we will consider its role as an 'electronic memo'. The layouts of a typical memo and equivalent internal e-mail message are set out below:

MULTI-TECH SERVICES EUROPE LIMITED

MEMORANDUM

To:	JOHN SMITH	Date:	4th Nov 199X
	AV Department		

From: Moira Jones   Copies: Mike Williams
        Press Office

Ref: VID098/JAS

Subject: **LOAN OF VIDEO EQUIPMENT – 11TH TO 15TH NOVEMBER**

Following our conversation today, I confirm our booking for the period Monday 11th to Friday 15th November inclusive. We will require the following items for the interview training sessions in room Q12:

- 1x VHS Camcorder and monitor
- 1x Tripod
- 5x VHS 240 minute cassettes
- 1x lighting unit
- 1x speaker's lectern

Please arrange for all equipment to be set up and tested by 09:00hrs Monday morning; call me on extension 5432 if you see any problems with the booking.

Figure 9.1 Typical memo format.

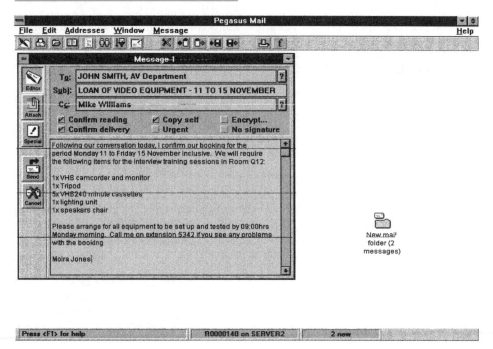

Figure 9.2 Typical e-mail format.

For reasons of consistency, businesses tend to have their own 'house style' for these documents. E-mail formats also vary depending on the software used. However, the following 'essential points' apply when drafting both memos and e-mails:

- **Subject headings** Include a brief, descriptive heading. Your receiver is probably scanning through a large quantity of memos or e-mail, so a heading can help them to spot important items.

- **No salutations required** Memos should be polite but brief, so you should omit the conventional salutations (i.e. '*Dear . . .*' and '*Yours faithfully / sincerely . . .*') that are found in business letters.

- **Signatures?** Some people like to sign or initial their memos. This is a useful way of ensuring that you have sent out the final version, and not an earlier draft. E-mail packages allow you to add address details as a kind of electronic signature.

- **Sensitive material?** If the contents is considered 'Personal' or 'Private and Confidential', note this on the memo or e-mail heading. A sensitive memo should be placed in a sealed envelope, which *also* needs to marked as appropriate. In a busy office, the most common lapse in confidentiality occurs when someone leaves a memo on the photocopier – it is very easy to do! Those receiving e-mail need to make other arrangements to ensure confidentiality. Your organisation will probably have a system of personal 'log-in' numbers and passwords to restrict access to your mailbox. However, if colleagues have access to your computer during the day, bear in mind that they may stumble across incoming mail.

- **State deadlines** If you require a response from the recipient, always state a reasonable, but specific deadline. This can be done politely, and may be reinforced with a brief explanation or incentive. For example: 'To guarantee a place, please confirm whether you will be attending before Wednesday 8th May.' Avoid vague statements such as '... *in due course* ...'. Recipients will interpret this as being a low priority item and are unlikely to reply. An 'urgent' heading can be effective in getting a response, so long as it is not used unnecessarily or too often.

- **Follow-ups** Unfortunately, there will be many memos and e-mails that do not receive a response first time. E-mail has the added advantage that senders can receive confirmation of reading, but it is still necessary to chase up those who do not reply.

EXERCISE 9A

Drafting memos and e-mail

Re-read the sample memo and e-mail message, illustrated above. Imagine that you are John Smith, from the AV department. Unfortunately, there are no video cameras available for Moira Jones's course, as one is being repaired and the other is on a three-week loan to Helen Brown in the Personnel department. You have the option of hiring another camera but the cost of this would have to be charged to the Press Office budget, requiring written confirmation from the department head. Draft a suitable reply:

(a) As a memorandum
(b) As an e-mail message

In practice, which communication channel would *you* prefer to use for this message? Give reasons for your choice.

9.4 ██ Business reports – types and purposes

Business reports come in all shapes and sizes:

- Written or oral
- Formal or informal
- Routine or original

- Single page or multi-volume
- 'In-house' or prepared by external consultants

Many companies use standardised formats for routine internal reports, such as a retailer's 'Weekly Sales Update'. In the following sections, we focus on how to write an **original** report, with relatively complex material presented in a formal way. The subject matter might be, for example, a new product proposal, office reorganisation plans or an industrial accident investigation.

Types of report: some practical examples

Executive briefing	The factory manager provides the managing director with a concise summary of the main issues and likely questions on health and safety prior to a shareholders' meeting when the issue is likely to be raised.
Research results	A market research executive at a food manufacturer is investigating a new ice cream. He presents the findings from a consumer taste panel to senior management.
Regular update	On a weekly basis, the management accountant of a major retail chain advises regional managers of their profitability performances by branch and geographic area.
Business proposal	An entrepreneur contacts a venture capital company to seek financial support (and offer of a possible equity stake) in her new leisure business. She provides them with a business plan to read before attending the verbal presentation.

The underlying principles of report writing are common to all types of document, so the advice given can be adapted to suit your particular purpose. Whatever type of report you are writing, there are three distinct production stages which are detailed in the following sections of this chapter:

(i) **preparation stage**
(ii) **drafting stage**
(iii) **completion stage**

9.3 ■■ Report writing: (i) preparation stage

A report is a kind of 'guided tour' through a jungle of ideas. It is important to plan your route in advance, but also to remain flexible; unforeseen changes are bound to arise once you get under way. To prepare successfully, it is worth asking some fundamental questions. Above all, clarify your terms of reference and establish which items really need to be included:

- **Initial questions** Before putting pen to paper, there are many basic questions to answer, regarding your prospective readers, your objectives, the context in which the report will be read and the sources that you plan to use:

Who am I writing for?	Named individual or a group of people?
	Aware or ignorant of the subject-matter?
	Positive, negative or neutral views?
What is my objective?	To inform the reader?
	To explain concepts?
	To persuade?
	To consult?
What is the context?	Urgent or important?
	Routine or original/'one-off'?
	Commercially/politically sensitive?
	'Stand-alone' or linked to a presentation?
What source material?	Is it readily available (e.g. location, confidentiality)?
	What quality is it (e.g. accurate, current, objective)?
	Are there any 'gaps' to fill?
	Do I need to do any primary research?

It is often tempting to skip or rush the planning stage, but poor preparation invariably causes time-consuming problems later on.

- **Terms of reference/project brief** One of the most common causes of bad report-writing is failure to obtain a clear brief. You may need to *revise* this brief as the work proceeds, but it is still important to *begin* with some clear objectives. As the following exercise demonstrates, people often find themselves struggling to extract a clear brief from their boss or client.

EXERCISE 9B

Terry Nebulous – getting a clear brief

Terry is the owner and managing director of Nebulous Electronics, a medium-sized manufacturing company. Terry is notorious for his vague instructions to staff, and he invariably complains whenever they produce something that fails to match his requirements. Read the following selection, taken from Terry's recent requests' and:

(a) note what you think is wrong with each of the briefs;
(b) redraft them to overcome the problems you have identified, inventing and inserting any necessary details.

1. *'Sally, sorry to interrupt your lunch. I need a report on the Blue Whale Engineering deal. Lots of graphs and things. Do us something impressive looking; it's for the Board of Directors . . . Anyway, enjoy the lasagne, I'll leave you to it.'*

> 2. *E-mail to Yusef (Treasury Manager): I need something on our main suppliers . . . you know, financial ratios and things. Can you bash it out for me, pronto? Terry.*
>
> 3. *'Is that Kay? Hello, Terry here. Sorry to bother you at the weekend. Look, I've just seen an OUTRAGEOUS article in the 'Sunday Enquirer'. A load of unscientific media hype about pollution! Kay, I want the facts. Can you please draft me a full-scale report, showing just how "green" and responsible we are at Nebulous Electronics?'*

- **What to include in the report** The next preparatory task is to collate the material you are going to use in the report. In a large report, selecting *relevant* information from an ever-growing pile of possibilities is often the main problem. Diagramming can be a useful tool (see Exercise 2C) to separate the 'forest' from the 'trees'. By writing out the topics to be covered on a whiteboard or large sheet of paper, you can uncover **logical links** between topic areas and identify **key points**. These should help to provide an outline structure for the written report.

9.4 ■■ Report writing: (ii) drafting stage

How do you approach the task of writing? Some people can settle down and write out an extended piece of text from beginning to end. However, for most of us, writing is a more gradual process, with many revisions and redraftings on the way to a finished article. Whatever your approach, there are three 'secrets' to successful drafting; organise the material, make the structure visible and use tables or figures where appropriate.

(a) Organise the material

A report is like a new building; it needs to have a clearly defined **structure** in place before any interior fixtures are installed. Start to organise the material once your initial preparation is complete, but *before* you begin to draft lots of text. Identify what the main sections and sub-sections are likely to be, and consider the order in which each topic should be placed. Ordering is a matter of judgement and there are a number of logical alternatives to consider, as illustrated below. If you are unsure which order to adopt, it is worth experimenting with the alternatives; some are bound to work better than others. In making a choice, you should always ask yourself: *Which sequence is most appropriate for the **material** being presented and for the **reader** who has to absorb it?*

Getting a report in order: the main alternatives

Order based on	Practical example
Importance	In a report entitled '*10 challenges for UK industry in the new century*', the three factors considered *vital* to future prosperity are covered before, and in more detail than, the other seven.
Urgency	The survey of a newly acquired building begins by identifying a leaky roof that needs to be repaired immediately, and moves on to discuss less urgent, longer-term maintenance work. Note that urgency is *not* the same thing as importance.
Date/Chronology	A progress report on a civil engineering project describes events over the past year period in date order. The educational background and employment history sections of a CV are usually written in **reverse** chronological order, with the most recent items first.
Simple to complex	The documentation supplied with an accountancy training course begins with the basic concepts of book-keeping before explaining more advanced topics, such as accounting adjustments and ratio analysis.
Global to specific	A report into a company's absenteeism problems starts by looking at broad social factors, gradually narrowing down to causes within particular factories and departments (nb: the opposite sequence, specific to global, may work equally well).

(b) Make the structure visible – use 'signposts'

Have you ever considered how other people might approach the task of *reading* your report? Do you expect them to sit down with a nice cup of tea and work their way religiously from the first letter to the last full stop? In practice, most managers begin by 'scanning' a report, absorbing the overall look of the piece and pausing over the occasional heading or bullet point. Bearing this in mind, you can help the reader by inserting some well-lit signposts. Use headings and sub-headings to guide the reader. These signposts also send a positive message, suggesting a competently drafted and valuable document. By contrast, poor signposting will give readers a poor first impression of your report. The contents page and index, section headings, numbering and typography are all useful signposts. Well-placed graphics, such as charts and photographs, can also help to emphasise the main subject areas.

* **Contents page and index** The contents page provides an overview of the entire report. An important signposting feature, it should be included in any report of more than five or six pages. A contents page lists section numbers and headings, with their respective *first* page numbers. Sub-section details may also be included. Indexes, which are only required in long reports, can be generated using the relevant function on most wordprocessing software.

- **Section headings and numbering** Keep headings short and to the point, making clear what material that section or sub-section contains. In formal reports, decimal numbering systems are normally used alongside the heading. Some legal and scientific reports writers may use up to four levels of sub-section, so that 'Section 1.9.3.1' is followed by 'Section 1.9.3.2', etc. This can be useful when it is necessary to refer to specific sections of text. However, multiple sub-sections can become confusing, for the report writer as well as the reader. In business reports, the numbering is best kept simple, using no more than three levels. If further levels are required you can switch to bullet points or lists based on lower case letters or Roman numerals ('a, b, c, d ...' or, 'i, ii, iii, iv ...').

- **Changing type** Bold text and larger font sizes can be used to identify the main section headings. You can also use upper case and lower case letters to create a logical 'hierarchy' of headings and sub-headings. This hierarchy should descend from larger font sizes to smaller, upper case to lower case or emboldened text to unemboldened text. In addition, it is important to use the structure consistently throughout the report. In the days when most reports were produced on a typewriter, underlining was commonly used for this purpose. However, in most wordprocessed reports it has been replaced by emboldened text, as illustrated below:

Good typography – a simple 'hierarchy' makes titles clear

Chapter title	**12**	**FIELD RESEARCH RESULTS**
Main heading	**12.1**	**INTRODUCTION**
	12.2	**REGIONAL BREAKDOWN**
Sub-headings	**12.2.1**	**East Anglia region**
	12.2.2	**South West region**
Lower levels		(a) Consumer sample
		(b) Producer sample

Structuring a typical business report

Title page	Your title should, like the rest of the report, be clear, concise and unambiguous. Writers commonly use a short 'main' title, followed by a longer explanatory sub-title (e.g. *'Project Equinox: a first year progress report'*). You may also include the author's name and publication date.
Executive summary	A summary should distil the *entire* contents of the report into a few words, providing busy executives with the essence of the report 'at a glance'; they can then decide

whether or not it is relevant to their needs. This is not to be confused with the introduction, which serves a different purpose.

Introduction

The purpose of an introduction is to lead the reader into the report. Like all 'reception areas', it should be welcoming. It may include the 'terms of reference', and/or the reasons for writing the report. Introductions are used to *'tell'em what you're gonna tell'em'*. However, this should be brief, otherwise you may pre-empt the rest of the report.

Main section(s)

The 'main body of the report', is divided into various logical sections and sub-sections. Help the reader to 'cross the borders' of each section by inserting some 'linking text', leading them out of one topic and into the next.

Conclusion

Here, the key arguments and/or findings of the report are drawn together and put in context. The concluding section should also relate back to the original objectives of the report (nb: this provides a useful check that you have met them all). NEVER PUT 'NEW' MATERIAL IN THE CONCLUSION. Any 'last-minute' findings must be either fully integrated into the text, or reported separately. If you simply 'tack them on' to the conclusions, your reader is likely to be confused and annoyed.

Recommendations

These may be combined with the Conclusion, and should always flow logically from it. For example, you might suggest a preferred option from several that were under consideration, make new proposals or recommend further research.

References

If external information sources are used, it is helpful to provide details for the reader. Academic research papers have full Bibliographies (listing books and other sources used) and referencing within the text (e.g. *'Kropotkin (1995) states that . . .'* or, *'. . . as suggested by recent studies (Schmidt & Jones, 1992a) . . .'*). However, references can 'clog up' the text, making it cumbersome to read. Hence, in business reports, referencing is usually kept to a minimum.

Appendices

Use the appendices for detailed data and analytical material that some readers are likely to need but which would obstruct the flow of your argument if inserted earlier. Do not use them to 'pad out' a report or to show how much research material you have collected; unlike the *human* appendix, they must be there for a purpose!

(c) Use tables and figures

Wherever possible, summarise your analysis or findings in the form of tables or figures. Tables are a block of figures set out in the form of labelled rows and columns; figures can include anything from a photograph or line drawing to a pie chart, summarising statistical data. A table is more concise than the same data presented as continuous text. However, a well-designed graphic and can be even more focused and revealing (see Chapter 4). You should position tables and figures as close as possible to the relevant section in the report, but to avoid confusing the reader they must always follow rather than precede that section. Include a brief reference in brackets, such as ' *An artists impression of the new staff restaurant has been prepared (Figure 18.3)* . . .'. This helps the reader to link the text of your report to the correct figure or table.

Table 1.1   Lager drinkers: by age group

Age band (years)	Sample size (number)	Sample size (percentage)
18–25	50	18.5
26–35	90	33.3
36–45	60	22.2
46–55	40	14.8
56–65	20	7.4
65+	10	3.7
	270	100.0

Source: Bacchus Institute (1996)

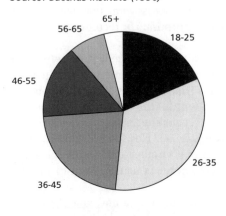

Lager drinkers: by age group
(Sample size: 270)

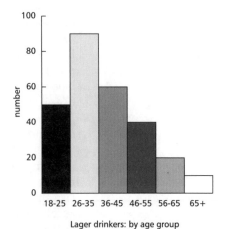

Lager drinkers: by age group
(Sample size: 270)

Figure 9.3   Data can be presented in the form of a table (above), or as a figure. Note the different impressions given by the pie chart (below left) and the bar chart (below right).

9.5 ▪▪ Report writing: (iii) completion stage

When you have been working on a report for a long time, it is difficult to judge it objectively. Be sure to get an independent opinion of the contents and format of your report before it is finalised. Ideally, you should ask a colleague or friend to read it through. They can then provide constructive criticism and ensure that it is readable. The software company *Microsoft* describe this review process as '*checking with Brad's mom*'; they ask themselves whether the mother of one of their executives would readily understand it. The next best alternative is to re-read the report yourself. Try to put it aside for a week, or at least a few days, since a period away from the material will give you a more realistic perspective. Another trick is to find a secluded spot and read sections of the report aloud. This simple technique is very effective at highlighting any unclear or long-winded passages.

In long, complex and multi-authored reports, it is very difficult to produce clear and consistent prose. The most common errors are:

- **Variable grammar** Agree at the outset, and then stick to, either present or past tense and either active or passive voice. The shortest and most direct style, present tense and active voice, is preferable in most business reports. See Chapter 3 and Appendix 1 for more details.

- **Incorrect cross-references** When a section is added or deleted during the drafting process, it is easy to forget to change earlier references to numbered sections in the text. Either use the referencing system on your wordprocessor, or leave your cross-referencing until the final draft stage.

- **Inconsistent style and labelling** If the report is being written by more than one person, appoint one of them to be the overall 'sub-editor', tidying up the differences in writing style, labelling of figures and tables, referencing system, etc.

- **Spelling errors** In long reports, proof-reading becomes very time-consuming. The 'spell-check' facilities, built into current wordprocessing packages are very powerful. However, you cannot rely on them exclusively as they are not yet clever enough to spot incorrect but similar-sounding words. For example, '*Kevin is a soul trader*' remains mis-spelt even though Kevin is an owner-manager rather than a disciple of Satan. Allowing your spell-checker to correct the text automatically is fatal, since it is replaces mis-keyed and unrecognised words with meaningless substitutes (e.g. the noun 'payphone' converts itself into 'puffin', offering ample opportunity for surrealist report writers).

9.6 ▪▪ Summarising: a vital business skill

Modern technology has made everyone vulnerable to 'information overload'. Top decision makers are increasingly reliant on 'executive summaries' and briefing papers, prepared by others. One vital characteristic of a successful manager is the ability to select and focus on key information, to get to the heart of a complex issue. The following six-point plan should help you to draft concise but accurate summaries of written material:

1. **Be sure of your brief** Do you need to summarise everything in a document (or collection of documents)? Does your recipient have a particular topic of interest? What level of knowledge is assumed?

2. **Read source material thoroughly** Do you understand the main themes and the structure of any arguments? Are you able to distinguish between reliable sources and more dubious ones (e.g. an objective, validated research study versus the unsubstantiated opinion of 'a person on a bus').

3. **Identify the key points** If the material is well written, each paragraph should contain a number of clearly identifiable points. Separate each major point from the supporting material that usually follows it – a yellow 'highlighter' pen is a useful tool for this task. Mark only those points that are relevant to your brief. Some of the material may be incredibly interesting, but if it is not required by the person reading your summary, leave it out. If you have a number of source documents, prepare 'key point' summaries of each, before moving to the next stage.

4. **Compose a rough draft** Keep the '*KISS*' principles in mind, outlined in Section 3.2, as you begin to write. Prepare the text in plain English, based around the key points and cutting out any supporting material. This includes all sentences beginning '*For example ...*' and all detailed statistics. Consider using simple graphics, a useful form of shorthand that reduces the word length and makes material easier to assimilate.

5. **Check draft against source material** Double check any facts and figures that you have copied from the source documents. Ensure that you have covered all of the areas specified in the brief and omitted any topics that were not specified. Re-read the whole draft summary. Does its overall 'balance' reflect that of the original source(s)? In other words, have you reflected the different arguments or perspectives equally?

6. **Prepare final version** With careful editing you may be able to shave off a few more words, omitting any repetition or 'waffle'. However, unless a 'note' or 'bullet point' format has been specified, you should retain full sentences and correct grammar. Finally, read it out to yourself to ensure that it flows smoothly. Practice and perfect this skill. It is an excellent way to demonstrate your 'star potential' to employers and clients!

EXERCISE 9D

Briefings and bullets – summarising skills

You have been asked to prepare **two** summaries based on either:

(a) the contents of Chapter 6 of this text book;
(b) a recent article from a journal or trade magazine, of 2,500 words or more.

One version should be a 'briefing' for the Sales Director, to fit on a single side of A4 paper, covering all the main arguments in plain English, using a 12-point font size; the other version should be in the form of 'bullet points', suitable for printing on a maximum of two overhead projector (OHP) transparencies.

9.7 ▪▪ Chapter summary

• Memos and e-mail are ideal for short internal messages (though e-mail can also be used externally). Keep the contents concise but assist the reader with subject headings, references and clearly stated deadlines.

• There is a wide range of report types, and writers need to adapt structure and writing style to suit the readership and topic area.

• The three stages in report writing are: preparation, drafting and completion.

• At the preparation stage, a clear brief is essential.

• At the drafting stage, writers need to consider logical sequence, ways of making the structure visible and use of figures and tables to summarise material.

• At the completion stage, proof-reading and an independent perspective are important. Ensure that grammar and writing style are consistent. Check cross-referencing.

• Summaries and briefing papers are widely used in business, and the techniques are worth practising.

Practical exercises

1. Reports & summaries

Select a business-related topic (or use one provided by your tutor). Prepare the following documents, based on this topic:

• A 2,000-word 'long' report, with contents page, executive summary, referencing and bibliography. Include tables and figures where appropriate.

• A 500-word 'short' report, suitable for use as a briefing document. Imagine that your boss had to give public talk on the topic and needed some background material.

* A bullet-point summary, suitable for use as an OHP transparency.

2. Presenting data in a report – images replacing words

Obtain sufficient raw data from one of the following sources to construct a report:

* Results from a questionnaire survey
* Financial accounts from a company report
* Technical data from a scientific report

Write a short report (maximum 1,000 words, include a word count). Prepare suitable business graphics (with headings, axes and legends fully labelled) to illustrate the data you have selected. Try to use graphics wherever possible in place of explanatory text. See Chapter 4 for guidance on business graphics. Refer to 'Further Reading' on page 000 for additional texts on statistics and data presentation.

Chapter ten

Making presentations

Your brain starts working from the moment you are born and never stops, until you stand up to speak in public

Sir George Jessel

Objectives

- To identify special characteristics and requirements of a business presentation (10.2)

- To learn how to prepare yourself, particularly voice and posture, and your materials in advance of the presentation (10.3–10.4)

- To identify and practice the best methods of remembering what to say (10.4)

- To consider advantages and disadvantages of various audio-visual aids (10.5)

- To develop a checklist on how to deal with the day itself, deliver the presentation and deal with any questions or disruptions (10.6–10.8)

10.1 ▄▄ Introduction

Students find themselves on the receiving end of many presentations. However, any request to *deliver* a presentation invariably causes a major panic. This dread of addressing an audience is also common amongst experienced managers. They often resort to reading out prepared scripts, and their audience sits through a dry and monotonous performance that communicates little. This chapter aims to help you improve public speaking and related presentation skills. It includes advice on preparing yourself and your materials in advance, using audio visual equipment and handling an audience successfully.

10.2 ▄▄ What makes presentations different?

The fundamental feature of this communication channel is *physical presence*; the sender and the receivers are together, in one room. Confronted with this, presenters often feel vulnerable and exposed. However, when giving a presentation, you are actually in a position of considerable power. There are few forms of communication where your audience is so entirely 'captive'. For example, in contrast to someone *reading* a report in their office or at home, those on the receiving end of a presentation cannot easily:

- Stop or 'pause' the communication flow
- Return to or re-read an earlier part of the message
- Scan through and skip ahead to the end

As members of your audience, they can do these things only by disrupting the presentation for everyone else. Most people, other than a few thick-skinned hecklers and strong-minded bosses, experience strong group pressure to 'sit tight' until the end of a talk. However, it is not enough just to have them tied to their seats. You also need to ensure that they are **willing** and **able** to absorb your message:

- **Willing to receive?** This is a useful point to review the material on persuasive communication (Chapter 5). Consider the best ways of securing the attention of your audience and holding their interest through the presentation. Whilst you may not want too many questions, these are a useful way of maintaining interest and involvement.

- **Able to receive?** Since audiences have little or no control over the information flow, it is important to allow pauses between your main points, avoiding 'information over-load'. Provide a clear framework at the beginning, frequent reviews as you proceed and a brief summary at the end.

The chapter goes on to consider the practicalities of delivering a presentation. However, there are two essential preliminaries: preparing yourself and your material.

10.3 ■■ Preparing your material

Though it uses some different media, a presentation shares many of the features of a written report, and often serves a similar purpose (e.g. briefing, reporting results, making proposals). As a result, the preparation process is similar, whether you are communicating in writing or using the spoken word. Sections 10.3 and 10.4 outline the five main stages in preparing the material. These can be summarised as follows:

1. Answer the 'basic' questions (audience? objective? context? source?)
2. Clarify your terms of reference / project brief
3. Decide what to include and what to cut out
4. Decide how to organise the material
5. Make the logical structure visible

If your presentation is going to be accompanied by a **written report**, ensure that the written version *complements* what you are saying rather than simply repeating it. Decide in advance whether to circulate the written report before or after the presentation, and structure the event accordingly. If your audience has already had a chance to read your report, the presentation provides an opportunity for discussion and focusing on specific issues of interest. However, if a report is distributed afterwards, the presentation may work best as 'broad brush' introduction to the topic, with the written report providing supporting detail. Incidentally, distributing the report at the start of your presentation is usually fatal – people will read it instead of listening to you!

Sound preparation of the material is, of course, essential to the success of your presentation. However, you should put just as much effort into preparing **yourself** for the occasion. This is especially true if you are new to presenting. Few of us are born business presenters. Fortunately, there are some useful 'tricks of the trade' that can help to make the whole thing more enjoyable, for presenters and audiences alike.

EXERCISE 10A

Presentation skills – self-assessment and critique

(a) Think back to the most recent talk or presentation you *delivered*. How did it go? What do you feel were your main strengths and weaknesses? What areas would you most like to improve?

(b) Now think of the most recent talk or presentation you *attended* as a member of the audience. How well did the speaker communicate his/her messages? Were you clear about the structure and objectives of the presentation? In what ways could the speaker's performance have been improved?

If you are working in a **group**, discuss your experiences in (a) and (b). What are the major presentation strengths and weaknesses within the group? How do these compare to those of the presenters you have listened to recently?

10.4 ▮▮ Preparing yourself: posture, voice and memory

Many people, who are happy to spend hours perfecting a pie chart on the computer, fail to invest more than five minutes on the most important communication tool of all; themselves. Like athletes, presenters need a training schedule to reach competition standard. In this section we work on three critical areas, the way people stand in front of an audience, the way they speak and how they manage to remember what to say.

(a) Looking right: posture and clothes

You are sending out messages from the moment your audience catches sight of you. These visual messages are based on your physical appearance, including your

Figure 10.1 Desperate measures add some sparkle to the finance director's presentation.

posture and even the clothes you wear. Many speakers adopt a head down, round-shouldered stance when addressing an audience (Figure 10.2). This has two negative effects. Firstly, the voice is projected into the floor, making it inaudible. Secondly, the speaker has minimal eye contact with the audience. These are basically **defensive** postures. Others include leaning on one foot, trying to blend in with the background, and folding the arms tightly across the chest to protect the 'soft underbelly' from attack. These postures usually have a negative impact on an audience. They signal, however unintentionally, that the speaker is hostile, ill-prepared or disinterested in the topic. If you want to communicate clear, confident and positive messages, it is essential to stand (or to sit) in a way that re-inforces them. Your body needs to be:

- upright and well balanced
- stable but not static
- reasonably relaxed!

Achieving this requires some practice, either in class or at home (see Exercise 10c below). After a few attempts, you should feel – and will certainly be perceived as – much more confident, positive and alert.

Figure 10.2 Common presentation errors. This unfortunate presenter is making a number of serious, but all too common, mistakes. Firstly, he is trying to read from his own OHP transparencies, rather than cuecards. As a result, he has lost eye contact with the audience and his voice is projected downwards rather than ahead. Secondly, he is blocking the projected image by standing behind the projector and between his audience and screen. Thirdly, there is his personal appearance. Few audiences will be impressed with the unshaven look, and the shirt is unlikely to help!

Your **clothes** can also help to project the right image as well as increasing self-confidence. However, there are no hard-and-fast rules. In the past, some companies had notoriously strict dress codes, but today there is much greater variety. As in all areas of communication, you may want to consider your what messages your clothes are going to communicate to a particular audience. For example, the same expensive suit could impress a group of overseas investors, but alienate an employee group who are being briefed about a cost-cutting programme. Having weighed up the argument, you might just decide to dress in the way that you prefer!

EXERCISE 10B

Look confident, feel confident

(i) **The 'before' test** Walk to the front of a class or meeting room and introduce yourself to your colleagues as though you were beginning a presentation on a topic of your choice (a 30-second introduction will be sufficient).

(ii) **The practice session** Make a conscious effort to stand upright, with both feet flat on the floor. Loosen up your head and shoulders; gently 'shake out' any tension in your neck and arms so that you are not standing there like a mannequin! Settle down with your shoulders back, your head centred and your chin up. Breathe slowly and deeply before you begin to speak.

(iii) You should notice the following improvements:

Your lung capacity is increased, so your voice is more resonant

Your voice projects impressively, and is not lost in the floor

You have better eye contact with your audience rather than the floor tiles

You feel happier and more 'in control' of the situation

(iv) **Consult the audience** Did they perceive you as more confident and competent, second time around? Check whether you 'over-did' the upright stance. It will *feel* very strange to you at first, but should *look* perfectly normal to them. Continue practising until you reach a happy compromise. If possible, make a video recording to demonstrate the 'before and after' effect.

(b) Developing your voice

Though our voices are in regular use every day, they are not always ready for the tougher demands of a business presentation. In contrast to informal one-to-one conversations, the presenter has to speak:

- for an extended period
- in a fairly structured way
- to many different people simultaneously

Voices are rarely inherently weak, but in many cases they are seriously under-used. A poorly prepared speaker will be mistreating an incredible piece of machinery, breaking the speed limit in his or her vocal 'sports car' without leaving first gear. To use the voice effectively, we need a basic understanding of how it functions.

EXERCISE 10C

Vocal mechanics

The preceding section places a lot of emphasis on the physical aspects of speech. Does it really make so much difference? Read the following sentence out loud:

Speech is an extremely complex cognitive and mechanical process which is probably unique to the human species.

Now try the sentence again: (a) Without closing your mouth; (b) Without moving your tongue; (c) Whilst pinching your nostrils shut.

These extreme cases help to highlight some very common weaknesses found in a 'poor' speaking voice. Most voices can be improved by a combination of deeper breathing (for better tone and projection) and more active use of the mouth, which really does need to be opened and closed! In addition, movements of the tongue help to ensure that individual words are spoken clearly. The objective is not to abandon your local accent, but simply to upgrade your voice for the greater demands of public speaking.

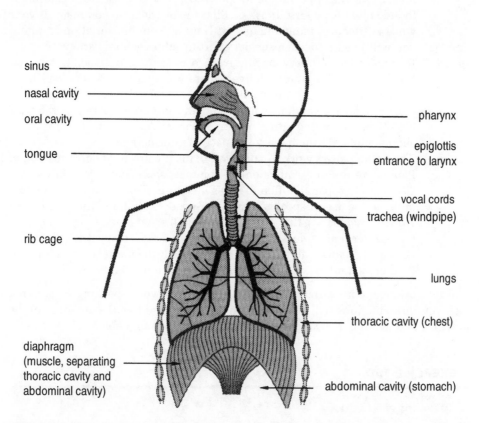

sinus

nasal cavity

oral cavity

tongue

rib cage

diaphragm
(muscle, separating
thoracic cavity and
abdominal cavity)

pharynx

epiglottis
entrance to larynx

vocal cords
trachea (windpipe)

lungs

thoracic cavity (chest)

abdominal cavity (stomach)

Figure 10.3 The vocal system. When breathing in, you draw fresh air into your lungs by tightening the diaphragm, normally an unconscious action. Breathing out is a reversal of this process; the muscles relax and air flows out through the narrow trachea. Here, the air passing over the vocal chords causes them to vibrate. These vibrations are amplified in the hollow areas of the mouth, pharynx and sinuses and shaped into different words by movements of your mouth, tongue and teeth.

Having considered how the voice is generated, and how posture affects it, you can begin to make tangible improvements in your overall public speaking performance. There are four main dimensions to consider – volume, pitch, speed and pauses:

Volume Speakers are more often too quiet than too loud. Clearly, the volume level has to suit the venue and size of your audience, but it is the *speaker's* responsibility to ensure that everyone can hear clearly. Key points can be emphasised with *either* an increase or a decrease in volume, just as upper case letters or italics are used in a written report.

Pitch Your natural voice may be a shrill *soprano* or deep *bass*, but you can still use variations in your tonal range to good effect. In general, you convey a more 'positive' message when your sentences end on a higher note. Doing the opposite sounds down-beat and depressing. It is difficult to judge this for yourself; ask a colleague or friend to comment. If your voice is literally 'monotonous', with no perceptible variation in pitch, you will need to make a special effort to achieve more variety.

Speed The major fault of nervous and excited presenters is speaking too fast. However, painfully slow deliveries are an equally serious obstacle to good communication, especially when combined with a monotonous voice! To keep an audience interested, the best option is to vary the pace of delivery, avoiding either of the extremes. Try a mixture of long and short sentences to help vary the pace of your delivery.

Pauses 'Dramatic' pauses work equally well in the theatre and conference room. Pauses are the oral equivalent of commas, semi-colons and full stops. Use them to separate different ideas, to emphasise a point, and to allow both audience and speaker that much-needed 'thinking time'. It is also worth remembering that a single pause will seem much longer to you as a presenter than it does to your audience. A skilled speaker will 'milk' the pause, using it to build eye contact with the audience or adding to its dramatic effect by moving from one position to another.

Aim to introduce more variety into all four aspects of your speaking voice. That way, your presentations will be much more powerful, holding the attention of the audience and making their underlying messages more memorable.

EXERCISE 10D

Speaking with variety

Trying to add more variety into your speaking voice can feel very strange and uncomfortable at first. To increase your confidence, repeat Exercise 10b in private. Record yourself as you make the 30-second presentation, sitting in a chair. Rewind and listen to the tape. Now repeat the presentation using the same words, but making deliberate use of pauses and variations in volume, pitch and speed. Listen to the replay again. Make the presentation a third time, standing up, as if addressing an audience, and exaggerating these variations as far as you can. Play all three recordings in sequence and compare their impact as if you were the listener.

(c) Remembering what to say

A stage actor's greatest fear is 'drying up', losing track and forgetting what to say next. There are four main options for the business presenter: reading a prepared script, memorising a script, improvising on the day or using a system of key words and cue cards. Only the final option, key words, is recommended for regular use:

- **Reading it out** Nervous speakers often make the mistake of reading from a script. With rare exceptions, this tactic results in a head-down, zero eye contact, monotonous dirge! Politicians and business leaders only *appear* spontaneous thanks to sophisticated technology and training. Former actor Ronald Reagan pioneered the use of two glass screens, either side of the podium, each of which projects the script from an **autocue**. By glancing from one screen to the other, speakers give the impression of simply turning to address each side of the hall.

- **Memorising** A few exceptionally gifted speakers can memorise their text as though it was the script of a play. However, in a business context, a memorised speech can easily sound artificial. It is also an inflexible system, and you can be caught out when the presentation is opened up to questions. Unassisted memorising is not a practical option for most people.

- **Improvising** This is a valuable technique for informal occasions, such as witty speeches at the office Christmas lunch. It is also necessary, and occasionally quite impressive, during question and answer ('Q&A') sessions, where the audience has an opportunity to keep you on your toes. In fact, most apparent improvisation is based on a lot of preparatory work. For example, it is worth having some ready-made responses to any questions or counter-arguments that are likely to arise from your presentation.

- **Key (or 'trigger') words** This is the most practical option for most business presenters. You should still *prepare* your material in a fairly detailed way, particularly where there is an accompanying written report. However, having become immersed in the subject, you can 'trigger' your recall using a short list of words or phrases. These can be written on a series of **cue cards**, usually postcard-sized, and tied together in the top right-hand corner in case you drop them on the floor. Alternatively, you can project the key words as 'bullet points' displayed via overhead projector ('OHP') transparencies or a computer-based display. These have the dual benefit of providing a reminder for you and re-inforcing the main points for your audience.

10.5 ▮▮ Audio visual aids

Audio-visual (AV) materials are an aid but not a cure. Well-produced AV materials can enhance a good verbal presentation but they cannot salvage an awful one! More importantly, AV-related errors, break-downs and crises are often the downfall of an otherwise capable presenter. The best advice is to plan and prepare your AV materials in advance, but not at the expense of preparing the most important AV resource, which is **yourself** (see 10.3 to 10.4 above). In the following sections, the main AV technologies available today are outlined. Each has its strengths, weaknesses and peculiarities. It is therefore worth experimenting so that you can select between a range of equipment and use your preferred alternative effectively.

Audio-visual equipment guide

- **Overhead projector** Can be used for prepared transparencies (text, illustrations and even photographs) and for writing 'live'. Liquid crystal (LCD) panels can be used to project images directly from a computer, though the display quality of some systems remains disappointing. Make sure that the text on your transparencies is large enough to be visible from the back of the meeting room. Use colour, wherever possible. *Weaknesses/user errors*: (1) Standing in front of the screen; (2) talking to the projector instead of your audience; (3) leaving OHP on once you have finished using it; (4) projecting your shaky hands as you point to an item on the slide; (5) not checking that all of the text on the slide is being projected; (6) OHP bulb failure – make sure there is a spare bulb in the projector or in your pocket.

- **Whiteboard** Useful in discussion and 'brainstorming' sessions, for building up diagrams, etc. Make use of coloured pens (e.g. alternating colours when writing a list on the board). A new breed of 'electronic' whiteboards allow the presenter to capture written material directly on to a stand alone or networked personal computer. *Weaknesses/user errors*: (1) Turning your back to the audience whilst writing on the board – practice writing 'from the side' whilst facing forwards; (2) illegible writing, also requires practice; (3) dried-out pens – make sure you have a functioning set available; (4) using indelible pens by mistake, making you very unpopular with the next user.

- **Flip chart** Can be used for pre-prepared sheets or for writing 'live'. Useful for group work (e.g. where your audience have an active role, preparing a flip chart sheet in a small group and bringing this back to the front; sheets can also be retained and pinned up around the room for future reference). You can impress an audience by preparing flip chart diagrams, etc. beforehand in pencil, so that you can quickly 'ink them in' during the presentation. *Weaknesses/user errors*: Similar to those for the whiteboard, plus the problem of removing paper and returning to previous flip chart pages; this is a matter of practice.

- **Video player/video projector** Short video 'clips' can be very useful to illustrate a point, but extended video playback is a waste of the 'live' aspect of your presentation. *Weaknesses/user errors*: Various technical problems can and do occur, usually due to faulty set-up of the equipment or tampering by other presenters. The most common problems include missing cables, players set to 'NTSC' instead of 'PAL' format and tapes running at different recording speeds. Always double-check in advance.

- **35mm slide projector** The traditional choice for highly visual presentations where image quality is a key issue. The drawbacks are inflexibility (slides are in a set order, within a 'carousel' container) and the preparation time required to design and process slides. *Weaknesses/user errors*: (1) Slides always seem to get out of order, upside down or back to front, so always check them yourself; (2) spelling mistakes cannot be altered at short notice; (3) projector bulb failures – make sure there is a spare.

- **Computer-based projector/display** Presentation software programs, such as *CorelDraw* are rapidly replacing 35mm slides, a process that will accelerate as digital cameras become more affordable. This software has all the benefits of wordprocessing programs, allowing relatively inexperienced users to produce 'professional' materials. *Weaknesses/user errors*: (1) Spelling errors can still slip in unnoticed; (2) software crashes and hardware failures can leave the presenter with no 'manual' back-up. Experience suggests that (until the technology is perfected) it is best to have hard copy OHPs just in case.

- **Props and 'take aways'** Liven up a presentation by introducing a 'prop'. These come in all shapes and sizes, including: food samples, scale models of a building development, fashion models, etc. In some cases, you may be able to provide the audience with an information pack to take away; this could include supporting details, a written report or a 'goodies bag' of samples. A well-chosen prop can act as a powerful persuader, re-inforcing your verbal messages. *Weaknesses/user errors*: (1) Handing out material at the beginning of a presentation; the audience look at it instead of listening to you.

10.6 ▪▪ On the day itself

Let us assume a 'worst case' scenario: you are giving an important presentation to a large audience of colleagues, senior managers and international visitors at an overseas hotel venue you have never seen before. How can you maximise your chances of success and minimise the risks of a disaster?

(a) ***Check the venue*** There are a number of basic practical questions to ask. Which room are you in? Is it well sign-posted? Are there enough chairs? Is the ventilation and lighting adequate? Is tea or coffee scheduled? You can check with staff at the venue beforehand, but always be sure to see the room for yourself at the earliest opportunity.

(b) **Check the equipment & materials** Again, the rule of experienced presenters is *never* to rely on others. Check for yourself whether the AV equipment is working properly. Is the projector focused? Do you have spare bulbs? Are your slides in order and the right way up? Is the video recorder set to the right channel? Is the software compatible? Are the power sockets the same shape and voltage? (see the AV equipment guide).

(c) **Check your appearance** Try to leave enough time for last-minute grooming, especially if you have spent the previous hour lugging AV equipment about. Find a suitable mirror! Do you look reasonably smart and relaxed?

(d) **Make a good entrance** This is likely to be the time when you are most nervous, but, unfortunately, first impressions do count. Before your presentation, breathe deeply: it is remarkably calming and it improves your voice. Do *not* rush into your first sentence. Look slowly and calmly around your audience, establish eye contact with everyone and **smile**. In that instant, you can communicate strong, positive messages before you have uttered a word. Allow everybody to settle down, and adjust to your being 'centre stage'. If someone has just introduced you, thank the person concerned briefly, focus on your **audience** and move into your 'opener', the first stage in your presentation.

Beating stage fright: 'fight or flight' syndrome

Why do some of us always get in such a state before a speech or class presentation? Because our brain and body are trying to prepare us for an imminent crisis. This 'fight or flight' response was essential when people lived in caves, had to catch their own supper and were in constant danger from wild animals or neighbours. However, its adrenaline-induced symptoms (heightened senses, excessive sweating, temporary memory loss and an urgent need to urinate) are particularly *unhelpful* in a packed conference hall. With practice it is possible to overcome stage fright, or at least minimise its symptoms. Make sure you have rehearsed the speech and are familiar with any audio-visual aids. On the day, a combination of controlled slow breathing and positive thinking are most effective. Avoid stimulants like coffee, for obvious reasons, and try to steer clear of the bar. Alcohol is a depressant, reducing activity in the central nervous system. In small quantities it may help to relieve anxiety, but drinking also slows the reactions, impairing your overall performance. Instead, find a quiet corner and try to visualise yourself giving an excellent presentation; this should help to encourage the right kind of behaviours.

10.7 ■■ The presentation: three key stages

This section focuses on the delivery of your presentation, but the issues raised here also need to be considered at the planning stage. Pay particular attention to your opening words, to the transitions between each topic area, and to your closing words:

1. *Creating an 'opener'* How do you secure the audience's attention? They will want to know two things: that your message is *relevant* to them; and that you have the *credibility* necessary to deliver it. Imagine, for example, that you are going to talk to a group of office managers about reducing waste in your company. They are very busy people, and have only attended the meeting reluctantly. What 'openers' could you use to get them on your side?:

   - Ask a relevant question: '*Let me begin by asking you a question: how much do you think our company spends on waste paper, in one year?*'
   - Create a powerful scenario: '*Imagine a warehouse about the size of a football pitch, and ten metres high. In six months, we will fill that warehouse with scrap paper*'.
   - Quote a surprising statistic: '*Last year, our company was spending in excess of £150 per employee on waste paper. We are going to halve that this year.*'
   - Share a striking anecdote: '*I was chatting to an office manager from another company last week about the waste paper problem. "Yes" she said, "we were in a similar position, but now I've got it sorted." "What's your secret?" I enquired. "Bought bigger waste bins," she replied!*'
   - Use a relevant quotation: '*You probably remember Sir Percy Scrimper's, our former Managing Director, famous statement that, "A penny saved from scrap is worth two pence earned from sales ..." Well, making money out of waste is exactly what we're here to discuss today.*'

   Follow this up with a brief explanation of who you are and what you are going to cover, emphasising what members of the audience will gain by listening. There must be a perceived benefit for them and in addition, **you** must be perceived as having the relevant skills or knowledge to help them secure that benefit. For example, in continuing the waste reduction talk, you might say:

   > For the last three years, I have been working with each of the company's subsidiaries to introduce our new environmental strategy. Of course there have been some teething problems, but we are now seeing a measurable reduction in waste. This morning I am going to discuss five simple and practical ways that you can reduce your office stationery costs, without affecting staff performance.

   Hopefully, the prospect of painless cost-savings will be attractive enough to keep these managers listening for the next few minutes.

2. ***Signalling 'transitions' and changing pace*** You can easily lose an audience by moving too quickly from one topic to another. Remember the inherent limitations of this communication channel (Section 10.2) and take time to emphasise transitions between each of the main points that you cover. Guide your audience by giving a brief recap of the last topic. **Pause** for a few seconds before introducing the next topic. Transitions can be further reinforced by moving to another part of the platform or by using visual aids. Frequent changes in the pace of delivery also help to keep an audience alert and interested.

3. ***'Closing' with a flourish*** The close is equivalent to the concluding section of a written report, where you draw your argument together. Remind everyone of the objectives of the presentation, and summarise your key points, showing how they combine to meet those initial aims. You can also use the unique feature of a 'live' presentation (i.e. physical presence, discussed in Section 10.2) to secure **commitment** and **action** from your audience by injecting some energy and motivation. Try to close the event with a '*bang*', not a '*whimper*'!

10.8 ■■ Dealing with questions

Questions, during or after a presentation, offer you the chance for a welcome dialogue with the audience. This does not need to be an inquisition, if you are well prepared.

During If you prefer to take questions at the end, say so at the outset; you can then side-step unwanted interventions. However, whilst unrelated or poorly worded queries can disturb your train of thought and distract the audience, a few well-handled questions can bring a presentation to life. If you feel that you are losing your audience – the main symptoms being whispering and 'EGO' (meaning 'eyes glazing over') – be ready to take control of the situation. Pause, look around the room, and ask for questions. Use open questions in order to generate some feedback, an example being, '*I see a few puzzled expressions out there ... how do people feel about the proposal?*' With luck, this will wake people up and bring the presentation back on course. If not, think seriously about bringing things to a speedy but dignified close.

After Many people find it difficult to switch smoothly from 'presenter' mode to an active dialogue with their audience. Help yourself by trying to predict the kinds of questions that might come up and having some prepared answers 'up your sleeve'. In a large audience, ask questioners to stand up, introduce themselves, and **speak clearly**. If they insist on mumbling or whispering, be sure to repeat the question, to ensure that everyone has heard it.

There are three main problems in question and answer sessions:

1. You do not know the answer
2. You do know the answer, but do not think it is of interest to everyone else
3. You do know the answer, but do not want to give it

In each case, honesty is the best policy. Tell them you do not have an answer to hand, but will obtain one if the person contacts you afterwards. Alternatively, you may be able to pass the question to someone else in the room. If the question is highly specialised, make it clear that you do have an answer, and will be pleased to discuss it with the questioner at the end. If giving the answer is going to be embarrassing or would breach some kind of confidentiality, the only real option is to state that you are unable or unwilling to respond to that point at this time, giving whatever justification you consider to be necessary. Being 'economical with the truth' in these situations is rarely more than a short-term solution.

10.9 ▪▪ Chapter summary

• Presenters must manage the flow of information to an audience, so that they are both willing and able to absorb it.

• Presentations can be planned, much like a written report. Decide whether you are going to have an accompanying report or hand-out and, if so, when it is to be distributed.

• Prepare yourself for the special demands of giving a presentation, paying particular attention to posture, voice and ways of remembering what to say.

• It is not a good idea to read from a script or to rely on pure improvisation. Use cue cards or bullet points on OHP slides to help trigger your recall.

• Select audio-visual aids according to the type of presentation and be aware of their strengths and weaknesses.

• Check the basic practical arrangements at the venue, including rooms and refreshments. Always double check any AV equipment and materials before you appear on stage. Also find time to check your own appearance.

• During your presentation, pay particular attention to three key areas: your opening words, transitions between the main topics and your closing words.

• Make the most of Q&A sessions by preparing answers to the most likely questions and by encouraging dialogue.

Practical exercises

1. Short presentations

Prepare a short (ten minute) informative business-related presentation on a topic of your own choice, such as a recent development in human resources management, finance or engineering. Allow five minutes at the end for Q&As. Prepare your own answers to anticipated questions in advance. Choose suitable AV aids and prepare the necessary materials. Design and distribute a short report as a hand-out. Decide and make it clear whether this is for distribution in advance or as a 'take-away' at the end. Ensure that the report complements rather than repeats the contents of your presentation.

2. Persuasive presentations

Repeat the previous exercise, but on this occasion you have to *persuade* your audience to accept the case that you are arguing. Refer to Chapter 5 for background material on persuasive communication. Select your own topic for this exercise, remembering that at least some of your audience must begin by disagreeing with you!

Suggested topics include:

- Vegetarianism/meat-eating is wrong/unsustainable
- Cannabis/all drugs should/should not be de-criminalised/legalised
- Restrictions on advertising (e.g. smoking) should be reduced/increased
- Private/state education should be abolished
- All health care should be privatised/in the public sector
- Computers have made UK business more/less productive
- Britain is better off inside/outside the EU
- The government should/should not invest in public transport

You will gain most from this exercise if you try to argue a case that is the *opposite* of your own viewpoint. For example, if you are a vegetarian, try to argue for the case for meat-eating. Do your best to stick to the main arguments 'for' and 'against', avoiding highly personalised attacks on members of the group!

Take a show of hands, before and after the presentation, to see how many people have actually changed their minds as a result of your performance.

Chapter eleven

Meetings, teams and negotiation

'Jaw, Jaw' is preferable to 'War, War'

Attributed to Winston Churchill

Objectives

- To identify the main types of business meeting, their functions and distinctive features (11.1–11.2)

- To outline formal business meeting procedures, including the planning and documentation required for a successful outcome (11.3)

- To discuss the key role and essential characteristics of the chairperson (11.4)

- To review the requirements for a less formal 'team' meeting, the value of 'brainstorming' and the key role of a 'facilitator' (11.5)

- To learn how to achieve successful 'win–win' negotiation (11.6)

11.1 ▪▪▪ Introduction

People are always complaining about meetings, but most of us are destined to spend a large part of our working lives taking part in them. Meetings are one of the most difficult communication channels to handle successfully, whether you are chairing, taking the minutes or simply participating. This chapter reviews the main reasons why meetings often become so infuriating and unproductive, generating more 'heat' than 'light'. It compares formal and informal meetings, emphasising the key role of the chairperson and, in less formal settings, the facilitator. By careful preparation and management it is possible to minimise the 'downside' and make the most of these gatherings, be they a top-level committee or an *ad hoc* project team. The chapter concludes with a brief look at negotiation, and the skills involved in securing a 'win–win' outcome.

Meetings: types and objectives

The matrix (overleaf) gives some idea of the range of meetings you may encounter in business. Problems often occur where the wrong type of meeting format is used, or where participants have different views on the objectives of a meeting. For

Meeting type (& objective)	◀── FORMAL ──────────── INFORMAL ──▶	
BRIEFING (to give information)	Chief Executive presents the company's financial results to investment analysts	Project manager explains the week's priority tasks to team members or voluntary workers
INVESTIGATORY (to gather information)	Royal Commission appointed to review the current structure of local government	Architect and structural engineer visit site to discover why roof beam has collapsed
ADVISORY (to provide information)	Panel of experts advise Government department on its new legislation	Personnel manager seeks advice from colleagues on a disciplinary problem
CONSULTATIVE (to air views/opinions)	Full public enquiry is held into a proposed motorway scheme	Head of department asks staff what they think of a new profit sharing scheme
PARTICIPATIVE or **EXECUTIVE** (to make decisions)	Board of Directors or Trustees of a charity meet to agree the annual budget figures	Marketing Director and her advertising agency agree the firm's new poster campaign

Figure 11.1 Meetings – types and objectives.

example, imagine the potential for conflict when the Sales Director thinks she is giving a *briefing*, the Regional Managers are expecting to be *consulted* and the Sales Executives are hoping to *participate* in some real 'executive' decisions. The degree of 'formality' (i.e. record-keeping and written procedural rules) varies widely, from a Main Board meeting to a project team briefing at the *Dog and Duck*. Typical illustrations of each type are given in Figure 11.1.

11.2 ▦ Advantages and disadvantages

Meetings share the benefits and drawbacks of any face-to-face communication. Benefits include instantaneous feedback and the potential for group synergy. The combined efforts of a group can often generate better solutions than individuals working alone or communicating through less intensive channels, such as letters or e-mail. Successful meetings can both *inform* and *motivate* those attending. Unfortunately, business meetings rarely succeed in exploiting these opportunities to the full. To understand why, it is necessary to consider the kind of communication that is going on.

Figure 11.2 Jemima tackles a busy meeting schedule with the help of new technology.

Meetings involve a complex pattern of information flows (Figure 11.3). Messages criss-cross around the meeting room and are highly vulnerable to noise and incorrect decoding. Each attendee arrives with his or her own information, ideas, feelings and prejudices. As the meeting grinds on, individual attention lapses, perceptions vary and people forget what has been agreed. Discussions and arguments can become highly personalised as individuals 'play politics' or identify themselves too closely with particular positions. Meetings often lose direction, either drifting into unrelated topics or being hijacked by a strong personality in the group. As a result, far too much time is spent on relatively minor agenda items. The hours roll by and important issues are rushed through by an over-tired chairperson who wants to get home for supper. A badly run meeting generally makes bad decisions; equally serious is its de-motivating effect on everyone concerned.

simple exchange between individuals   informal social event

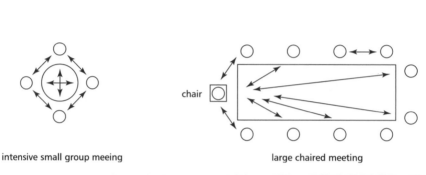

intensive small group meeing   large chaired meeting

Figure 11.3 Different information flows. Note the special problems of managing information flows in a chaired meeting. Some people may begin private conversations whilst others may feel excluded, withholding potentially useful information.

EXERCISE 11A

Me and my meeting

Think back to a meeting that you have attended fairly recently (either in business, a sports club or similar). Try to identify the following:

(a) What were the objectives?
(b) How were they communicated?
(c) Were they achieved?
(d) How was the meeting controlled?
(e) What were the 'best' and 'worst' aspects of the meeting?
(f) How did you feel: before, during and after the meeting?

Discuss your conclusions with other students or a colleague. Are their experiences similar? If you have limited experience of business meetings, arrange to attend a meeting of your local council, or one of its sub-committees. This will provide a useful insight into the procedures and practice of a formal meeting.

11.3 ■■ The formal meeting

The main features of a formal meeting are: established rules and procedures, written records of previous meetings and usually a specified membership who are able to participate. Many organisations are operated through a system of **committees**, whose members act as representatives for different departments or interest groups. These members may be appointed to their posts or elected by a wider group. The board of directors of a public company, for example, is elected by the shareholders. Below the 'main board' (or equivalent) level may also be various **sub-committees** dealing with more narrowly defined subject areas, such as finance, social services or directors' remuneration. The decisions and recommendations of sub-committees are then reported to their 'parent' committee. Each committee, sub-committee and ad hoc working group must have clear terms of reference and lines of reporting. It is important to clarify the levels at which decisions can be made, otherwise operations can be paralysed by the slow process of referring back to senior committees.

Figure 11.4   Typical sub-committee structures.

This section describes the main rules governing formal meetings and then shows how to produce useful business agendas and minutes.

(a) Rules and order

Most large organisations have a written constitution (or 'standing orders'). Limited companies, for example, are governed by their principal legal documents, the Memorandum of Association and the Articles of Association. The Company Secretary is responsible for seeing that the rules are followed, and that statutory meetings (e.g. the Annual General Meeting) are held, with appropriate notice given. If a Board of Directors acts outside its rules or powers (i.e. *ultra vires*: see below), its decisions are invalidated, and the individual Directors find themselves in a vulnerable position (they have a 'fiduciary responsibility' to act in the best interests of the company's shareholders). Similarly, local authority councillors can be 'surcharged' (i.e. fined) if their spending decisions exceed centrally imposed limits. The following specialist terms are used in and around formal meetings:

Meetings: the terminology explained

- **Ad hoc meeting/group** Temporary grouping, for a particular purpose (e.g. a one-off project or investigation)

- **Adjournment** A break in the meeting before all of the agenda items have been covered. This may because it is inquorate (see below), to obtain information or simply to allow participants to have a break. An adjournment is normally a temporary postponement with an agreed date and time for resumption. However, adjournment *sine die* means that it is for an indefinite period.

- **Any other business (AOB)** Members should submit items for the agenda in advance if possible; this allows them to be scheduled in a logical order. However, genuinely 'last minute' items can usually be notified to the chairperson at the start of the meeting. If time permits, they are taken as 'AOB' at the end.

- **Ex officio members** Individuals appointed to a committee by virtue of the office they hold, rather than by direct appointment or election.

- **Matters arising** A standard agenda item, referring to items from the previous meeting's minutes that require further discussion.

- **Motions and amendments** Some meetings have complicated voting arrangements, and a skilled 'politician' will know these in detail! Motions and amendments both require a 'proposer' and a 'seconder'. If accepted for debate, an amendment is always voted on before the original or 'substantive' motion. In politics, amendments are often used to block unpopular policy.

- **Points of order** If someone thinks that the meeting is not following its written rules, they can point it out to the chairperson by calling 'point of order'. Examples include: quorum, *ultra vires*, and speaking on items which are not on the agenda.

- **Proxy** A proxy refers to someone acting on behalf of another person who is unable to attend the meeting. Proxies are most commonly used when a vote is called at an Annual General Meeting.

- **Quorum** The minimum number of members or delegates required for a meeting to proceed. If attendance falls below that number at any time in a formal meeting, it is deemed to be *inquorate* and business must be suspended.

- **Speaking 'through the Chair'** It is normal practice for all comments to be addressed to the Chairperson, rather than directly to another person at the meeting. In theory, this allows the Chairperson to exert some control on the meeting.

- *Ultra vires* From the Latin, 'outside the powers', it refers to decisions or actions that are beyond the remit of a particular committee or council.

(b) Preparing the agenda

The agenda, listing the topics to be discussed, provides a structure for the meeting. It may be a useful route map but if poorly constructed it can lead everyone astray! A fortnight or so before the meeting, the Secretary circulates members, requesting agenda items. The Chairperson and Secretary normally plan the 'running order', based on the items submitted. The following factors should be considered when deciding on this order:

- *Logical sequence* If the outcome of one decision is going to affect another, ensure that the 'dependent' topic is further down the agenda.
- *Simple items first* Get the straightforward items out of the way before going on to more complex issues.
- *Consensus items first* Uncontentious items at the top of the agenda should be dealt with speedily. However, a seemingly bland item can cause unexpected controversy and time-consuming arguments. It is wise to check, before the agenda is finalised, that the item really is as innocuous as it sounds.
- *'Where's Gordon?'* There may be a topic that can only be discussed with a particular individual present. Hence, it may be necessary to defer or advance an item where 'Gordon' is going to be late, or has to rush off to *another* meeting.
- *Less important/less urgent last?* The Chairperson and Secretary may be tempted to place 'minor' items towards the end of the agenda, but this is not good practice. If you have a full agenda, it is best to defer these items to a subsequent meeting or, better still, deal with them via another channel. For example, it is much less time-consuming to circulate a draft report, asking for written comments, rather than to proof-read the whole thing, page-by-page, during a meeting.

Items of business may simply be numbered from '1' onwards, though many organisations use an annual referencing system comprising the current year, followed by the item number, such as: '97/01', '97/02' etc. This series of numbers continues from one meeting to the next. It is illustrated in the examples below. There are two further points for agenda-setters to consider.

- **Chair's agenda** The Chairperson often has an extended version of the agenda, with notes to help him/her run the meeting smoothly (e.g. reminders to provide an update, before opening a discussion). The Chair's agenda should also include a provisional time allocation for each agenda item.
- **Circulating the agenda** Committees and Boards usually have a regular pattern of meetings, scheduled well in advance. However, some 'extraordinary' meetings may also be needed to deal with urgent matters, whilst others may be rescheduled or cancelled. Once the agenda is drawn up, the Secretary sends out copies, normally including details of the date, time and venue (people invariably need a reminder!). It is important to ensure that everyone is included on the circulation list, particularly where the meeting has voting powers.

Sample agenda and notice of meeting:

Yellowtec plc

MEMORANDUM

To: All Finance Sub-Committee members

From: Jean Lafitte (Secretary)

Date: 20th December 1995

Subject: **FINANCE SUB-COMMITTEE: JANUARY MEETING**

The next meeting of the Finance Sub-Committee will take place on Monday 8th January 1996 at 15:00hrs in Room K383, Ryton Tower.

AGENDA

96/01	Apologies for absence	
96/02	Minutes of last meeting	
96/03	Matters arising	
96/04	Response to internal audit report	PJH
96/05	Capital investment proposal: project Alpha	ADR
96/06	Financial information system update	LPN
96/07	Software purchases: 1996/97	LPN
96/08	Any other business	
96/09	Date of next meeting	

(c) Writing up the minutes

The Secretary takes the minutes, which subsequently become the definitive record of the meeting. There is a balance between recording every detail, and the cost of record-keeping.

- *Verbatim minutes* 'Word-for-word' accounts of the proceedings. The records of Parliamentary debates (Hansard) and those of some public inquiries are verbatim. However, for obvious reasons, these are not widely used in business.

- *Narrative minutes* A more or less detailed summary of the discussions taking place on each item, followed by a note of the decision taken. Narrative minutes usually include an **action** column on the right hand side of the page, with the name or initial of the person responsible for carrying out any matters agreed by the meeting. Meetings tend to agree things with little thought of how they are to be implemented; the action column counters by putting someone's name 'on the line'.

- *Resolution minutes* These are the briefest type of minute, stating only what was agreed. Resolution minutes are used primarily for statutory meetings (e.g. those required to form or make changes to the legal status of a company). The wording is normally in the form:

  RESOLVED: That Frederick George Wilson be appointed a non-executive director of Yellowtec plc, with effect from 1st January, 1996.

  or alternatively:

  It was resolved that Frederick George Wilson be appointed a non-executive director of Yellowtec plc, with effect from 1st January, 1996.

It is essential that minutes are an **accurate** and **unbiased** record of the meeting. Minutes of the previous meeting must be circulated before the next one. If the issues were contentious, they are sure to be scrutinised carefully, and may even be corrected during the subsequent meeting.

Sample narrative minutes:

Yellowtec plc

Minutes of the Finance Sub-Committee meeting held on Monday 8th January 1996 at 15:00hrs in Room K383, Ryton Tower.

Present: Daniel Felton
Peter Harris (Chairperson)
Jean Lafitte (Secretary)
Neema Patel
Lisa Nolan
Adrian Robertson

		Action
96/01	Apologies	
	Apologies for absence were received from Martin Smith and Kerry Jones.	
96/02	Minutes of last meeting	
	The minutes of the meeting held on 20th November, previously circulated, were signed as a true record.	
96/03	Matters arising	
95/13	Computer security: Neema Patel reported that the anti-virus program was updated, effective from 1st December. No further problems had been reported, but a review was to be carried out in June.	NP

96/04	Response to internal audit report	
	A response was submitted on 20th December, covering the substantive points made. Kay Rodgers of internal audit would report back formally to the next sub-committee meeting.	PH
96/05	Capital investment proposal: project Alpha	
	Following Adrian Robinson's presentation, the sub-committee recommended that project Alpha go forward to the February Board meeting.	AR
96/06	Financial information system update	
	A detailed report, accompanying Lisa Nolan's presentation is appended to these minutes. It was agreed that a regular update be presented during the development phase.	LN
96/07	Software purchases: 1996/97	
	The provisional list was agreed, with the addition of the updated virus-checker. Department heads would be asked to provide a list of their requirements by 31st March.	LN
96/08	Urgent business	
	No urgent business was notified.	
96/09	Date of next meeting	
	The next meeting is scheduled for 8th April 1996 at 15:00hrs in room K383, Ryton Tower.	

EXERCISE 11B

Draft the agenda and minutes

Read the sample agenda and minutes of Yellowtec plc's Finance Sub-Committee, and put yourself in the role of the Secretary, Jean Lafitte.

(a) Create an imaginary agenda and the subsequent set of minutes for the next meeting of the Finance Sub-Committee. You have been advised that the following items need to be included in the discussion:

> A decision on whether to purchase an upgrade for the spreadsheet package
> A report by Lisa Nolan on departmental software requirements
> Neema Patel's update on computer security (following a theft in March)
> Lisa Nolan's update on the financial information system
> Martin Smith's request for air conditioning in the Accounts office
> Kerry Jones's report on the Treasurer's annual conference in Torquay

(b) How did you decide on the 'running order'?
(c) Do you anticipate any problems in the meeting you have scheduled?

11.4 ■■ On being a successful Chair

The task of a Chairperson is to manage a 'live' flow of messages without either stifling useful discussion or showing obvious bias towards one or other viewpoint. This can be a challenging task, particularly when you are faced with 'personality clashes' and controversial issues. The successful Chair needs three key attributes; diplomacy, assertiveness and organising ability. In conjunction with the Secretary, the Chair will need to consider the following issues:

1. **Before the meeting – plan & prepare** Even where a meeting is scheduled on a regular basis, ask yourself: '*what is the purpose of this meeting?*' and '*what are my tactics for achieving it?*' If there is insufficient business, or key personnel are unavailable, take the initiative and either cancel or postpone the meeting. If the agenda is over-full, it is better to drop items in advance, rather than trying to 're-jig' them once the meeting is underway. Check that you have a suitable venue, with enough seats and reasonable heating, lighting and ventilation. If audio-visual equipment is required, such as flip-charts and overhead projectors, ensure that it is in place and functioning. Read all the relevant background papers and reports, so that you are aware of the main issues under discussion.

2. **During the meeting – diplomacy & time management** Keep strict control of the time, ensuring that all business is covered adequately. The Chairperson is responsible for stopping anyone who insists on repeating old arguments, jumping ahead

or digressing from the current item. Be aware of those signalling a wish to speak, and ensure that everyone has a fair opportunity to contribute. Try to remain calm and objective, setting a tone for the meeting. Ensure that both you and your Secretary have a sound knowledge of the 'rules', otherwise you will waste hours arguing over 'points of order' and technicalities. Ensure that proper minutes are being taken by the Secretary. If the Secretary thinks a decision has not been expressed clearly, ask for it to be re-stated 'for the record'. From time to time, the Chairperson may also need to get a 'sense' of the meeting. This is often done by summarising the arguments that have been stated, and seeking or proposing a consensus view. If you have agreed to finish by a specified time, be sure to do so. Otherwise, the tail-end of the meeting is likely to become inquorate, as people drift away for other engagements. Ensure that all the business is either fully dealt with, or held over until a specific date. Try not to leave any ambiguities or 'loose ends', especially regarding those responsible for taking agreed actions after the meeeting.

3. **After the meeting – follow-up action** Ensure that the minutes are written up, checked and circulated promptly to all concerned. Do not leave this task until a few days before the next meeting. The Secretary should remember to circulate minutes to non-attenders; this is one reason for including 'apologies for absence' in the minutes. Check the 'action' column before the next meeting and confirm whether the named individuals have done what was required.

Practical issues, such as seating arrangements and adequate ventilation, may sound trivial. However, these can have a significant effect on the success of a meeting.

EXERCISE 11C

Seating your meeting

Seating arrangements have a major impact on the way people interact in a meeting. The famous Cabinet table in number 10 Downing Street, for example, has slightly curved sides, so that Ministers can see the faces of colleagues to either side of them.

Prepare brief comments on the seating plans illustrated overleaf, covering the following issues:

(a) What do you see as the advantages and disadvantages of each seating plan?
(b) Would some layouts be more suitable for particular types of meeting?
(c) Are any layouts undesirable *whatever* the purpose of the meeting might be?

You can also 'test' your conclusions by using some of these layouts during your next meeting or team-based project.

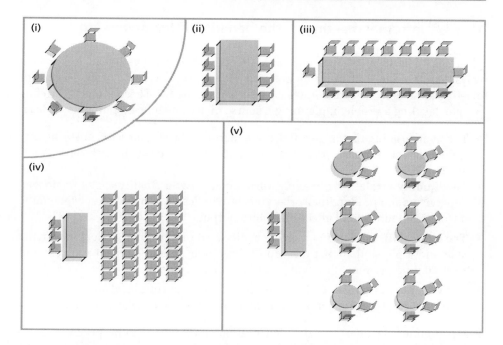

Five possible seating plans

Committees and sub-committees are an important and inevitable part of business life. This section has covered many of the potential pit-falls, showing how they can be avoided with the help of a well-prepared Chairperson and Secretary. However, some other faults in committee-based systems are more difficult to overcome. Among the most common are:

- confusion over the respective roles of particular committees or sub-committees. As a result of this some issues are 'bounced' between them, delaying any decisions that need to be made. Committee members will get irritated and the agenda will be over-burdened with items that keep re-appearing without being resolved.

- undermining of the authority of certain committees or sub-committees. Members find themselves 'rubber stamping' decisions made elsewhere, which can be a very disheartening experience. It is likely to result in members 'voting with their feet', so that attendances fall and the meeting becomes weakened and inquorate.

In these situations, any solution lies outside the meeting room. The Chairperson and other participants will need to address the underlying structural or political problems that have resulted in these 'symptoms' of poor quality communication.

11.5 ■■ Informal meetings – the benefits of team-working

Meetings come in all shapes and sizes. People often get together in less formal ways than those described in the previous section. However, the basic reasons for meeting are much the same, however informal it may be. These include: briefing people, tackling a problem, planning a course of action and generating new ideas:

- **The team briefing** In a large retail store, managers brief their staff, ensuring that individuals are properly prepared, well motivated and clear about the task (Adair 1983).
- **The 'quality circle'** At a manufacturing company, a small team of engineers, supervisors and production workers meets to re-design a component, overcoming a technical fault that is affecting factory output.
- **The clinical discussion** In an orthopaedic ward of a hospital, a doctor, nursing staff and a physiotherapist meet to discuss their patient's recent progress and treatment programme, following a serious road accident.
- **The voluntary organisation** In a church hall, members of a local sports club plan their next fund-raising venture, a float at the forthcoming town carnival.

Pre-determined agendas and detailed minutes may not be appropriate in these situations, though there is clearly a need for some degree of preparation and note-taking. Even in the most informal business meetings, a little time spent on structure and procedures is likely to generate better results. However, the most important requirement is for the individuals concerned to work together as a **team**. There are many situations where a team is likely to achieve better results than individuals working independently. A good team can:

- *Solve complex problems* Management problems are often wide-ranging and multi-disciplinary, requiring a combination of skills, knowledge and experience. Such combinations are rarely found in one person.
- *Stimulate creativity and innovation* Lively interactions between people can spark off new ideas and provide original perspectives. This often occurs when one person mentions something they have seen recently, prompting someone else to recall a related memory, and a third makes a link between the two.
- *Increase motivation* Most people have a need to belong, and enjoy mixing with others rather than spending all their time working alone. Today's field sales forces, for example, could theoretically spend all of their time on the road, communicating with the office through a laptop computer and mobile 'phone. However, productivity is likely to increase if they can meet and identify with a team on a regular basis.

By contrast, a badly functioning team will cause all kinds of problems for the managers concerned. The symptoms of dysfunction are easy to identify. These include: expressions of frustration and negativity, unhealthy competition (or 'in-fighting') between team members, lack of involvement or commitment, dishonesty, a climate of 'back-stabbing' and a general lack of direction. These problems are both serious and widespread, attracting the attention of researchers. One of the most constructive approaches to emerge from the research has been **teambuilding**. This suggests that many problems can be overcome by selecting a balanced team. During the 1970s, Dr R. Meredith Belbin conducted experiments with industrial managers who were attending short courses at a management school. He compared the performances of different teams who were competing against one another in a series of business games. By measuring the behaviour of individuals and then experimenting with teams comprising different mixes of people, Belbin isolated eight distinct team **roles**. He argued that a successful team needs a balanced combination of these roles. You can actually identify your own 'primary' and 'secondary' roles using Belbin's 'self-perception' questionnaire, which is based on a well-known personality inventory. Unfortunately, building an ideal team is complicated by a number of practical constraints. For example, a person may be needed for his or her technical expertise, irrespective of team role. In addition, some teams are simply too small to be 'balanced', and there may be structural or cultural barriers that constrain these roles. As a result, team composition is usually a compromise. However, if you accept Belbin's argument that team members adopt alternative roles when it becomes necessary, his general conclusion remains valid:

Teams are a question of balance. What is needed is not well-balanced individuals but individuals who balance well with one another. In that way, human frailties can be underpinned and strengths used to full advantage. (Belbin, 1981)

	Name	Key role
LEADERS	Chair Shaper	Team controller and co-ordinator/'slave driver'
NEGOTIATORS	Resource-investigator Team worker	Entrepreneur, diplomat and 'networker' Internal facilitator, maintains the team
INTELLECTUALS	Innovator Monitor-evaluator	Creative and original thinker Problem analyst and 'trouble-shooter'
MANAGERS AND WORKERS	Completer-finisher Company worker	Guarantees completion and checks detail Effective organiser/administrator

Figure 11.5 Belbin's eight team roles.

EXERCISE 11D

Brainstorming for results

Brainstorming is a popular and well-established technique for problem-solving and generating novel ideas. However, it is often conducted wrongly, leaving people disappointed with the results. If you make an effort to follow the principles outlined below, the ideas should really start to flow:

(a) Appoint a 'facilitator' to write ideas on the board and encourage participation; make sure they can write quickly and legibly!

(b) Call out any ideas that come into your head, keeping them concise (insist on a maximum of two words).

(c) Encourage everyone to participate

(d) Do not reject or criticise any ideas at the first stage, no matter how crazy they might appear. Accept and acknowledge every contribution.

(e) Once the initial flow of ideas is exhausted, move to the second stage; begin linking similar words on the board and drawing out common themes.

Bearing these principles in mind, prepare and run a 10 to 15 minute brainstorming session with half of the group, tackling one of the following topics:

- How to promote your college or organisation to a new market segment (you may want to specify one in advance)

- Solutions to either: city centre congestion, air pollution, the drugs trade, world poverty, car crime, or any current social issue.

- Alternative uses for (or ways to improve) a selected product or service.

Ask the other half of the group to spend the same amount of time working on the problem individually (and in another room). Bring the sub-groups together and compare the 'brainstormed' ideas with those generated by the individuals working alone. Did the 'brainstormers' manage to achieve any 'synergy' or creative energy?

11.6 ■■ Negotiations

The principles behind a negotiation are much the same, whatever its scale. It is a process of discussion, proposals and counter-proposals that eventually leads to a mutually acceptable compromise. The basic principles of negotiation are learnt in early childhood, when proposals like, 'Can I have another biscuit?', are countered with, 'Not unless you put those toys away'. Subsequently, there are many occasions in business and personal life when some kind of negotiation is required:

- Buying or selling a car
- Agreeing the terms of your employment contract

- Agreeing terms for supplying products or services to a major customer
- Deciding who is going to cook the meal or wash up

A blunt refusal to negotiate is sometimes seen as a sign of strength. In the 1980s, Prime Minister Margaret Thatcher's admirers gave her the nickname *TINA*, which stood for '*There Is No Alternative*'. Such single-minded resolution has its place, but most business relationships rely on a more flexible, long-term approach. This applies to the private sector, just as much as to public or voluntary sector organisations. Skilful negotiation is frequently more effective than simple-minded aggression, even when you appear to be in a position of strength. For example, it is a central feature of modern supply chain management, where major retail firms such as Marks & Spencer or J. Sainsbury are developing long-term relationships with their key suppliers, rather than simply pressuring them towards the lowest price. Of course, if you are the weaker party, well-rehearsed negotiating skills become essential to survival.

Forms of negotiation

The most common form of negotiation is described as **positional**. Typical examples include the annual pay rounds between trades unions and large industrial employers, and some ceasefire meetings between warring factions. Each party to the negotiation consists of a small team with a tightly defined mandate, giving them limited authority to act on behalf of their respective chiefs. The negotiation proceeds as a series of shifts in position, proposals and counter-proposals. If each party's ultimate point of compromise overlaps, an agreement may be reached. However, this form of negotiation often results in deadlock. Another common feature of traditional negotiations is where one party makes a kind of 'pre-emptive strike' against the other. For example, a politician makes selective 'leaks' to the media in order to undermine an opponent, or anti-road protestors occupy a construction site before a public enquiry. This tactical action, which can also be taken once 'face-to-face' negotiations are underway, is designed to exert additional pressure. In practice, it is usually countered by the other party and can result in a breakdown in negotiations. Responding to the perceived problems of positional negotiation, a group of Harvard Business School researchers developed an alternative approach, known as **principled** negotiation (Fisher and Ury 1982). This is based on a search for the objective principles underlying each Party's position. The aim is to achieve more creative and positive outcomes. A key feature of this is the separation of the issues and arguments from the personalities (and egos) of those involved in the negotiations. Above all, it recognises the importance of achieving a 'win–win' solution.

Advantages of 'win–win' negotiation

Since most negotiations are part of an on-going relationship, success does not usually mean 'beating' the other party. If you achieve a deal that is highly

	'A' loses	'A' wins
'B' loses	lose/lose	win/lose
'B' wins	lose/win	win/win

Figure 11.6 Alternative negotiation outcomes.

unfavourable to a valued customer or key supplier (i.e. 'win–lose') they are unlikely to do much business with you in the future. However, it is equally important not to be 'ripped off' (i.e. 'lose–win'). Hence, the best outcome for both parties is referred to as 'win–win'.

Negotiation and power

Parties to a true negotiation will have some freedom of manoeuvre. However, this does not necessarily mean that they will come to the negotiating table as equals. In most cases one party is in a stronger position than the other. For example, the large multiple retailers can exert substantial buying power over their smaller suppliers. However, as skilled negotiators recognise, it is the other party's **perception** of their power that is the key factor. By influencing these perceptions, an apparently 'weaker' party can alter the course of the negotiations in its favour.

The negotiation process

The skills required to manage a negotiation are similar to those used in other types of meeting, but the negotiation itself has a distinctive shape. There are four stages:

1. ***Prepare the ground*** Carry out background research on your own proposals. Assess your positions from the other party's point of view, and try to anticipate their likely positions and counter-arguments. Identify your own maximum realistic expectations and minimum 'worst case' acceptance level.
2. ***Create the climate*** You need to get the meeting off to a good start by creating a climate that is likely to lead to agreement. Experience suggests that this should be cordial, collaborative, brisk and businesslike. The location is important, it needs to be quiet and free from interruptions; for example, many of the Cold War meetings between the USA and USSR were held in Iceland whilst Israelis and Paelestinians negotiated in Norway. On arrival, pay attention to basic good manners: handshakes, eye contact, non-threatening gestures and uncontentious 'ice-breaking' conversation. As the memoirs of international politicians demonstrate, good inter-personal relations can often play a crucial role in the outcome of a negotiation.

3. *Make tentative proposals* The bargaining phase should be used to reduce substantive differences between the parties. Emphasise areas where you already have consensus, and avoid 'personalising' any remaining disagreements. Your proposals should always be **conditional** (i.e. *'If you offer us "X" ..., then we could offer you "Y" ...'*). Identify the factors that are most important to the other party, and value all your offers in their terms. For example, a busy customer may value 'door-to-door' delivery very highly, even though it costs you very little to add them to your existing round. By contrast, your offer of 'instant credit terms' may be of little value to a cash-rich retailer, though to you it would be a costly concession. Sometimes it takes a truly creative team of negotiators to put together a proposal that offers a solution satisfying all parties. This creativity rarely emerges from a confrontational approach.

4. *Reach and record an agreement* Both parties need to spot when it is time to stop the exchanges and move to firm proposals. Make sure that the terms are absolutely clear to both parties, taking time out if necessary in order to check that everything has been covered. When you are satisfied, seal the agreement with a handshake and be sure to **record** all the mutually agreed conditions and undertakings in writing. Many commercial and diplomatic agreements have broken down because the terms were drafted ambiguously and disputes subsequently arose over the 'small print'.

EXERCISE 11E

The negotiation game

Split into two teams and spend 20 minutes preparing your position. This may be based on your own scenarios, or using case materials provided by a tutor. Appoint a 'team negotiator' to represent you. The negotiation should run for about ten minutes, with each team acting as observers (i.e. not interrupting the negotiation). You may also allow the negotiators to request a short 'time out' during the discussions, giving them an opportunity to consult in private with the rest of their team.

At the end of the negotiation, return to discuss the outcome. Was it a 'win–win'? Did the discussions get bogged-down? Were both parties able to develop creative offers, valuing them in the other party's terms? Most importantly, do both parties agree on what has been agreed? !

11.7 ■■ Chapter summary

- Managers spend a large part of their lives attending meetings. This investment is only productive when meetings are well planned and managed.

- There are important differences between the objectives and format of briefing, advisory, consultative and executive meetings.

- Formal meetings have procedural rules, agendas, minutes and (in many cases) a specified membership. Agendas must be carefully planned and circulated in advance. Minutes must be accurate and objective.

- A successful Chairperson should be calm, objective and a good time-manager. The Chairperson provides a structure for the meeting by planning the agenda, and manages the 'flow' of the discussion once the meeting is underway.

- The Secretary also has an important role, assisting in the preparation of the meeting, advising on points of order and ensuring that clear and unambiguous minutes are taken.

- Many informal meetings are based on teams. A well-balanced team can be creative and highly motivated, but managers should look out for the danger signs of a malfunctioning team.

- Negotiations are a specialised type of meeting. In modern business relationships, 'win–win' strategies are usually most effective. It is essential to develop a professional, yet cordial atmosphere and to evaluate your offers from the other party's perspective.

Practical exercises

1. Meeting observation and discussion

Arrange to attend a meeting of a local council, chamber of commerce, trade union ranch, voluntary body or professional organisation. Observe the actions of the Chairperson, Secretary and other participants. In particular, look out for the following:

Did the Chairperson . . .

- start the meeting at the stated time?
- ensure that each item received sufficient time for debate?
- control anyone who strayed from the subject-matter of the item?
- allow those who wanted to speak to do so?
- get clear and unambiguous decisions?
- remain calm and diplomatic throughout?
- close the meeting on time (if stated)?

Did the Secretary . . .

- distribute copies of all the reports and papers under discussion?
- advise on any points of order?

- ask the Chairperson to clarify the wording of any decisions?
- take any other part in the discussions?

Note: The role of the Secretary will vary depending on the type of meeting. Much of his/her work tends to be 'behind the scenes' rather than in the meeting itself.

Did the other participants ...

- make positive and well-considered contributions to the discussion?
- allow others to speak without interrupting?
- appear to understand the arguments that were being put forward?
- reach an agreement on items, or resort to a majority vote?
- become agitated or visibly bored by the proceedings?
- stay until the end of the meeting?

take notes on these items at the meeting and discuss the findings with other group members on your return. What are the main lessons to learn from this experience?

2. Better meetings – idealistic or realistic?

Most managers despair of meetings and their procedures, yet realistically few alternatives have ever been proposed. The following advice on managing a meeting was written three centuries ago by members of a religious group known as the Quakers. Some of the United Kingdom's most famous and successful companies, including Cadburys, Rowntrees, Lloyds, Barclays and Friends Provident, were founded by Quaker entrepreneurs. Their emphasis on employee involvement and decent working conditions has influenced industrial relations practice around the world. Today, most of the successor companies have reverted to more conventional decision-making methods. However, the Quakers' own business meetings are still based on seeking agreement from all of those attending, rather than on majority votes; this general approach has been adopted by a number of other organisations.

(a) Read the following extract and list the main points in modern language.
(b) How far is the advice on behaviour in meetings applicable to a modern business in the public, private or voluntary sectors? What do you see as its advantages and disadvantages? Is it entirely idealistic or realistic?
(c) What do you see as the main advantages and disadvantages of meetings based on majority votes and those that rely on achieving agreement amongst all those present? What is the difference (if any) between decisions based on agreement and those based on compromise?

For the preservation of love, concord and a good decorum in this meeting, 'tis earnestly desired that all business that comes before it be managed with gravity and moderation, and in much love and Amity, without reflections or retorting ... let whatsoever is offered, be mildly proposed, and so left with some pause, that the meeting may have opportunity to weigh the matter, and have a right sense of it, that there may be a unanimity and joint concurrence of the whole. And if anything be controverted that it be in coolness of Spirit calmly debated, each offering their reasons and sense, their assent, or dissent, and so leave it without striving. And also that but one speak at once, and that the rest hear. And that private debates and discourses be avoided, and all attend the present business of the Meeting. So will things be carried on sweetly as becomes us, to our comfort: and love and unity be increased: and we better serve Truth and our Society.

Wiltshire Quarterly Meeting, Religious Society of Friends (Quakers), 1678

Source: *Quaker Faith & Practice* (1995), section 19.57

Chapter twelve

Adverts, news releases and displays

Advertising is the cave art of the twentieth century

Marshall McLuhan

Objectives

- To discuss external communication in the specialised but inter-related fields of advertising, public relations and promotion (12.1)
- To consider practical aspects of commissioning an advert (12.2–12.4)
- To consider practical aspects of drafting a news release (12.5–12.6)
- To consider practical aspects of designing an exhibition stand (12.7)
- To place each method in the wider context of a co-ordinated promotional campaign (12.2–12.7)

12.1 ▪▪ Introduction

Many managers become involved in commissioning advertisements, drafting news releases and designing displays. Together, they form part of the 'promotional mix', the ways that an organisation communicates with the world around it. The task of *producing* promotional materials is often contracted out to specialists, advertising agencies, public relations (PR) firms and exhibition consultants. However, experience suggests that it is worthwhile gaining an understanding of what these professionals are up to. As a result, you will be able to:

- Prepare a better brief for the agency (or the in-house team)
- Identify the best 'pitch' (i.e. when two or more agencies compete for a job)
- Deal more effectively with those selected to carry out the work
- Measure the cost-effectiveness of their efforts
- Take appropriate action to change and enhance promotional strategies

By contrast, vast amounts of money can be wasted if, as a client, you are unable to communicate your requirements clearly to an agency. This invariably results in the production of unsuitable advertising, PR and exhibition materials. The chapter therefore focuses on the practical aspects of communication through each of these channels. You may also wish to review the underlying principles of persuasive communication which are covered in Chapter 5. Direct mail, another important element in the 'promotional mix' of many businesses, is considered in Chapter 8.

12.2 ▪▪ Advertising – an overview

Markets have existed from the earliest times, and wherever people have sold goods or services, they have advertised. However, the advertising *industry* is a more recent phenomenon, a mid nineteenth century response to mass production (creating products and markets) and mass literacy (creating the books and magazines in which adverts were placed). Annual expenditure on display advertising in the United Kingdom is now estimated at about £7 billion, most of which is represented by television, newspapers and magazines. A further £3 billion is spent on classified advertising and directory entries (Advertising Association, 1996). All this activity means that adults and children are exposed to hundreds of advertising messages every day. Many of these are both highly sophisticated and expensive to produce. For example, Rover Group's 15 second *Englishman in New York* commercial reportedly cost £0.75 million to record, plus many thousands of pounds required for airtime. However, there are less expensive forms of advertising; straightforward '10 per cent off' promotions in a regional newspaper could cost less than a £100 per insertion. Whatever your budget, the key test of an advert is whether it achieves its purpose, which may include one of the following:

- To create or renew awareness (e.g. of a new service, brand name or social issue)
- To inform or educate (e.g. how to use a product properly or minimising health risks)
- To stimulate 'purchase' decisions (e.g. buy a product or service, select a brand, donate to a specific charity)

Success depends on presenting the organisation's messages to a specific audience in such a way that they, along with other influences, are able elicit the desired response.

12.3 ▪▪ Planning an advertising campaign

One isolated advert is unlikely to have any lasting impact. To be effective, it needs to be part of an integrated 'campaign'. Promotional campaigns are run much like the a war, with a vocabulary based around 'strategic targets', 'hit rates' and 'pre-emptive strikes'. To illustrate some of the key elements of a campaign, imagine that you are the product manager responsible for launching '*Vegigrub*'. It is a new, vegetable-based high protein food that is being positioned as an attractive alternative

Case study

Persuasive advertising for Oxfam

UNITED KINGDOM AND IRELAND

Oxfam was founded in the United Kingdom in 1942. Its work with people around the world includes emergency relief, long term development and research. One of the organisation's basic aims is to work in partnership, helping people to help themselves, rather than just giving short-term handouts. Oxfam is also involved in public education programmes, lobbying and campaigning in the United Kingdom and Ireland. Oxfam International now comprises a number of independent partner organisations, including Oxfam America, Oxfam Quebec and Oxfam Hong Kong, each with a shared mission to overcome the suffering caused by poverty, conflict and natural disasters.

Oxfam
Save lives in Central Africa

Up to one million people in Eastern Zaire are dying from starvation and disease. Some refugees have been able to flee into Rwanda, Burundi, Uganda, and Tanzania. **Oxfam can help them.**

We are providing clean water for thousands of those who have escaped the turmoil. You can help us to save more lives.

We are doing everything possible, but we need extra funds **now** to respond as this crisis unfolds.

Please, give a donation today.

credit card donations ✆ **01865 312231**

Yes, I want to help Oxfam's work in Central Africa. Here is my donation of:

£25 ☐   £50 ☐   £100 ☐   £250 ☐   £_____

Mr, Mrs, Miss, Ms _____

Address _____

_____ Postcode _____

Please send to: Oxfam, Room BA01, FREEPOST, Oxford OX2 7BR.

Oxfam United Kingdom and Ireland is a member of Oxfam International.
Registered Charity No.202918

This stark but powerful press advertisement (left) appeared in a number of national newspapers during the horific mid-1990s conflict in Rwanda and surrounding countries. Whilst emergency programmes of this kind are an essential part of the organisation's work, funding is also required for its equally important though less newsworthy development programmes, such as digging wells in Sudan (above left), literacy training in Guatemala and training voluntary health workers in India. A range of communication channels, including: news releases, free information leaflets, supporters' newsletters, poster displays in Oxfam stores and public events, are used to develop these broader messages.

Source: Sarah Errington, Oxfam; Press advertisement: WWAV Rapp, Collins, Oxfam.

to meat. How would you get from the 'drawing board' to the final 'roll out' in the shops?

1. *Marketing research* You could begin by investigating the market, its principal characteristics and long-term potential. Who buys food for the household? What are the recent trends in meat consumption? What are the existing alternatives to meat, and how are they perceived by both users and non-users? What do people already know and think of '*Vegigrub*' and your company's other products?

2. *Identifying target market(s)* Market research, together with your own instincts, should suggest who is in your sights. In the case of a product launch, the initial focus is likely to be on so-called 'early adopters', the sub-group who are first to experiment with a new product. In the '*Vegigrub*' example, your research suggests that these are likely to be females aged 20 to 35 from socio-economic groups A, B and C1 (professionals and skilled workers).

3. *Developing campaign objectives* What are you aiming to achieve? Objectives are usually quantified, so that the success (or otherwise) of the campaign can be measured. Advertisers are particularly interested in the level of awareness of a product, and how far this is converted into trial purchases. You have decided to aim for a 25% unprompted recall of 'Vegigrub' in your target market, by the end of a three month media campaign. Unprompted recall means that, in a follow-up survey of the target group, respondents can describe the advertisement without being given a brand name or a similar prompt by the interviewer.

4. *Planning and budgeting* In most organisations, budgets are tight, and campaigns have to be designed within these constraints. Planning decisions include the channels to be used (e.g. newspaper and television adverts, direct mail, in-store promotions), and the timescale of the campaign. Project management techniques, such as 'Gantt' are used to schedule and co-ordinate the different activities. For '*Vegigrub*', you decide to run full colour adverts in six women's magazines, with accompanying 'advertorials' (i.e. sponsored editorial articles, describing the product), a series of local radio adverts and a month-long programme of in-store tastings. You may also decide to experiment with delivering samples of '*Vegigrub*' to selected addresses, as part of an on-going market research survey. This is known affectionately in the trade as a '*knock and drop*'.

Case study

Delivering product samples – pros and cons

One of the best ways to communicate a message is to involve the receiver directly. Product samples are a good example of this technique, and have been used to deliver 'trial size' shampoos, perfumes, computer software and even food products, direct to the home or workplace. However, this channel has some obvious limits. In the 1960s, a seriously misguided promotional campaign for razor blades was halted when inquisitive children started opening product samples that had been dropped through their letterboxes.

5. ***Drafting material – key messages*** Alongside the campaign planning, you need to recruit people to create the advertising materials. Individual adverts are built around 'key messages', and the real skill of advertising agencies is to convert these messages into memorable words, sounds and images. For example, your key messages might be that '*Vegigrub*' is a new, nutritious low-fat product, derived entirely from natural vegetable ingredients, which can be prepared much like meat and which has a similar texture to veal. How do you convey this to your audience?

EXERCISE 12A

Creating the '*Vegigrub*' campaign

Take up the role of the advertising agency designer (sometimes called a 'creative'), working on this promotional campaign:

(a) Suggest a more appropriate alternative to the client's proposed product name, bearing in mind their target market and the benefits that the product offers to the consumer.
(b) Convert the key messages, outlined above, into three concise and attention-grabbing slogans that can be used as the campaign develops.
(c) Draft a fax to your client, explaining your proposals and requesting a response.

12.4 ■■ Communicating with an advertisement

An effective advert is likely to have to two distinguishing features: messages summarised briefly, and messages re-inforced using more than one medium. With their emphasis on the target audience and their creative approach, adverts display many of the best features of effective business communication, many of which can be applied elsewhere in management. When devising an advert, it is worth considering the wide range of possible formats or 'treatments' that are available:

Some popular advertising formats

• **Slice of life** Commonly used on television adverts for food (e.g. the *Bisto* family) and mass market domestic products such as washing machines. Short dramatised excerpts can be used to link a product with a lifestyle that is familiar to the target audience.

• **Humorous** Visual and verbal humour secures audience attention and generates positive reactions. Humour is used for all kinds of products, including very 'dry' ones, such as financial services. The electricity industry's famous *Creature Comforts* campaign (using ordinary customers' voices with an animated 'family' of animal characters) was a response to research suggesting that customers perceived electric power as less 'friendly' than gas.

- **Aspirational** Used for 'luxury' and other heavily branded products (e.g. *Chanel* perfumes and *Levis 501* jeans). Imagery is used, either to enhance a brand identity, or to suggest that consumers can obtain some element of a fantasy lifestyle by purchasing the product.

- **Celebrity endorsement** This can work at various levels. There is the simple 'if she says so and/or uses the stuff, it must be ok' proposition. Beyond that, a celebrity can be perceived as 'humanising' your message. For example, the brewers Guinness used actor Rutger Hauer (star of the film *Bladerunner*) to re-position an 'old man's drink' for a new generation. Dressed in black and with bleached hair, he literally 'embodied' a younger and more sophisticated pint of Guinness. Celebrities do not even have to be alive! With the help of computer animation, Alfred Hitchcock was recently resurrected to promote insurance policies. Celebrity cartoons have three advantages over live stars: they are immortal, they cannot become embroiled in a scandal and they demand no repeat performance fees.

- **Demonstration** The most effective way of introducing novel or difficult to understand products and services is to show them being used. Demonstrations are often used on television, but with some imagination, they can be applied to other channels, such as newspaper advertisements. They can educate potential consumers, and reduce their fear of the unknown. A common trick with technology is to show a non-specialist or a child using the product quite happily.

- **Surreal/post-modernist** There has been a recent increase in bizarre and self-parodying adverts, where the message seems obscure, if not unintelligible. Tobacco companies pioneered this format when regulators began to restrict the content of their adverts. Over many years, the *Silk Cut* campaign has played on the brand name 'silk' and 'cut' in many different ways. Surreal advertising has been introduced because audiences are now so 'visually literate' that they can see through, and 'deconstruct' traditional adverts. Hence, more sophisticated and puzzling content is needed to secure their attention.

The best way to explore these options is to design your own advertisement. Use brainstorming techniques (outlined in Chapter 11) to generate as broad a variety of ideas as possible. When selecting your preferred treatment, keep the target audience in mind and package your messages in ways that attract them. Avoid the easy trap of using material that appeals to *you* rather than to your audience.

EXERCISE 12B

Design a display advertisement

The 'Vegigrub' campaign has gone well, and the product is now in the shops, with a growing consumer base consisting predominantly of young ABC1 women (nb! use your replacement product name for 'Vegigrub', as selected in Exercise 12a). The advertising agency has now been asked to design a new advert, targeting health-conscious, recently retired people. The key messages are unchanged, but the client's own research suggests that there will be greater resistance to a novel food product amongst older people.

(a) Select a treatment from those described above and prepare a short (maximum 200 word) justification for the client. Feel free to combine two or more of these formats, or introduce novel approaches of your own.

(b) Sketch out a 'rough', a hand-drawn design showing how the proposed advert will look. The illustration below identifies the main elements you are likely to include in a typical 'display' advertisement, but these can appear in many different guises, so feel free to adapt it to meet your needs.

visual image(s)

main slogan (bold type)

body text (optional), the advertising copy, describing the product

product brand or logo

return slip (optional), for further information

12.5 ■■ Public relations – an overview

Public relations (PR) has only developed as a unified profession in the last 40 years. It draws on a variety of fields, including: publicity agents and promoters from the entertainment industry, political lobbyists and advisors, journalists, management consultants and advertisers. This is a profession which, ironically, seems unable to escape a bad and disreputable image. The main criticisms are that PR is used to give a false impression of an organisation, or an issue, and that it is all about 'corporate hospitality', lavish entertainment for important clients and sleazy politicians. In reality, whilst there are examples of dubious practice, PR has proved to be a valuable form of communication. It is used by all kinds of organisations, including charities, pressure groups and political parties. Today's PR professionals talk in terms of developing a long-term dialogue with their 'publics', each of which has different information needs. The Institute of Public Relations defines this role as: '*The deliberate, planned and sustained effort to establish and maintain understanding between an organisation and its public.*' In the next section, we consider how this mutual understanding can be achieved.

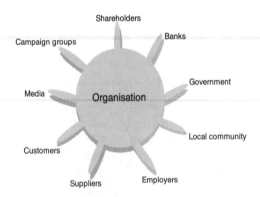

Figure 12.2 An organisation and its 'public'.

12.6 ■■ Successful PR: long-term commitment vs. short-term fix

Imagine that you are running a large manufacturing site in a rural area and are planning to expand the factory. If your track record is poor, with pollution and safety scares, the local community is unlikely to be sympathetic. If automation is leading to local job losses, you have an even greater image problem to handle. In this situation, a short-term PR exercise, such as sponsoring the village carnival, will be counter-productive, since everyone will see it as cynical and 'cosmetic'. By contrast, long-term PR involves greater commitment, with regular 'open days', consultative groups, efforts to keep the workforce informed and a genuine, sustained investment in community activities. However, once you *are* investing in long-term

PR, the 'pay-off' can be substantial. Accumulated goodwill from the public provides you with some degree of protection against short-term crises, like a factory fire or a financing problem. This more substantial and ultimately more effective form of PR can only be achieved if certain principles are followed:

1. **Get senior management commitment** PR must be seen as a top-level matter, based on real changes in your operations. Otherwise it will become a worthless cosmetic 'gloss'.
2. **Link PR to strategic objectives** This follows from point one; communication objectives should flow from the organisation's underlying business strategy.
3. **Understand your publics** The organisation must research and listen to its various publics, and express its messages in their terms – a fundamental communication principle.
4. **Plan and budget** Effective PR is an on-going, rather than 'ad-hoc' crisis management. Therefore, it must be planned and adequately financed.
5. **Monitor and adapt** PR should act as a continual monitor on the 'world outside'. If the other four principles are followed, it can help the whole organisation to adapt to new situations. Hence, PR can be about much more than external 'image'.

Public relations: a users guide

There are many types of PR activity that an organisation might use. The choice, much like that of advertising strategy, should be based on a combination of research into the needs of the various publics and an awareness of the organisation's objectives:

- **Corporate advertising and brochures** Organisations sometimes promote themselves, rather than specific products or services. Brochures and annual reports are sent to major customers, suppliers, financiers and shareholders.

- **Sponsorship** This can range from supporting an opera company or a sports event (with the added incentive of prime seats for corporate hospitality, entertaining important clients) to a simple charitable donation, based on employee interests or initiatives, such as sponsoring your company's team when it takes part in a fund-raising half-marathon or cycle race.

- **Lobbying** Lobbyists have an important role, providing decision-makers with well-researched briefing materials, technical advice and arguments in support of their respective positions. Governments often make use of these 'expert' briefings when drafting complex legislation. However, the activities of some lobbyists are highly suspect; rewarding politicians for asking specific questions in Parliament is morally dubious, whilst paying them to vote in a particular way is simply corrupt.

- **Internal communication** It is essential to keep employees informed, involved and motivated, not only for the internal health of the business but because employees are an important channel to the outside world. Proud, satisfied employees will tell relatives and friends what an excellent organisation they are working for, whilst disgruntled ones will do the opposite. As 'insiders', their views (either positive or negative) always carry considerable weight.

- *Day-to day procedures* Seemingly routine activities, such as the time taken to answer an external telephone call, can have a big impact. For example, if in-coming callers with simple queries are passed from department to department, the organisation soon gets a poor public image. Staff training programmes and improved computer databases could reduce this particular problem, but all organisations need to be vigilant to ensure that similar procedures are operating satisfactorily.

- *Other methods* Press briefings & news releases are considered in Section 12.7 below. Exhibitions, events and displays are discussed in Section 12.8. Like the other methods discussed here, these can be used to achieve both product/service marketing and broad public relations goals.

12.7 ▪▪ Media relations – planning a news release

The 'media', which in this context means television, radio, newspapers and magazines, can be seen as a kind of indirect route to the public. Journalists research your business and listen to your briefings, then report their findings to a wider audience as news stories. These stories are powerful messages, since the 'media' – and the trade press in particular – are perceived as informed and impartial. Because of this, their reports and editorials will be accepted more readily than any material you issue directly. The other advantage of this form of communication is its cost-effectiveness. You have to pay for advertising, but any messages that a journalist communicates are essentially free. There is only one catch; you have to deliver the kind of stories that make news.

So what makes a story newsworthy? The popular definition of a non-story is '*Small earthquake, nobody hurt*'. Similarly, '*Dog bites man*' is unexceptional and therefore uninteresting, whilst '*Man bites dog*' is front-page news. In addition, different types of story are likely to get coverage depending on whether local, national or specialist media are being used:

- *Local media* The local press, TV and radio are usually 'hungrier' for stories, but they do have strict selection criteria. The main factor is the **local angle**; is the story about people from the area, celebrities who are visiting, local controversies or events? Due to their limited resources, local newspapers are more likely to reproduce your news releases rather than rewrite them. They are also more likely to select a story if you can provide a strong monochrome photograph to accompany it.

- *National media* With a few exceptions, only the largest organisations are likely to merit national media coverage (e.g. via broadcasters such as the *BBC* and *ITV*,

Town & Country PR

Organisation name/logo

INFORMATION

Release date/time/reference

4 October 1996

Short descriptive heading

1995/6 MDC levy collection nears completion

Main news point

The Milk Development Council is very close to completing its collection of the 1995/6 levy. By the end of August, more than 96% of that due via wholesale milk buyers was received. Steps are being taken to chase the 4% outstanding, mostly due from small scale milk buyers.

Subsidiary news point

Data from the Intervention Board shows a total levy, based on actual production, of £5.484m. At 0.04 ppl, this equates to around £180/yr from the average milk producer.

Short quotation

MDC finance manager Patrick Morris says the organisation will be robust in pursuing outstanding money. "MDC exists to benefit all producers via its funding of near market research, the National Dairy Council and the Animal Data Centre. Fairness requires that we collect everything that is due."

- ends -

Notes to Editors

Notes to editors

The Milk Development Council was formed in 1995 to continue funding near-market research and development and other priority areas, such as enhancing the public image of milk, following the abolition of the milk marketing boards in 1994. Dairy farmers supported its formation in a referendum and its funding by a statutory levy on all milk production in England, Wales and Scotland. Currently, the levy is set at 0.04p/litre.

Dairy farmers' interests in the use of the MDC's £5 million budget are looked after by a ruling council of 11 people, of whom seven are active milk producers. MDC has a full-time staff of three to administer the organisation.

Further information from Peter Merson, Chief Executive, address & telephone number below

Contact names and numbers

Issued by Phil Christopher, Town & Country PR, Telford, telephone 01952 291911.

Milk Development Council
5-7 John Princes Street London W1M 0AP

1 of 1

Ref: mdcj44
Job no: mdc0129

Telephone: 0171 629 7262
Facsimile 0171 629 4820

Figure 12.3 Structure of a typical news release. This press release, designed for specialist trade publications, was produced for the Milk Development Council by Town & Country PR as part of a corporate public relations campaign. It is aimed at dairy farmers and other influential people in the dairy industry. To be effective, news stories need to be well timed, clearly expressed and relevant to the target readership. They should also support the organisation's stated objectives.

or newspapers such as *The Guardian* and *The News of the World*). It is therefore a waste of time sending them a news release about a local prize-giving, or a *minor* dispute. The national media are also more pro-active, telephoning you for comments on a particular issue and sending out their own journalists and photographers. The 'down-side' of this is a loss of influence over the end product; PR managers and executives are often horrified to see their relaxed 45-minute interview turned into a 'wholly unrepresentative' ten-second clip! To overcome this, interviewees and writers of press releases create '*sound bites*', short and memorable phrases that journalists are more likely to use uncut. Another way to obtain and control national media coverage is to stage a newsworthy event. The environmental campaign group, *Greenpeace* has perfected this technique with its 'abseiling down Nelson's column'-style of photo-opportunity. The nationals also monitor local media for suitable stories, offering another point of entry for those wanting more extensive coverage.

- *Specialist media* Even the smallest organisations may be able to get into one of the many specialist programmes and publications (e.g. *Computer Weekly, Hotel and Caterer, Yachting Monthly, Food & Drink, Gardeners' World, The Clothes Show*) with a relevant story. The main advantage of specialist media is that you can target a message at specific audiences. Some may offer 'advertorial' space (as in the earlier '*Vegigrub*' example), where a paid advertisement is linked to an feature article that also helps to promote your product or service.

EXERCISE 12C

Making news

Based on the advice given in the previous sections, select one of the following as a potential **national, local** and **specialist** story. Draft news releases for each story. In each case, you have the luxury (unavailable in real life) of inventing any necessary detail to turn a mere event into a real news story. Follow the news release layout described above.

- Museum hosts a travelling exhibition
- New shop opens in the High Street
- Company chief executive retires
- Canteen manager retires
- New product line launched
- Charity begins a new fund-raising effort
- Hospital expands (or threatens to close) paediatrics unit
- County's tourism strategy unveiled

12.8 ■■ Exhibitions, events and displays

Exhibitions are big business, with total annual expenditure in the United Kingdom of about £600 million (ISBA). For the exhibitor, there is a wide range of 'business to business' trade fairs and consumer events, such as *The Ideal Home Exhibition* and *The Boat Show*. Venues can range from 400 square metre parish halls to 158,000 square metres of floor space at Birmingham's National Exhibition Centre (NEC). Many organisations invest in expensive exhibition stands, which require considerable staff time. But is this an effective promotional technique? Exhibitions certainly offer unique communication opportunities. In particular, you have direct and simultaneous contact with many existing and potential customers. Exhibitors can therefore obtain immediate feed-back, simply talking with visitors on the stand. Exhibitions are also a popular venue for new product launches. Dramatic 'roll outs', accompanied with the obligatory musical fanfare, dry ice and lasers are something of a cliche. In the 1990s there has been an increasing interest in alternatives such as company-only events, including 'open days' for a company's network of distributors or agents. Whatever the format, trade shows and events are a rare opportunity to demonstrate new products to a specialised audience, including prospective customers and journalists. They can also be a good way to:

- Entertain key clients and suppliers
- Monitor competitor activity
- Build lists of 'prospects'
- Obtain media coverage and develop media contacts

The keys to effective exhibiting are similar to those for advertising and for PR. Exhibitions and events must fit into a coherent promotional strategy. Your objectives must be clear, and the whole exercise needs to be carefully planned and budgeted. The following case illustrates what can happen, if these factors are not addressed:

Case study

Super-Cadeaux '98 – the exhibition from hell!

The directors of Dozeytoys plc decided it was time to get into Europe. Janet Dozey, the MD, had spotted an advert for *Super-Cadeaux '98*, a major three-day toy trade fair to be held in Paris in two months time. They were pleased to secure the last available exhibition space and set to work constructing a world-beating stand. Arriving in Paris two days before the opening, Dozeytoys' marketing assistant was horrified to find that their space was too narrow to take the stand and it had to be hastily re-designed. They were located in the centre of a section *loisir-sportif*, devoted to children's sports equipment; but unfortunately their speciality was furry animals. It was day one of the fair and the newly translated product brochures had still not arrived. When the courier finally reached Paris, they found an embarrassing spelling error. The stand was very quiet for two days. This was unsurprising, since none of the key continental retailers had been invited to visit. By the end of day 2, there were five 'prospects' on the list, but two company names were illegible and one just said '*C'est tres jolie ! j'aime les petits animaux. Marie-Claire xxx*'. Day 3 was a complete contrast, and life on the stand became hectic. The exhibition had opened to the public and a large army of Parisian school children descended on to the stand and scooped up an entire stock – some 20,000 – brand new, full-colour French/German language brochures; these had cost the company about £2.50 each to produce. The management of Dozeytoys plc went home sadder and wiser. Most of all, they blamed the French.

As the *Super-Cadeaux* case study highlights, exhibitions and trade shows present some major pitfalls for the unwary. These can be summarised as follows:

- *Choosing the wrong show* It is easy to spot the company making this mistake as the crowds rush past their stand and their staff look longingly at the busy exhibitors across the aisle. Expensively produced brochures are handed out to school trips or disposed of, to hide the embarrassment of the organisers.

- *Wasting time on 'time wasters'* Most trade exhibitions have restricted admissions. However, exhibitors need to focus their efforts on those who can make or influence a buying decision. Sales staff should be trained to establish 'buying potential' and to prioritise their visitors accordingly.

- *Logistical problems* Have you sent an 'advance party' to set up the stand? Do you have enough brochures and other display items, communications links to head office, food and drink (if running a hospitality suite), spare OHP bulbs? Can you meet a short-term surge in orders, generated by this promotion?

- *Failing to 'follow-up'* As with any promotional activity, it is essential to assess the effectiveness of the exhibition in getting your message across (e.g. by taking a count of new prospects added, sales enquiries, etc.). Prospects must be followed-up promptly. Hence, an integrated promotional strategy is essential.

Nine steps to a successful exhibition stand

1. Decide what you are aiming to achieve, quantify it, and set a realistic budget.
2. Appoint an exhibition manager to co-ordinate and take overall charge of the project.
3. Decide whether to use a specialist designer: if so, obtain competing quotations and try to see examples of their work.
4. Obtain information on events well in advance, including audited attendance data.
5. Decide when and where to exhibit, and think about your location within the exhibition hall.

6. Plan the stand with a clear idea about staff and visitor numbers.
7. Select an appropriate group of staff to run the stand: for example, technical specialists and sales people may be needed; ensure that staff are well briefed and motivated.
8. Develop complementary advertising and PR programme.
9. Be sure to record, classify and follow up leads promptly.

Figure 12.3 An exhibition stand in position at the London Boat Show, with video monitors, comfortable seating and a strong corporate identity. (Source: Quartz Presentations, Shrewsbury/Mercantile Credit)

EXERCISE 12D

Making an exhibition of yourself

You have been asked to promote your college or another organisation of your choice, using a portable display stand, suitable for use by two members of staff.

(a) Where would you exhibit and why?
(b) What are your key messages?
(c) Who is your target audience?

Design a trade stand to meet these requirements. This should include a preliminary sketch of the layout, slogans for the main headings and a description of the artwork (photographs, drawings, etc.) that you plan to use.

12.9 ■■ Chapter summary

- Managers need to be aware of the practical aspects of advertising, public relations, exhibitions and events, even where outside agencies are used.

- An effective advertisement needs to be part of a co-ordinated promotional campaign. It should summarise and underline your key messages in a way that is memorable for the target audience.

- News releases should be one part of a long-term public relations effort, including corporate advertising, sponsorship, lobbying and consultation.

- To be newsworthy, a story must meet the specific needs of either local, national or specialist media.

- Exhibitions and events are an important element in the 'promotional mix', allowing organisations an opportunity to meet customers and others 'face-to-face'. However, they require careful planning and follow-up in order to justify the investment.

Practical exercises

1. Advertising campaign – presenting a client brief

Develop an advertising campaign for a product or service of your choice, based on the guidelines provided in this chapter. Consider ways of integrating some public relations activity, such as an newsworthy event. Prepare a ten-minute presentation, making use of suitable audio-visual aids (refer to Chapter 10 for advice on presenting your arguments).

2. Public relations – re-building a reputation

You have just been appointed as the new public relations manager at AOK Chemicals (refer to Chapter 5, Exercise 5c for the background information). The company has a new board of directors who are keen to re-build AOK's reputation with a number of key audiences:

- **The 'City'** – financial analysts and institutional investors who sold their shares in AOK following its recent, well-publicised, difficulties.
- **The general public** – including those who have been upset by reports of environmental pollution and bird-lovers who are outraged by the demise of the 'Bay Gull'.
- **The employees** – who are concerned about jobs and extremely unhappy to be working for a company with such a poor public image.

Prepare a report (maximum 1,500 words) summarising your assessment of the problem and proposals for a public relations campaign. Try to distinguish your short-term objectives from longer-term goals. If a number of individuals of teams are working on this exercise, arrange short verbal presentations and compare the different solutions that have been developed.

Chapter thirteen

Interviews and listening skills

It takes two to speak the truth, one to speak and another to hear

Henry Thoreau

Objectives

- To review the various types of interview used at work, noting the differing requirements of each situation (13.1 to 13.2)

- To examine and improve listening skills and to consider the practical arrangements for a successful interviews (13.3)

- To identify and develop questioning techniques in order to produce useful responses from an interviewee (13.4)

- To provide practical advice on preparing to attend an interview (13.5)

- To discuss the role of counselling interviews at work (13.6)

13.1 ■■ Introduction

Interviews have been usefully described as 'a discussion with a purpose'. In business, they serve all kinds of purposes, from recruitment and employee appraisal to marketing research and public relations. In communication terms, interviews are particularly rich in messages. The words spoken are often less important than the 'non-verbal' signals that are exchanged. These include: facial expressions, eye contact, gestures and posture. As a result of this complex mixture of stimuli, interviews also offer considerable scope for misunderstanding and confusion. Hence, it is important for all managers to develop strong interviewing skills. Fortunately, the skills required by an interviewer are similar to those of a successful interviewee. By building on past experience 'in the hot seat', it is possible to prepare yourself for a subsequent switch in roles.

The chapter begins with a brief review of the main types of interview, describing their distinctive characteristics. Two practical sections deal with the essential, but poorly practised, skills of listening and questioning. These are followed by suggestions on how best to prepare for an interview, looking from the interviewee's perspective. Lastly, there is a short discussion on the role of counselling techniques at work.

13.2 ■■ Types of interview

As a manager, you will almost certainly become involved in the four typical interview situations described below. The level of formality (i.e. the established procedures and paperwork) is likely to vary depending on the organisation and the individuals involved. However, some common features can be identified:

(a) Recruitment and promotion interviews

Interviews are normally used at the second or third stage of a recruitment process. Prior to this, applicants are 'screened' on the basis of information provided in CVs and application forms. Screening is essentially a *rejection* process. It is used to produce a 'shortlist', reducing the initial numbers to a more manageable size. Some larger organisations then ask shortlisted candidates to take part in psychometric tests, 'in-tray' exercises, etc. The final stage, where *selection* takes place, is almost always a personal interview. Selection, unlike screening, is about choosing the most **suitable** candidate from a shortlist, most of whom could probably do the job very well. Interviews can also be used to clarify and check up on the candidate's 'paper' achievements and interests (e.g. '*So tell me, Felicity, did you really cycle from Moscow to Beijing?*'). However, for many managers, the principal function of a face-to-face interview is to see whether the candidate would make a decent colleague, fitting in with those already employed. As a result, recruitment interviews can become highly subjective, no matter how objective the rest of the process has been. Interviewees are not the only ones who use persuasive techniques (Chapter 5); prospective employers may also be seeking to influence the outcome, encouraging a 'star' candidate to accept their offer rather than taking up an opportunity with the competition.

Recruitment interviewers should ensure that all interviewees, successful and unsuccessful, are left with a positive impression, perceiving the organisation as efficient, fair and a decent place to work. After all, unsuccessful candidates may subsequently become customers or suppliers. In any event, they will certainly influence other people who deal with, or apply to join, your organisation. Promotion interviews operate in a similar way to recruitment, with internal candidates competing for a more senior post, the key difference being that applicants will continue to work for the organisation, whether or not they are successful at the interview. You may also interview candidates for a 'sideways move', a change in work task or location which does not involve an increase in salary or status.

(b) Employee appraisal interviews

Thanks to the current emphasis on Total Quality Management, and to initiatives such as the UK Government's '*Investors in People*', more businesses are establishing a regular system of appraisal interviews. An appraisal interview should provide an opportunity for employees to review with their line manager performance and progress. An open and honest discussion can highlight the person's achievements, probe the reasons behind any 'problem areas' and identify training or work experience needs. The interviewer prepares a summary of the discussion and outcomes, and both parties agree an 'action plan' for the next period. If the manager ensures a climate of openness and trust, the appraisal interview can be highly motivating. By reviewing the results of a number of interviews, underlying structural or procedural problems in the organisation can be identified and corrected. Unfortunately, many companies make the fundamental mistake of linking appraisals to performance-related pay schemes or bonuses. Obviously, this is not likely to encourage an open or self-critical approach in the employee!

(c) Coaching/mentoring interviews

Coaching is a kind of on-going appraisal for newly appointed and recently promoted staff, where employees are asked to discuss progress on current projects with an experienced senior person, sometimes known as a 'mentor'. In these interviews, the emphasis is on making the employee more self-aware, encouraging them to discuss how things have gone since the previous meeting. Here, the role of the interviewer is not primarily to instruct or to give advice, but to encourage the interviewee to take on increasing responsibility at work. Mentors and coaches can help the interviewee by agreeing targets and encouraging reflection upon what has been learnt.

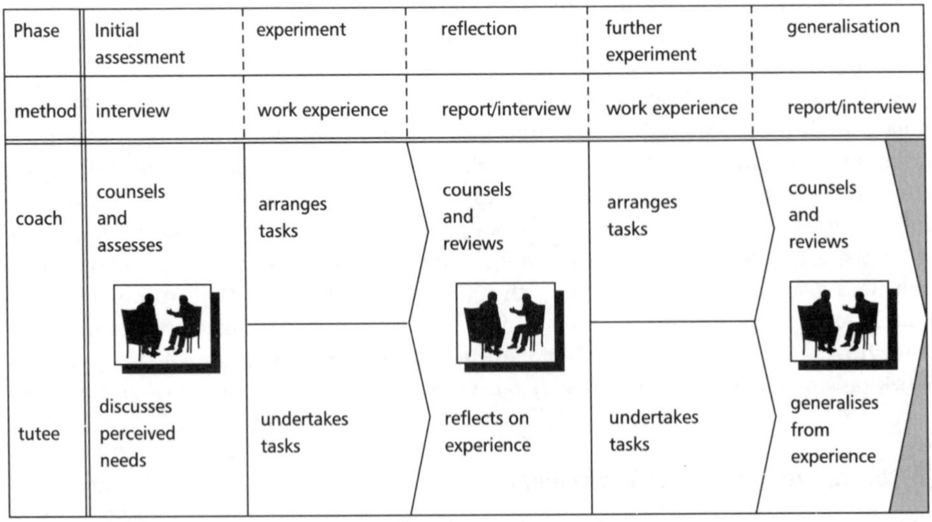

Phase	Initial assessment	experiment	reflection	further experiment	generalisation
method	interview	work experience	report/interview	work experience	report/interview
coach	counsels and assesses	arranges tasks	counsels and reviews	arranges tasks	counsels and reviews
tutee	discusses perceived needs	undertakes tasks	reflects on experience	undertakes tasks	generalises from experience

Figure 13.1 The coaching process.

(d) Disciplinary interviews

With children, the threat of being 'sent to the headteacher's office', or of more specific punishments, is sometimes enough to ensure reasonable behaviour. However, disciplining adults is a different matter. Ideally, problems should be identified and remedied in appraisal or coaching sessions. Minor 'one-off' incidents (e.g. an unscheduled extended lunch break) should be dealt with quickly and with minimal fuss. In the case of a more serious, complex, or long-running problem, a more formal interview may be necessary. Procedures for this type of interview should be clearly stipulated in the individual's employment contract, and these must be closely followed. In the worst case, you might subsequently need written evidence to defend against an unfair dismissal claim before an employment tribunal. During a disciplinary interview, the interviewer's main priorities are to establish the facts and to remain calm and objective. You should not resort to personal abuse, even when provoked, but seek to secure a commitment from the employee to acknowledge the fault and to overcome it voluntarily.

13.3 ▪▪ Listening techniques

Our ears play an important role in the communication process. Biological design, based around two ears and one mouth, suggests that listening could be twice as important as talking! However, compared to the years we spend perfecting the powers of speech, very little time is devoted to listening skills. In this section, we focus on six things that a receiver can do in order to become a more effective listener:

1. *Avoid prejudice* Prejudice acts like a filter on the ear, cutting out those things that do not fit in with a person's original viewpoint and reinforcing anything that does. In order to cope with a complex world, we have put our experiences, and the people we meet into pre-existing 'pigeon holes'. However, these rough and ready categorisations can become an obstacle, distorting the more detailed information that we subsequently receive. If we are to deal with our prejudices, they need to be recognised. One way of increasing awareness is to consider previous occasions when you have formed an incorrect opinion based on someone's nationality, gender, age, politics, educational qualifications or similar factors.

EXERCISE 13A

Examine your prejudices – Elite Fashions

Your company, which manufactures a range of expensive fashion accessories, is recruiting a new secretary, who would also spend some time working as the headquarters receptionist. What thoughts do the following candidate details provoke?:

Name	Age	Status	Qualifications	Experience	Born
Marjorie Jones	58	Married	Secretarial/PA	25 years	UK
Natalie Brown	21	Single	Secretarial	3 years	UK
Andy Smith	33	Divorced	Graduate	5 years	Kenya
Sasha Pruzik	27	Married	Secretarial	7 years	Poland

Did you find yourself identifying a 'most likely' candidate, based on these details? Would your choice alter if Marjorie was younger, if Natalie was a single parent of five, if Andy was female or if Sasha spoke with a 'home counties' accent and had five years' experience in a rival London fashion house?

2. **Show interest** It is not enough to concentrate on your interviewees, you must demonstrate a real interest in what they have to say. Interest can be signalled in a number of ways. Interviewers should adopt an 'open' posture with arms *unfolded*, facing towards the person and perhaps leaning forwards slightly. Eye contact, facial expression and tone of voice are also influential. These signals of interest serve to re-inforce the words that are spoken.

3. **Listen for feelings** A good listener operates at two levels simultaneously. At a 'surface' level, there is information that needs to be absorbed (e.g. '*Yes, I have completed the report*', '*No, we did not receive the training materials*'). However, some of the key messages communicated by an interviewee are more to do with personal feelings and emotions. In a culture where feelings are notoriously difficult to express, they tend to be hidden 'between the lines' of a conversation. In the following extract, what do you think the office supervisor, Jack, is trying to communicate to Jill, his immediate line manager?

JACK: Do you realise, those contractors we hired have still not finished. I've spent *five* hours today trying to chase them up and the painting job is still not completed. You wouldn't believe it, Jill, they always have a brilliant excuse for not turning up, but I really don't think it's on.

JILL: So, will the restaurant be ready for next week's opening?

JACK: Well yes, Jill, it will be ready ... if I have anything to do with it!

JILL: Oh fine, so that's alright then.

At the 'emotions' level, Jack is clearly annoyed. In addition, he appears to be seeking some (well-deserved?) recognition for his efforts, and is perhaps expressing disappointment that Jill is failing to provide the expected level of support? If Jill continues to miss these cues, she is likely to have a demotivated and hence less effective colleague to manage.

4. **Avoid interruption and distraction** One of the most difficult challenges for a 'hands on' manager is to keep their mouths shut! Speaking over another person will usually stop them in their tracks. In effect, you are announcing that '*I don't*

want to listen to this any more'. Interviewers should only 'cut in' where they are sure that interviewees are either repeating themselves or digressing from the subject matter of the interview. Shuffling paperwork or reading while an interviewee is speaking are equally distracting and should therefore be avoided.

5. ***Signal encouragement*** There are ways to maintain the momentum of a conversation without distracting the interviewee. Occasional nodding of your head, eye contact, smiling and the use of vocal cues like '*mmm*', and '*uh huh*' are strong signals for the other person to continue. The reverse is also true. If you stop using these cues, the effect can be dramatic, particularly where the interviewee is either nervous or reluctant to speak.

6. ***Clarify and summarise*** Towards the end of the interview, you can draw everything together in the form of a summary. This is likely to include paraphrases of what the interviewee has said, and of your own comments. Summaries help to ensure that both parties have a similar understanding of what has been covered. They also provide an opportunity to specify decisions and action. However, there is a danger of 'leading' the interviewee. Always check whether your clarifications and summaries accurately reflect what the person was trying to say.

INTERVIEWER: So, to summarise, would it be fair to say that your main reasons for applying for the post are: (a) because you want a company car, (b) because our offices are close to home, and (c) because you fancy our Sales Director?.

EXERCISE 13B

Active listening practice

Perhaps the easiest way to understand the importance of these techniques is to experiment with their opposites. Arrange for two interviewees to leave the room, and have an interviewer call them in one at a time. The rest of the group act as observers. Use exactly the same list of questions in each interview, but vary the listening techniques as follows:

Interview A   Try to follow the six guidelines described in section 13.3.
Interview B   This time, do the opposite. Try to keep a fixed expression on your face, have your arms tightly crossed, interrupt the interviewee mid-sentence, write notes and gaze out of the window from time to time.

Ask the observers to comment on the outcomes. Discuss how the experience felt for the interviewer and each interviewee? Are there occasions when you might *want* to make interviewees uncomfortable?

Effective interviews – practical arrangements

(a) ***Seating*** Layout does affect the atmosphere of the interview (Figure 13.2). It is often better to move away from your desk, with its distracting piles of work. Putting your interviewee in a lower or less comfortable chair sends out a message of superiority and distance. However, if you are aiming to retain some degree of businesslike formality, relaxing armchairs are best avoided.

Figure 13.2 Effective interviewing – seating makes a difference.

(b) ***Interruptions and distractions*** Managers tend to have frequent telephone calls and visitors, so divert calls (or unplug the phone) and put a 'do not disturb' sign on the door. If your offices are open-plan, book a small meeting room or borrow someone else's office. Try to sit in sight of a wall clock, so that you can then keep track of time without glancing at your watch.

(c) ***Before and after*** Especially in the case of recruitment interviews (where the person is a visitor), basic courtesies convey a positive image of the organisation. Do not leave people waiting in a busy corridor! Find a suitable room, offer them a coffee, keep to stated times if possible and ensure that any agreed follow-up action is taken.

13.4 ■■ Questioning techniques

An interview is punctuated by questions and answers. The same question can be asked in many ways, and each of these can actually generate a *different* response. By considering the types of questions people ask, it is possible to improve your questioning technique.

(a) Open & closed questions

One of the most important distinctions is between 'open' and 'closed' questions. Closed questions demand a short pre-determined response, often a simple 'yes' or 'no' (e.g. '*Have you called the office this morning?*'). Open questions, by contrast, encourage the respondent to think for themselves and thus allow for a wider range of responses (e.g. '*How should we tackle this production problem?*'). Consider how using a closed question limits communication in the following dialogue:

PETER: So anyway, Helen, was that training course OK?
HELEN: Well yes . . . , I suppose so . . .
PETER: Excellent, see you later!

An 'open' version of the same basic question produces a much more informative (and therefore useful) answer from the interviewee, since it encourages them to speak for longer, and to give a more considered response:

PETER: So anyway, Helen, how did you feel about the training course?
HELEN: Well . . . , the tutor was excellent, but she was repeating a lot of the material we covered during our induction sessions in September.
PETER: Ah, that's unfortunate. Looks like we need to revise the programme.

Closed questions are useful for establishing the basic facts (e.g. '*How many people do you employ?*'). You can also use them to 'close down' an overly wordy or rambling interviewee, forcing them to give more concise responses. Open questions, with occasional closed questions for clarification, are a very useful way to investigate complex issues, especially where your own knowledge of the area is limited.

(b) Probing questions

These are open or closed questions that build on the interviewee's previous response(s). Probing needs to be tackled carefully. It can easily sound aggressive, prompting an unhelpful defensive reaction from the 'victim':

PETER: So anyway, Helen, how did you feel about the training course?
HELEN: Well . . . , the tutor was excellent, but she was repeating a lot of the material we covered during our induction sessions in September.
PETER: Oh really, so which topics were repeated?
HELEN: The presentation skills, and the session on company organisation.
PETER: And did you tell the tutor about this?
HELEN: No, actually . . .
PETER: Was there a feedback session?
HELEN: Hang on a second. It wasn't **my** fault they messed up!

(c) Hypothetical questions

Hypotheticals are an excellent way to make your interviewee reflect on things. This type of question is often used to test the mental agility and creativity of prospective employees (e.g. *'Imagine you're in charge of our Japanese export marketing operation. The Tokyo stock exchange has just collapsed. What would you do?'*). Hypotheticals are also used in coaching and counselling, to help a person explore previously unconsidered options (e.g. *'So, if we could arrange the extra language tuition, how would you feel about spending two years in Romania?'*).

(d) Leading questions

These are questions that encourage the interviewee to respond with the answer that you either desire or expect. Leading questions are the interviewers' most common fault. They are always communication failures, their one-way messages masquerading as an exchange of views. An extreme example illustrates the dangers:

PETER: So what did you think of that 'so-called' training course?
HELEN: Well, it's difficult . . .
PETER: And as for the tutor! – a complete waste of space, don't you think?
HELEN: I'm sure she . . .
PETER: Means well?
HELEN: No, not really.
PETER: Helen, I couldn't agree more. Have to dash. See you!

Leading questions are sometimes disguised, but can be identified by any kind of prompt towards a particular answer. Use Exercise 13c to find out whether you have a tendency to ask leading questions. If you do, make a conscious effort to *listen* to the interviewee, *focus* on them and try to keep your own opinions to yourself!

EXERCISE 13C

Question spotting

Either arrange a mock interview during a tutorial, or make a tape recording of an interview from television or radio. Use the grid shown below to record each type of question used, noting other interviewer behaviour, such as encouraging, clarifying and summarising. Compare the performances of different interviewers using each of these criteria.

questions										
open										
closed										
probing										
leading										
hypothetical										

behaviour										
interrupting										
encouraging										
clarifying										
summarising										

13.5 ■■ The interviewee's perspective – making the best of it

Interviews can be nerve-wracking occasions, bringing back memories of sitting outside the head-teacher's office or waiting to see the dentist. However, from the interviewee's point of view, they are best viewed as just another channel of communication – given practice and preparation, they can be handled more effectively. How, for example, might you improve your performance during everyone's favourite nightmare, the job interview? There are a number of things that you can do, in advance and on the day itself:

(a) *Practice and review* Try to attend as many interviews as possible, so that you can rehearse your interview technique. Take up every opportunity for mock interviews, ideally with a video recording so that you are able to look back on your own performance and that of other 'candidates'; look out for any nervous habits (such as wringing your hands or ear scratching) and try to un-learn them. Get hold of one of the many interesting 'fly on the wall' documentaries that include a sequence on job interviews; these usually feature doctors, vets or paratroopers, but the basic principles are much the same. Accept every invitation for an interview that you receive; even if your chances are slim, the experience is going to be invaluable. After each interview, review your performance objectively. Do not waste time complaining about the way you were treated, but focus on how well you responded to the questions that were asked. If possible, try to get some informal feedback from the interviewer.

(b) ***Prepare and organise*** In a job interview, you are obviously involved in persuasive communication (Chapter 5). The interviewers are going to be looking for a range of personal attributes (e.g. enthusiasm, social skills, creativity, decisiveness) plus evidence to support your application. Prepare by finding out as much as possible about the subject of the interview – in this case, the company and the job itself. Ensure that you are ready to reinforce the information contained in your written application. For example, if your form mentions that you are a keen mountaineer, be ready with anecdotes from expeditions that you have organised. If you have stated a particular ambition, be prepared to explain how you intend to realise it. There are also more practical aspects to consider: do you know how to get to the interview address? Have you left sufficient time to cover a delayed train or traffic jam? What clothes are going to give the right impression? Have the interviewers asked you to prepare a short presentation (see Chapter 10).

(c) ***On the day*** Always arrive in good time; you may pick up some useful information while waiting for the interview, or simply have a chance to chat to other candidates. When you enter the interview room, always remember to smile at the interviewer(s) and try, if possible, to shake hands. You should be aiming for that difficult combination of calmness and focused attention. When you are asked a question, take a few seconds to consider your answer; that pause always seems far longer to you than it does to the interviewer. Always answer honestly but concisely. At an appropriate moment, try to insert a few questions of your own, demonstrating your interest in the organisation and awareness of relevant issues. When the time comes to leave, do so with another smile and handshake rather than scrambling for your coat and rushing out of the door.

With suitable practice and preparation, plus a better understanding of the inter-viewer's task, the whole process of attending an interview can become more enjoyable as well as producing a successful outcome.

13.6 ▦ Counselling techniques and the manager

Counselling techniques are now widely used in business, with many courses aimed at both personnel 'professionals' and those with a general interest in people. Managers are often criticised for taking insufficient interest in the problems faced by their staff, either due to time pressures or a reluctance to become involved in the private lives of their employees. While these objections are understandable, human resource specialists are keen to promote 'workplace counselling' as a positive development, benefitting both the individual concerned, the manager and the wider organisation.

In what is known as a 'person-centred' counselling interview, the role of the counsellor is simply to listen and to 'facilitate'. Above all, this means that a counsellor should *not* give advice (i.e. telling the interviewee how to solve the problem). Instead, the primary objective of counselling is to provide a climate in which the person is able to resolve problems for themselves. However, there are some important obstacles to successful counselling at work. Employees are understandably unwilling to share personal problems with line managers, whilst managers often find emotions difficult to handle, and (as professional 'problem-solvers') are unable to avoid giving advice. Hence, for many practical reasons, the following areas need to be distinguished:

- Advice and instruction
- Befriending
- Workplace counselling
- Professional counselling

Counselling is clearly different from giving advice or instructing employees. In practice, it is extremely difficult to switch between these roles, so your counselling session can easily revert into a 'lecture'. Counselling is also different from the role played by a friend who might take time to share a person's problems, acting as a 'shoulder to cry on'. Perhaps the key distinction for a manager is between workplace and professional counselling. It is essential for all concerned to recognise the dividing line between work-related personal issues, where the manager (or Personnel department) has the relevant skills and experience to handle things, and those more serious problems (e.g. drug and alcohol abuse, clinical depression) requiring urgent professional support. Managers must be ready to refer such cases to outside agencies.

13.7 ■■ Chapter summary

- Interviews are a widely used communication channel, but their rich messages are open to misinterpretation. Future interviewers should learn from their own experiences as interviewees.
- Interviews are used within an organisation for a variety of purposes, including: recruitment, promotion, appraisal, coaching and disciplinary problems.
- Listening is a skill that can be improved with practice. It is important to focus on interviewees and to show that you are interested in what they have to say. Try not to interrupt them, but be ready to clarify and summarise the conversation.
- Be alert to the differences between: open, closed, probing, leading and hypothetical questions. The way that a question is framed can have a material effect on the answer you receive.

- Workplace counselling can be a helpful activity, using many of the listening techniques discussed in this chapter, but its use in a work situation needs to be defined carefully.

Practical exercises

1. Interviews on tape

Using a video-recorder, you can practice the roles of interviewer and interviewee. Try to make the setting as realistic as possible by setting up desks and chairs and by wearing appropriate clothes. Select one of the following scenarios:

- A job interview
- A promotion interview
- A disciplinary interview
- A media interview (e.g. relating to a real or invented news story)

Allow five minutes for the interview, play it back and discuss the outcomes with colleagues. Try to identify specific strengths and weaknesses. You may also want to use the interview grids provided in Exercise 13c to record what occurred during the interview.

2. Where does it hurt?

The interviewer takes the role of a placement student or volunteer visitor in a hospital. The interviewee is a patient being visited, and takes up one of the following roles (or others developed by the group):

- You have suffered a mild stroke.
- You have just had a baby prematurely.
- You are undergoing tests, having had repeated stomach pains.
- You have suffered concussion in an accident and have lost your memory.

The objective is for the interviewer to discover as much as possible about the patient's condition, without upsetting or annoying the 'patient'. Of course, the interviewee should try to be as reticent and unhelpful as possible, providing ambiguous answers or straying from the question. Observers should pay particular attention to the interviewer's use of open, closed, probing, hypothetical and leading questions.

Chapter fourteen

Future communication: the role of technology

Mr Watson, come here; I want you

Alexander Graham Bell: first words spoken by telephone, 7 March 1876

Objectives

- To review recent developments in communication and computing technologies, including the advantages of converting information into digital formats (14.1–14.2)

- To assess the emerging role of intranets, the Internet and digital office equipment, and to explain some widely used specialist terminology (14.3)

- To identify the different ways that information can be collected, processed and shared using the new technologies, noting some practical implications for the 'electronic office' (14.4–14.6)

- To consider critically the potential advantages and disadvantages of these innovations, including the skills required to exploit them successfully (14.2–14.6)

14.1 ▦ Introduction

This closing chapter is about technology, the tools that people use. It focuses on the ways that recent developments in computing and telecommunications are transforming the ways that we do business with one another. The undoubted opportunities of the 'information age' are considered, along with its potential problem areas. The chapter begins with a brief historical review, putting the short-term changes into some kind of context. Another important task is to demystify the language of information and communications technology. As Chapters 2 and 3 suggested, cultural differences and the jargon of technical specialists are major causes of communication breakdown. In the world of computing, these barriers have led to many millions of pounds of wasted investment, and a great deal of unnecessary stress. Poor consultation has led to unsuitable computer systems being installed. It has also resulted in users who do not understand and cannot therefore fully exploit the hardware and software that their organisation has purchased. Technologists and business managers need to learn more of each others' language. With greater mutual understanding, the technological innovations of the future could be much more exciting and productive than those of the recent past.

A note about the 'FUD factor'

Whether intentionally or not, the jargon-ridden language of computers and communications has created 'Fear, Uncertainty and Doubt' in the minds of many everyday users – the so-called *FUD factor*. This chapter has been written with the non-specialist in mind, but in some cases technical terms are unavoidable. Some of the more commonly used initials and acronyms are described briefly in the glossary (p. 217). The Further Reading list includes suggested texts for those requiring more detailed technical information on the topics discussed. However, due to the sheer pace of change, it is worthwhile referring to current magazines, journals and Web sites.

14.2 ▓▓ Computing and communication – the technologies converge

Recent changes in business life are dominated by a convergence of two technologies, computing and telecommunications. As a result, information can be handled in far greater volumes, and at far greater speeds, than was possible in previous generations.

Communications technology was the first to advance. As early as the mid nineteenth century, it was transformed through the use of electricity and cables. By 1870, for example, merchants and civil servants enjoyed direct telegraph communication between Bombay and London. In contrast to this, computing technology has been a very late starter. Today, it is difficult to imagine life without them. However, until very recently, computers would have been considered largely irrelevant to the average manager.

Before the arrival of electronic calculators in the mid 1970s, most people worked out their sums using an ingenious seventeenth-century device called a slide rule. Letters and reports were either dictated to secretaries, or typed from a hand-written draft; even minor amendments involved the retyping of whole pages of text. Similarly, brochures and presentation materials had to be prepared by a specialist art department using traditional 'cut and paste' techniques. So where were the computers? The majority were locked away in air-conditioned 'data processing' departments, enormous and highly temperamental 'mainframes' which carried out routine number-crunching tasks like payroll and accounting. 'Mini-computers', which were actually about the size of a wardrobe, offered limited data processing facilities, but they tended to remain under the control of accountants and researchers. The intervening years have seen a real revolution. In terms of memory capacity and processing power, the old mainframes would be comprehensively beaten by any of today's desktop or laptop computers, at a tiny fraction of the cost. As a result of this, most office workers have one of their own. Microprocessors, the heart of a modern computer, have become a commodity item. They are found in all kinds of business and domestic equipment, from fax machines to tumble driers. Insert a microprocessor into a 'smart card' and it records every detail of your supermarket or petrol station purchase; slip one into a 'musical' birthday card and it can play an irritating tune. Computer technology has clearly come a long way in the last 25 years. The scale of change is well captured by an *Apollo 13* astronaut who pointed out that the computing power of his multi-million dollar space craft, leading edge technology in the 1970s, was about that of today's average family saloon car.

The digital revolution: what does it really mean?

The advances in computer memory and processing power are impressive, but the fundamental transformation in recent years has been the linking of computing and communications technologies. The key to this convergence is making information 'digital'. In other words, converting it into a series of binary numbers. The idea of expressing information as binary code was first proposed by the mathematician, Claude Shannon (Gates 1996: 32). 'Data compression', another building block of the digital revolution, was also Shannon's idea. The data in a file are compressed by omitting 'redundant' coding (i.e. material that is not essential in order to make sense of a message). Thanks to compression techniques, computers and networks can cope with more demanding tasks, such as multi-media presentations. Incidentally, you may recall Claude Shannon as co-author of the model of communication outlined in Chapter 1. With these other important ideas, he conveniently returns us to this book's initial topic: the links between messages, channels and media.

What will be the effect of new technologies on the form and content of our communication? A partial answer can be found by contrasting today's digital formats with their 'analogue' predecessors. This comparison highlights some of the novel and interesting things that you can do with information, once it is in binary form. Information can be stored, copied, manipulated and accessed in ways that were unimaginable a few years ago:

- **Storage** Vast quantities of information can now be held in tiny spaces. The most familiar example of this is the compact disc, with billions of binary 'switches' embedded in its shiny surface. Originally limited to about 70 minutes of music, this format has been extended with the introduction of higher capacity and recordable discs. One CD-ROM can hold the contents of a large encyclopaedia, for example.

- **Copying** Each time you make a copy using 'analogue' technology, such as a video recorder or conventional photocopier, there is always some deterioration in quality. However, digital sources are simply lists of binary numbers. As a result, your original file, first copy and millionth copy will be identical. This is good news for software pirates as well as for genuine publishers.

- **Manipulation** Conventional typewriters had a single typeface. The most you could do to your text was to use upper case letters or underline particular words. The font, point size and colour of *wordprocessed* text can be changed at the touch of a button. More elaborate manipulation can be seen in many of today's feature films. The life-like dinosaurs in *Jurassic Park* and the earth-shattering tornadoes in *Twister* were constructed with the help of computer-based animation techniques.

- **Access** Conventional storage systems tend to make information inaccessible. Paper documents get lost at the back of filing cabinets, the local library does not stock the book you want, and it is always difficult to find your favourite track on a music cassette. Once the same information is held in digital form, it has the potential to be accessed instantly by anyone with a suitable communications link. Stored items can be indexed, much like the tracks on a compact disc. They can also be delivered anywhere on (or above) the planet.

Communications & computing: some key events

The technologies of computing and communication have developed separately over many centuries. With the arrival of digital technologies in the last few years, they have converged, resulting in the dawn of a so-called 'information age':

c.830	Hindu-Arabic numbering system brought to Europe by al-Khwarizmi
1614	Logarithms, discovered by John Napier, simplify multiplication and division
1615	Slide rule invented by William Outghtred, creator of 'x' symbol for multiply
1801	Punch card operated automatic loom devised by Joseph-Marie Jacquard
1839	Electric telegraph invented by Charles Wheatstone and William Cooke
1840s	Steam-driven computer ('analytical engine') devised by Charles Babbage
1843	Universal telegraph coding system introduced by Samuel Morse
1843	First public telegraph line laid between Paddington and Slough in England
1847	Principles underlying computer programs established by George Boole
1858	First transatlantic telegraph cable laid
1873	First typewriters sold by US gun-makers, Remington and Sons
1876	Telephone invented by Alexander Graham Bell
1891	First telephone cable laid between England and France
1892	First commercial adding machine patented by William Burroughs
1896	Founding of the Tabulating Machine Company, precursor of IBM
1901	First 'wireless' signals transmitted over the Atlantic by Guglielmo Marconi
1922	First radio (or wireless) transmissions by the BBC
1926	First practical demonstration of television by John Logie Baird
1929	First experimental television broadcasts by the BBC
1936	Concept of a digital computer established by mathematician, Alan Turing
1943	Electronic code-breaker 'Collosus' built by Thomas Flowers and Alan Turing
1946	First general purpose electronic digital computer, the 18,000 valve 'ENIAC'
1948	Concept of data compression first described by Claude Shannon
1951	First 'business computer', 'LEO' introduced by Lyons Teashop Company
1954	COBOL programming language developed by Grace Murray Hopper
1958	First silicon integrated circuit constructed by Texas Instruments

1962   First transatlantic satellite broadcast of live television pictures
1965   First commercial 'minicomputers' launched by Digital Equipment Corporation
1969   ARPAnet, forerunner of the Internet, set up by US Department of Defense
1971   First microprocessor developed, the Intel 4004, based on a silicon chip
1975   First 'microcomputer' marketed, the Altair 8800 (4Kb memory)
1977   First optical fibre cables first installed for commercial purposes
1981   IBM launch its first personal computer (upgradeable 256Kb memory)
1981   IBM licence the operating system MS-DOS from the fledgling Microsoft
1984   Apple Macintosh launched, with the first commercial 'graphical user interface'
1983   Digital compact discs introduced, initially for pre-recorded music
1983   IBM launches PC-XT with 10Mb hard disk; IBM-compatibles ('clones') arrive
1989   ARPAnet loses US government funding; users re-invent it as the 'Internet'

1990s   PC market growth continues, still dominated by IBM-compatibles or 'clones'. Parallel expansion in the equally competitive computer software market. PC memory and speed, is improved, ready for multi-media applications. Accelerating Internet usage, mainly via the graphical 'World Wide Web'. Internal corporate networks re-designed as Web-like 'intranets'.

14.3 ▪▪ Information age essentials – nets and digital machines

This section looks at how computing and communications technologies have converged in three key areas: corporate 'intranets', the global Internet and the re-design of familiar old office equipment as networked digital machines.

(a) Corporate 'intranets' – the internal network

Local area networks (LANs) are a combination of hardware – basically, file servers, personal computers and cabling – and controlling software. They can link a large number of computers situated in one building or across a single site, such as a college campus. Wide area networks (WANs) carry out a similar task across a number of different sites, such as a company's various manufacturing locations. Company-wide internal networks are being redesigned using Internet-standard software to turn them into 'corporate intranets'. Intranets offer a 'seamless' connection between the internal network and the wider world. This two-way communication via a 'Web server' gives staff, customers and suppliers easy access to in-house data – sometimes referred to as 'data warehouses' – plus the ability to search external sources on the Internet (see below).

A 'server' is basically a high-powered computer with a fast microprocessor and sufficient memory capacity to store networking software, shared application software (e.g. wordprocessors, spreadsheets) and a large amount of data (e.g. incoming e-mail and company databases). The additional role of a 'Web server' is to provide a 'bridge' between the internal network and the Internet. Of course, once an organisation creates an electronic link to the outside world, security and confidentiality become critical management issues. There are many ways to protect precious data from spies or saboteurs. The first line of defence is a 'firewall'. This can be either a piece of hardware, or a software program, that aims to stop unauthorised access to the internal network. Before confidential data are sent out, it may be 'encrypted'. This means that the contents of a message are rendered meaningless to everyone except a recipient with the relevant conversion code.

The most popular form of sabotage is the unleashing of a software virus. Once inside a network, the virus can spread its self-reproducing codes from machine to machine, destroying data. Virus-checking software is now used routinely, but it cannot provide complete protection; regular updates are needed to take account of newly emerging viruses. Assuming the 'worst case scenario' many organisations have a disaster recovery programme in place. 'Back-up' copies of all essential data are stored at a remote location. In the event of data being irretrievably corrupted by a virus, or destroyed by fire, explosion or natural disaster, it could be largely reinstated using the back-up storage. As in other areas of life, demands for individual privacy and corporate security do sometimes conflict. For example, when the network manager monitors staff access to the Internet, employees perceive it as intrusive. These are difficult issues that each organisation needs to resolve.

(b) The Internet – revolutionising external communication

The celebrated global network actually consists of an *ad hoc* combination of linked file servers and transmission lines. The 'backbone' (i.e. the Internet's main long-distance connections) is provided by the major telecommunications companies, and paid for by 'service providers'. These service providers (e.g. *Compuserve, Virgin Net* and *Pipex*) act as wholesalers, selling access on to companies and individuals. Current estimates suggest that there are more than 5 million 'host' computers on the Internet, of which about one million are in Europe. However, when you realise that many of these 'hosts' are actually network servers, with perhaps a further 50 or more computers attached, the sheer scale of the Internet becomes apparent. This network has developed over a number of years with no overall control. It originated in a United States Department of Defense network called *ARPAnet* which was designed to provide a link between the country's widely dispersed university research teams. One of the arguments for a loose network of this kind was that, unlike conventional systems, it could survive the effects of a nuclear war. In 1983, the so-called 'Internet Protocol' (IP) was introduced, a common standard that allowed one machine to communicate with another, by routing messages to its unique address. When, in the late 1980s, the US Government ceased funding the network, existing users began to re-position it as the 'Internet'. This coincided with the massive expansion in personal computing, which attracted many new users. Today, activity on the Internet is still concentrated in the United States, particularly amongst academics and individual enthusiasts (the much-lampooned computer 'nerds' or 'anoraks'). However, commercial businesses and other organisations have begun to experiment with this once-anarchic communications system. Navigating is much easier and more orderly, thanks to the 'World Wide Web' (WWW). This graphical interface treats the information on each Web site as a series of pages; users can jump from one site to another by simply clicking their mouse on highlighted words, known as 'hypertext links' (see Figure 14.1 below).

Figure 14.1 Prentice Hall Web Page.

As its longer-term potential is recognised, retailers, financial institutions and the entertainment industry are busy seeking Web-based commercial opportunities, including subscription services. In the meantime, access to the Internet has remained remarkably open and equal. With a budget of around £1,500, it is now possible for anyone to link a personal computer to the local telephone network, design a professional-looking Web page, pay a modest subscription to a service provider and make contact with millions of potential customers – or like-minded individuals – around the globe.

Case study

E-commerce over the Internet

There are more than 80,000 commercial sites on the Internet (*Yahoo!* estimate 1996), but electronic commerce is still in its infancy. Revenues generated by European Web sites is forecast to rise from around 50 million ECU to over 56 billion ECU between 1995 and 2001. Business-to-business sales are likely to develop faster than the consumer market, which is currently focused on luxury and niche products. At present, only 6.3 per cent of the UK's 23 million households have an Internet connection. However, the introduction of hybrid television-computers may help to increase consumer participation. A wide variety of products and services are already being sold via the World Wide Web, including:

- *Sunglasses* The Rome-based optician, Ottica Meloni set up its Web 'store' in 1996, hoping to reach consumers who lived outside the larger cities and had difficulty in finding the most fashionable products. It also gave this small company low-cost access to international markets, without the need for catalogues and distributors (http://www.meloni.com/).

- *Music* Cerberus is a UK-based company which sells music tracks via the Internet. The Digital Jukebox was launched in 1996 after extended negotiations over copyright regulations. After registering, consumers can download selected tracks on to a hard disk. This offers independent and unsigned artists a new outlet, free from the restrictions of record labels and conventional music retailers (http://www.cdj.co.uk).

- *People* An Internet-based recruitment service is provided by another new UK business, PeopleBank. The company has created a large database of CVs by advertising in national newspapers. However, the database is accessed by clients via the Internet; an on-line search produces a shortlist within a few minutes, rather than the month or more required by traditional methods (http://www.peoplebank.com).

Source: Romtec

(c) Digital office equipment – linking activities

Office equipment, such as photocopiers, flipcharts, filing systems, answerphones and telephone switchboards, may not seem an obvious target for revolutionary change. However, these products are leading the next phase of the convergence process. In each case, the common element is the **digitising** of information. At this stage, original medium becomes largely irrelevant; it may have been written words on an electronic flipchart (a 'copyboard'), spoken words recorded as 'voicemail', or an application form that has been fed through a digital scanner (see Section 14.4 below). Once the content of these messages is converted into binary code, it can be stored, manipulated and transmitted anywhere on the network. Consider, for example, the advantages that arise once you have a photocopier that operates digitally. By linking copiers to your network, multiple copies of a document can be requested from and produced at whichever location you prefer, with no need to feed in a paper 'top copy'. Copiers can tell you when they are busy, or re-route your job to the nearest available machine. One result of this is that old boundaries between the copier and the (software-driven) printer industries are beginning to disappear.

Do the three broad areas discussed above really represent the dawn of an 'information age'? It is certainly clear that further technological changes are underway. In the early days of business computing, everything was centralised around a mainframe computer. In the 1970s and 1980s, processing became distributed, firstly with the arrival of the minicomputer and more dramatically with the proliferation of personal computers. Initially, most personal computers were called 'stand-alones' since they could not communicate directly with other machines. To transfer data, you had to save it on a floppy disc, and then re-load it into the other machine; in some cases, this meant that data were being sent by the conventional postal service. Improvements in networking technology, plus the much-publicised commercial potential of the Internet, are leading to a new emphasis on linking people, software applications and information sources electronically, irrespective of their physical location. In the following sections, some implications of these changes for tomorrow's businesses are considered under the following inter-connected headings:

- Extracting information (Section 14.4)
- Processing information (Section 14.5)
- Sharing information (Section 14.6)

An information age glossary

Communications and computing technologies are constantly sprouting new jargon. The following list gives a brief explanation of some current initials and acronyms. Technical specialists need to bear in mind how easy it is to confuse audiences with an over-dose of unexplained terms. The best advice for the non-specialist is: 'Do not allow yourself to be intimidated.' People with a good command of their subject should be able to provide meaningful explanations in straightforward terms.

CTI	Computer Telephony Integration: linking telephones to computer systems
DIP	Document Image Processing: scanning, storing and retrieving documents
dpi	Dots per inch: e.g. current laser printers operate at a resolution of 300dpi
DBMS	Database Management Software: turns raw data into useful information
EDI	Electronic Data Interchange: system used to trade, exchange or share data
FTP	File Transfer Protocol: the 'rules' allowing data to move between computers
Gb	Gigabyte: one thousand megabytes of data – see 'Mb' below
GSM	Global System for Mobile communications: the digital cellphone system
GUI	Graphical User Interface: e.g. Microsoft's Windows software
HTML	Hyper-Text Mark up Language: used with HTTP to write 'Web' pages
HTTP	Hyper-Text Transfer Protocol: used with HTML to link 'Web' pages

IP	Internet Protocol: the 'rules' ensuring compatibility on the Internet
ISDN	Integrated Services Digital Networking: the new digital telephone network
Kb	Kilobyte: approximately one thousand bytes, or 8,000 bits of data
LAN	Local Area Network: linked computers in an organisation, sharing printers, etc.
Mb	Megabyte: one million bytes, or 8 million bits of data
Mbps	Megabytes per second: data transmission speed – similarly Kbps and Gbps
MHZ	Megahertz: the 'speed' of a micro processor – such as a 200Mhz Pentium Pro
OCR	Optical Character Recognition: 'scanning' – converting text to digital form
PDA	Personal Digital Assistant: pocket-size or 'palmtop' computer (e.g. Psion 3c)
PIMS	Personal Information Management Software: diary / scheduler / address book
PCMCIA	Personal Computer Memory Card: 'slot-in' computer memory for laptop PCS
RAM	Random Access Memory: the 'active' memory used in a PC (e.g. 16Mb RAM)
ROM	Read-Only Memory: the 'stored' memory found, for example, on a CD-ROM
SVGA	Super Video Graphics Adaptor: current quality standard for PC screen display
TFT	Thin Film Transistor: current technology for laptop computer screens
URL	Uniform Resource Locators: the unique site addresses used on the Internet
WAN	Wide Area Network: links computers in various geographic locations
WORM	Write Once Read Many (i.e. describes type of data storage, cannot be updated)
WYSIWIG	'What You See Is What You Get': screen images look just like printed output
WWW	'World Wide Web', or 'Web': the popular page-based section of the Internet

EXERCISE 14A

Picturing the future

Flight by machines heavier than air is unpractical and insignificant . . . if not utterly impossible.

Simon Newcomb, astronomer (1902)

As Simon Newcomb discovered, attempting to predict the future can be spectacularly embarrassing. However, if you want to make an educated guess at the future of business communication, it is worth considering the forces that are already affecting the ways that we communicate, both at work and in our leisure time. Chapter 4 includes a discussion on the advantages of diagramming techniques when you are dealing with complex issues (see page 000). Here is an opportunity to test that approach. Using a whiteboard or a large sheet of paper, spend 30 minutes developing a diagram to illustrate the likely pressures on a manufacturing or service business over the next decade. Choose a specific organisation and try to identify both the general trends and the key forces affecting its industry sector (e.g. food manufacturing or financial services). Try to show logical linkages, whereby a development in one area is likely to affect what happens elsewhere in the business.

If you are working in a group, split into two or more teams and prepare separate 'predictions'. Present your results to the other team(s) and discuss the reasons behind any similarities and differences that emerge.

14.4 ■■ Extracting information: scanning and searching

It is very easy to *collect* information. There are piles of it in every library, bookshop and record store. The real challenge is to *extract* information; the process is like mining a mountain for gold, sifting it from the accumulated dross. How far do the new technologies assist in this task? As the following examples illustrate, they have undoubtedly increased our capacity to pursue specific items. However, though we now have better digging equipment, those same technologies have conspired to make the mountain many times higher.

(a) ***Electronic data capture*** One of the most widespread forms of data capture is based on bar coding. At most supermarket checkouts, the bar code on each purchase is scanned across a laser light source, and the details are recorded automatically. This Electronic Point of Sale (EPOS) technology offers retailers the opportunity to monitor sales in enormous detail. Proponents say that you can even track changes in local weather conditions by watching, in real time, sales volumes for soup or ice cream. When EPOS data are combined with 'smart cards', purchase details can be correlated with information about each customer. In theory, this turns the checkout into a kind of on-line marketing research laboratory. However, the sheer volume of data is overwhelming. How much of it can be turned into meaningful information? The other methods of capturing data electronically include Computer Aided Telephone Interviewing (CATI) and document scanning (see Section 14.5).

(b) ***Search tools*** The simplest search tool is an index. In a traditional book, the author identifies the subjects that seem most important, puts them in alpha-betical order and provides the reader with a series of page references. Informa-tion stored electronically is also indexed, but searching becomes much more sophisticated. For example, at the local library you might ask for every reference in a particular journal that includes the words 'industry' AND 'bicycle' AND 'China' OR 'Japan'. The computer then searches all of the relevant databases and returns every item matching your criteria. 'Search engines' (e.g. Web *Crawler* and *Yahoo!*) carry out a similar task on the World Wide Web. In both cases, the filtering process is known as 'Boolean logic' (after its originator, George Boole). It is impressive, but still requires a certain amount of thought from the person conducting the search. For example, current searching tools are unable to spot a spelling error, so keying in 'bivycle' is unlikely to return any items. One of the most exciting innovations for those who do not have time to search is the so-called software 'agent' (or, worse still, a 'knowbot'). These will be programmed to go out and track down the information you need. The user may specify the kind of material that is wanted, or the agent may simply monitor the user's standard requirements (e.g. obtaining stock market prices or an entertainment service) and then take over the task automatically. Some commentators expect agents to become increasingly important as or-ganisations and individuals make greater use of the Internet. Cynics may wonder whether people will ever trust a computer with their credit card.

Case study

COPAC – library searching goes on-line

Until recently, locating a particular book or periodical could involve long and sometimes fruitless searches around the country, visiting libraries and thumbing your way through endless card files. Today, life is considerably easier, with most major libraries having converted their catalogues into computerised databases. Apart from the increased speed of access over card-based records, an electronic filing system allows you to specify more than one search criterion, such as 'author's name' plus a word from the title. In 1997, a new on-line catalogue called COPAC was launched, combining the benefits of a computerised database with Internet access. Already, the COPAC database provides bibliographic information on approximately 3.5 million records, based on the merged online library catalogues of six leading universities in the United Kingdom and Ireland. However, this number is set to increase as more library catalogues are added. COPAC can be accessed via the Internet at: **http://copac.ac.uk/copac**. Online search assistance and user guides are available. Check the site, or consult your own library for further information.

Note: COPAC is funded by JISC and uses records provided by the Consortium of University Research Libraries.

Source: COPAC/University of Manchester Computing (e-mail copac@mcc.ac.uk)

14.5 ▪▪ Processing information – the workflow concept

Businesses are involved in a continuous 'paperchase'. A typical insurance company or government agency may be handling over 2,000 items of incoming mail per day; it is also maintaining hundreds of thousands of semi-permanent files, containing details of clients and on-going projects. Workflow software could yet make the unrealised dreams of 'paperless offices' into everyday reality. It combines the scanning technologies, described above, with document handling software. In theory, it should open up all of the advantages that can be gained from digitised documentation, including:

- More rapid processing of documents
- Reduced clerical staff costs
- Reduced materials and storage costs
- Fewer clerical and 'keying-in' errors
- Document tracking and searching facilities
- Easier sharing and integration of file data

In combination, these factors should lead to improved customer service and lower prices. The first step in setting up a workflow system is to analyse in detail the organisation's routine and predictable processes, such as the processing of invoices or stock reordering. Software is then customised to provide an automated version of the process. Many clerical tasks, such as keying-in customer details, filing paper documents and checking for overdue payments, can be streamlined. Digital scanners are used to convert incoming 'hard copy' (e.g. a letter, report or form) into electronic format. At this stage, each document needs to be indexed. Indexing software creates a database with a unique record of each document, and a series of index fields – such as the date, originator, subject or key words – to enable people to retrieve it subsequently. The file containing the document is then compressed before it is stored; data compression can reduce a 20Mb file (typical of an A4 page of text and graphics) to around 100Kb. Once the data are stored, it can be retrieved by anyone who has been given access via the organisation's computer network. An electronic version of the yellow *Post-it Note* can be attached to a file, recording the comments or actions of those who have worked on the file.

The 'structured' form of workflow, outlined above, must be planned and implemented in a 'top-down' way; in other words, it has to work in the same way throughout the organisation. However, much of the paperwork in a business arises from non-routine and 'one-off' projects, such as developing a new product or arranging a special event. 'Unstructured workflow' can support these kinds of activity. It shares many features with its more structured cousins, including the emphasis on digitising of information and routing it to colleagues around a network. However, because it needs to suit the changing requirements of a relatively small group, an unstructured workflow system need to be developed 'bottom-up', by the users.

Case study

Romtec plc – delivering business intelligence

Romtec is a market research and direct marketing company, specialising in the computing and telecommunications industries. It was founded in 1982 and has grown to be a market leader, with 'blue chip' clients in Europe, the United States and Japan. In order to monitor and report on such rapidly developing sectors, Romtec's own information systems have to be under constant review.

In late 1996 a new network infrastructure was installed, including re-cabling of the company's offices. In 1997, a range of remote access services were introduced, enabling staff to use networked software and databases, either from a PC at home or (via a portable computer and GSM mobile phone) when travelling. Information is collected in a variety of ways. Computer aided telephone interviewing (CATI) enables questionnaire responses to be input directly, speeding up the analysis process; this is equipped for a range of European languages. Other sources include depth interviews and database

Computer-aided telephone interviewing (CATI) at Romtec, and the company's 'home page'.

searches. A newly established Web site provides existing and potential clients with information on Romtec and its services; the company is also exploring ways of using the Web as a delivery mechanism for its products. However, a number of services (such as market monitoring information) are already sent to clients electronically, as e-mail, CD-ROM or diskette. Reports and presentation materials are designed and published in-house. E-mail and on-line faxing software is used extensively for contacting clients and international research partners. This is supplemented by a video-conferencing facility which cuts down on travelling time. Romtec uses a sales and marketing information package incorporating a database of the company's clients which provides regularly updated ordering details. There are also extensive research databases, or 'data ware-houses' which are used to provide customised information in response to client enquiries.

Other initiatives include a project logging system (to keep track of data relating to a particular research project) and the provision of remote back-up

Source: Romtec plc. (http:\\www.romtec.co.uk)

14.6 ■■ Sharing information – workgroups and teleworking

Workgroup computing is closely related to the concepts of workflow, discussed in the previous section. Software products (e.g. Lotus *Notes* and Microsoft *Exchange*) allow people who normally work together to do so through personal computers. Instead of simply *sending* information to one another via e-mail, users are able to *share* information. For example, a number of people can work together on the same financial forecast. Each person's screen displays the same spreadsheet page, and individuals can make changes for other workgroup members to consider. They may also discuss the changes using a video-conferencing system that inserts small video images of each participant at the edge of the screen. If additional information or calculations are required, workgroup members have instant access to the organisation's databases and computing power, via the internal network. They may also be able to bring in people from outside the organisation, via the Web. Even the most committed technophiles accept that a conventional meeting around a table is sometimes going to the more appropriate option. However, this technology does open up the possibility of working equally well together, irrespective of whether you are next door or a continent away.

The idea behind 'teleworking' is that employees can spend some or all of their working time away from their employer's premises, usually in their own houses or using the shared facilities of a 'telecottage'. Early adopters of teleworking were those in traditional 'out-of-the-office' jobs, such as management consultancy and sales. However, a combination of technological developments and external pressures has led to a wider interest in this approach. Teleworking offers many potential benefits to employers, employees and the wider world, though these have yet to be confirmed through detailed research:

- Lower capital and revenue costs for staff offices and facilities (e.g. canteens)
- Reduced wages bills, by using staff based in regions where labour costs are lower.
- Increased productivity, combined with reduced staff turnover and sickness.
- Reduced environmental damage from commuter travel.
- More flexible working hours and no travel time, benefitting families with children and enabling some people to operate a second business or to do voluntary work.

Against this, there are a number of costs and other concerns. Computers and networking equipment has to be provided for home use, though the now widespread use of laptops may reduce the need for a second computer at work. In addition, there is the recurrent cost of phone line rental and call charges. More importantly, some managers question the impact of teleworking on employee motivation; will isolation and the home environment affect morale and employee effectiveness? Furthermore, will reduced informal contact between work colleagues lead to a lack of coordination or loss of direction? In many cases, the best solution is likely to be a combination of teleworking plus regular meetings 'back at the office'. Many consulting firms already use the 'hot desking' approach, where visiting staff make use of any available desk in an open plan office; each desk has the necessary network connections, though it is bound to lack the individual touch (e.g. family photos, cartoons, plants, etc.) found in more traditional office environments. As video-conferencing technology becomes cheaper and more refined, this may provide another way for teleworkers to keep in touch with their work colleagues, though it remains a poor substitute for a squash match at lunchtime or an after-work visit to the local pub.

Case study

Rural Development Commission – teleworkers and telecottages

The information age appears to offer rural communities a number of challenges and opportunities. Rural England already benefits from a fairly high standard of telephone communication, including digital exchanges. However, the newer digital telephone lines (ISDN) and the 'broadband' services provided via fibre optic cable have not yet extended far beyond the urban centres. Thanks to legislative controls, rural users pay similar prices for telecommunications, irrespective of location, but there is concern that this 'Universal Service Obligation' (USO) will not be extended to the newer services. Recent initiatives in rural areas include an e-mail service to support small and isolated schools and teleconferencing to link medical consultants with doctors' surgeries in remote communities. Telecottages are shared facilities, often located converted rural buildings, offering a full range of modern office equipment, including networked computers, scanners and printers. Together, these developments can help to maintain and develop the economic and social life of our rural communities.

The Rural Development Commission advises the Government on economic and social matters affecting rural England and takes measures to further their development. Its prime aim is to stimulate job creation and the provision of essential services in the countryside.

Training in computing and communications technology is provided 'on-site' at two small rural-based enterprises, an artist's studio and a manufacturing business.

Source: Linda Bradbrooke / RDC

EXERCISE 14B

The electronic office

When compared to a paper system, the advantages of a fully electronic, 'intranet'-based office are clear. They include: instant access to information; remote access when away from base; shared access with work colleagues; easier analysis and manipulation of data, and so on. Unfortunately, experience suggests that the future is unlikely to be this rosy! What, therefore, are the likely disadvantages of the new technologies?

(a) Prepare TWO diagrams comparing the flows of information around a small company.

As a paper-based system, with no computers
After the introduction of a computer network

You can either base these on a real business or invent an outline of its activities and management structure (e.g. a local builder or manufacturer).

(b) Divide a sheet of paper into two columns. On the left-hand side, list the main PRACTICAL advantages of your computerised system over its paper-based and mechanical predecessor. In the right-hand column, against each 'advantage' try to identify a potential 'disadvantage' arising from the same technological change.

A telephone user's guide

The telephone is a nineteenth-century technology, yet many people still find it intimidating. Voicemail and mobile phones have added to the practical challenges of using this communication channel in business. The best way to improve your telephone technique is through supervised practice – tutors or colleagues may be able to help you to 'play act' a variety of types of call using an internal phone system. Try to arrange for calls to be recorded, so that you can review your performance. As with other communication channels discussed in this book, the key to using the telephone is to recognise its special features, such as the absence of visual information, and to consider the needs of the person at the other end of the line. The following guidelines should help you to avoid some of the more common pitfalls.

1. **Answering a call** Always pick up the phone within the first few rings; this conveys a good first impression of efficiency. However, do not destroy this effect by blurting out an unintelligible greeting. Remember that it takes the caller a few seconds to adapt to your telephone voice. Begin with a brief but clear introduction, such as 'hello' or 'good morning' before stating your name and (for external calls) your organisation or department; most business phones have different ringing tones for internal and external calls, so you can adapt your greeting appropriately.

2. *Making a call* The main points are to be well prepared and to choose a suitable time. If your message is a complex one, prepare some notes summarising what you need to say. If the caller is likely to require further details, have the relevant information available – either as hard copy or readily accessible via your computer. Have a brief and clear introduction prepared, saying who you are and explaining the reason for your call. If you have a specific contact in an organisation, ask for that person by name. Alternatively, be ready to outline the nature of your call to the receptionist. If possible, try to find out who you are being directed to *before* the call is transferred. Otherwise, you are likely to find yourself listening to the answerphone message: '*Hello there, it's Sarah. I'm away from my desk right now, so please leave a message.*' Since you have no idea who Sarah is, which department she works in, or even whether she is the person you need to contact, the call is wasted. At the start of some types of call (e.g. telephone sales and market research) it is usually worthwhile checking whether the timing is convenient and, if necessary, making arrangements to call back later. There are some obvious times to avoid, such as early on a Monday morning, late on a Friday afternoon, the first days after an extended summer holiday or *any* days during an annual audit inspection.

3. *Taking a message* If you are taking a message for a colleague, ensure that you get all of the relevant details, including the caller's name and number, the action required and – in some cases – a time when it is convenient to return the call. If possible, take action to avoid a wasteful exchange of messages; deal with the query yourself or obtain sufficient information to enable someone else to resolve the issue.

4. *Dealing with a query* If you the caller needs an immediate response, consider how long it will take you to obtain the necessary information or decision. Never leave a caller waiting on a line; to them a few seconds' wait will feel like hours! Always tell the caller what you are doing and always offer to call back if there is likely to be any kind of delay. Never re-direct a call without checking that the person is both available and able to deal with the problem; there is nothing worse than being passed between offices each of which claims that, '*it is the other the people you should be speaking to*'.

5. *Dealing with complaints and anger* The biggest mistake here is to take the caller's anger personally. In many cases, you will begin with insufficient background information on the caller to know, for example, whether they are a difficult personality or simply an otherwise reasonable individual who is having a very bad day. The key here is to stay calm, let the caller talk herself out, then ensure that you clarify and collect all of the relevant facts in an understanding (but not overly apologetic) way. Your tone of voice plays a key role here – never allow it to signal that you are angry or upset with the caller. If the caller refuses to stop talking, do not raise your voice in an attempt at drowning her out; silence is a more effective tactic. Before ending the call, try to make it clear to the caller that either you or a colleague will take specific action to remedy the cause of the complaint and, if possible, secure the caller's agreement to that action.

| Case study |

Telemarketing at 'Save the Oceans' – the right technology?

A number of charities and other campaigning organisations have begun to employ external 'telemarketing' companies to handle their fund-raising efforts. Telemarketing frequently involves the use of 'hard sales' techniques, based on a combination of computerised databases and trained callers whose carefully prepared scripts are designed to produce a 'sale' – or in this case a charitable donation. In a world where each charity is competing for a limited purse, telemarketing is said to be justified by its readily quantifiable results. However, this ignores the potentially damaging effects that the indiscriminate use of an external telemarketing company could have on the client organisation. The long-standing supporters of the (imaginary) charity 'Save the Oceans' may be alienated by an aggressive 'sales' approach which has nothing to do with the core values of 'their' organisation. By adopting and communicating a hard commercial approach, 'Save the Oceans' could be compromising its principal messages, which relate to sustainable fisheries policies and increased controls on industrial pollution. Can you identify any alternative ways of using the new communications technologies that are likely to avoid these longer-term problems?

14.7 ■■ Chapter summary

- The convergence of computing and communications technologies in the late twentieth century has had a major impact on communication at work and in the wider world; further dramatic changes are inevitable.
- The most important change is the ability to transform any communication medium (text, voice, visual image) into digital form. As a result, there is almost limitless potential for transmitting, copying, sharing, storing and manipulating information.
- At the business level, high profile developments include the growth of electronic communication through internal networks (or 'intranets') and the global Internet. Though less newsworthy, the introduction of digital office equipment, such as copiers, will also have an impact on the work environment.
- Technological convergence has been accompanied by a mass of specialist jargon. In order to achieve some mutual understanding, non-specialists should make some attempt to grasp the basic principles and key terms. At the same time, technical experts must learn to provide straightforward explanations that relate to business objectives.

- The new technologies are affecting the ways that information is collected, processed and shared. It is therefore essential for managers to assess the practical implications of developments such as: scanning, search tools, workflow, workgroups and teleworking.
- Irrespective of the technology, effective communication depends on a number of core principles (as discussed in Part I of this text). As new technologies are introduced, the wisest approach is to focus on 'benefits' rather than 'features'. As (nineteenth century) telephone technology has proved, people also need to experiment in order to make the best use of novel communication channels.

Practical exercises

1. New technology: a blessing or a curse?

During the 1990s, portable phones have quickly become a mass consumer product as well as an 'essential item' for business people travelling away from the office. Writing in 1995, the Italian novelist Umberto Eco argued that, far from being a status symbol (the classic 'yuppie' accessory of the late 1980s), portable phones mark out their owners as subordinates, always at the 'beck and call' of others.

Do improvements in technology actually improve business communication, or do they simply change the 'rules of the game'? What are the effects on those who use the technology to send of receive messages? Discuss with reference to one or more of the following:

(a) The portable phone/fax/modem
(b) The photocopier
(c) The portable computer
(d) The Internet/Intranet
(e) Retail scanning systems

2. Going electronic

WholeFeeds Limited is a small food manufacturing business, operating out of converted farm buildings in a remote rural area and employing 25 local people. Its owner-manager, Gretel Hughes, markets a specialist range of luxury vegan ready-meals, using local produce, and also publishes her own recipes and advice. At present, both food and book sales are concentrated within a 100 mile radius of the farm. Each month, her administrator prepares approximately 70 invoices by hand, ranging in value from a few pounds to several thousand. Stock control and accounting are also carried out manually. Though she finds little spare time to consider the future, Gretel is keen to expand her business. She thinks that this 'niche' product could interest a wider audience, and is thinking of preparing a leaflet to send to potential customers.

Prepare a short report (500 words maximum), outlining how communications and computing technology could help WholeFeeds to expand and become more competitive. Identify the key communication issues that Gretel and her management team would need to consider.

Grammar, punctuation and spelling guide

We don't need no education,
We don't need no thought control . . .

Pink Floyd, The Wall

All human languages are based on rules of grammar, punctuation and spelling. In particular, each language has its own system of grammar, which governs the ways that words can be combined. Without agreed rules, people would be unable to express or share their thoughts. Instead, we would be like the proverbial tourist abroad, hopelessly lost and struggling to obtain directions from a bemused 'local'. There are also rules governing punctuation, the marks and symbols that clarify language in written form. Punctuation replaces the many pauses and changes of tone that people use to express themselves when language is spoken. Correct spelling is important because it avoids confusion over the meaning of written communication; spelling errors interrupt the flow of a message and make a poor impression on the reader.

Grammar and punctuation

Traditionally, the rules of grammar and punctuation were taught in the early years of schooling. Today, due to changes in teaching practice and less book-based study, there are many people with little formal training in their native language. Some argue that there is no longer any need to learn or to follow what they see as 'out-dated' and 'irrelevant' rules. In fact, despite today's increased reliance upon visual media, the need for correctly structured language has never been greater. If you remain unconvinced, consider some common problems associated with poor grammar and punctuation:

- Receivers misinterpret the message, leading to incorrect responses and actions.
- Receivers waste time trying to check the intended meaning.
- Errors give a negative impression of the sender, who appears poorly educated, careless and un-professional.

On a more positive note, there are benefits to be gained from learning more about grammar, punctuation and the use of words:

231

- With a better understanding of its underlying laws, communicators can employ language in more focused, flexible and creative ways. In a world that is increasingly filled with bland and sloppy messages, this is bound to result in more effective communication.

- Fluency in language is also associated with clear thinking, which benefits individuals, organisations and the wider public.

To check on the current state of your grammatical knowledge, complete the following 'back to basics' exercise.

EXERCISE A1A

'Back to basics' – grammar

(a) Write down a brief definition and two examples of each of the following:
   abstract noun
   adjective
   verb
   adverb
   proper noun
   pronoun
   conjunction
   preposition

(b) Express the following sentence in the **passive** form:

   Isabel threw the armchair carefully out of the upstairs window, but it missed her timid husband.

(c) Identify the following 'parts of speech' in the sentence above:
   the subject
   the object
   the main (or 'independent') clause
   the subordinate (or 'dependent') clause

The terminology explained

- **Noun:** the so-called 'naming words', of which there are four main varieties.

Concrete noun	e.g. *book, alligator, sunglasses, bicycle*
Abstract noun	e.g. *love, recession, humour, wisdom*
Proper noun	e.g. *Dublin, Tesco, Rosemary, Manchester United*
Collective noun	e.g. *team, crowd, flight (of swallows), pride (of lions)*

- **Pronoun:** words that take the place of a noun, often when referring to it a second time.

Personal pronoun	e.g. *he, she, us, them, it*
Demonstrative pronoun	e.g. *this, that, these, those*
Relative pronoun	e.g. *who, which, whom, whose*
Possessive pronoun	e.g. *mine, yours, hers, theirs*

- **Adjective:** words that describe or explain a noun or a pronoun.

Descriptive adjective	e.g. *the **enormous** mess, the **red** balloon*
Possessive adjective	e.g. ***our** company, **her** pet albatross*
Quantitative adjective	e.g. ***twenty thousand** customers, the **first** place*

- **Verb:** so-called 'doing words' that bring the sentence to life, and appear in various guises.

Finite verbs	e.g. *he **speaks** to the sales force . . . Jill **danced** the tango . . .*
Infinite verbs	e.g. ***speaking** to her mother . . . after **opening** the brandy . . .*
Transitive verbs	e.g. *I **cut** the cake . . . the policeman **kissed** the Judge . . .*
Intransitive verbs	e.g. *the sun **shines** . . . the Mona Lisa **smiles** . . .*

Finite verbs are so-called because they are limited by person and by the time of the action (i.e. past, present or future tense). Transitive verbs involve an action being 'passed on' to an object, whilst intransitive verbs do not (i.e. the policeman kisses the Judge, but the sun does not 'shine' on anything in particular).

- **Adverb:** words that describe or modify a verb in various ways, answering questions such as:

How?	e.g. *the accountant spoke **monotonously***
When?	e.g. *our train left the station **early***
Where?	e.g. *but I was waiting **outside***

Many adverbs can be obtained from the equivalent adjective by the ending '-*ly*' (hence, 'bright' becomes 'brightly') though there are certain exceptions.

- **Preposition:** words that explain the place of a noun or pronoun in the sentence.

How?	e.g. *leaving the country **without** a visa . . .*
Where?	e.g. *the protesters sitting **on** the roadway . . .*
When?	e.g. *the fax that arrived **after** the deadline . . .*

Prepositions can be confusingly similar to adverbs. In general, they proceed the word which they are helping to explain.

- **Conjunction:** words that link words, phrases and the clauses of a sentence, in two ways:

Subordinating	e.g. *we worked all night **because** you wanted the report . . .*
Coordinating	e.g. *this orchestra is famous **and** the venue is spectacular . . .*

If a conjunction is 'subordinating', it mean that the meaning of one part of the sentence is dependent on another. For example, 'you wanted the report' is dependent on 'we worked all night'. By contrast, coordinating conjunctions link words of equal value (e.g. bacon and egg) and clauses that can stand on their own (e.g. We sell houses and they sell jam).

Building blocks of a sentence

The easiest way to understand the various ways that sentences can be written is to construct one from scratch. The raw material of any sentence is a selection of words and pre-fabricated phrases. These can be assembled into a series of **simple** sentences, or alternatively into one **compound** or **complex** sentence.

Phrase	In the morning
Simple sentence	It is time for work
Simple sentence	George gets out of bed
Simple sentence	George gets dressed
Compound sentence	In the morning, George gets out of bed *and* gets dressed.
Complex sentence	In the morning, George gets out of bed *and* gets dressed *because* it is time for work.

Simple sentences are short, clear and easy to understand. However, to give the language greater interest and dramatic effect, it is important to use a variety of sentence constructions. Compound sentences are created by combining 'free-standing' clauses using conjunctions ('*and*' in the example above). Complex sentences are similar, but consist of one main (or 'independent') clause and one or more subordinate (or 'dependent') clauses. Hence, '*It is time for work*' depends on the preceding clause for its meaning.

Sentences can be expressed in active of passive forms. In the *active* form, the subject does something to the object. In the *passive* form, this order is reversed. The subject of the sentence has something done to it by the object:

Active: Isabel (*subject*) threw (*verb*) the armchair (*object*)
but it (*subject*) missed (*verb*) her timid husband (*object*) . . .
Passive: The armchair (*subject*) was thrown (*verb*) by Isabel (*object*)
but her timid husband (*subject*) was missed (*verb*) by it (*object*) . . .

So what? Making use of sentence structure

Once you have learnt to identify the various elements in a sentence, it is possible to write more varied and interesting prose. For example, you might want to introduce shorter sentences by replacing selected conjunctions with full stops. Other effects can be created by swopping the order of main and subordinate clauses. You should also find it easier to edit other people's text, in order to make it more readable and appropriate to its target readership.

EXERCISE A1B

Sentence construction

Prepare examples of compound and complex sentences containing two, three, four and five clauses. In each case identify the conjunctions plus (in the complex sentences) the main and subordinate clauses. Rewrite each sentence as a series of simple sentences, punctuated with full stops. Note how the meaning and readability changes, depending on the sentence construction.

Correct punctuation

As the name suggests, punctuation is concerned with the 'points' or marks that are added to the text. Some people seem to distribute punctuation marks randomly, whilst others manage to avoid punctuation altogether. The aim of punctuation is to guide the reader, highlighting pauses and identifying the ending of one idea and the beginning of another. Punctuation marks are also used to identify spoken words, show 'belonging', emphasise a point and ask a question.

EXERCISE A1C

Getting to the point

Try adding the necessary punctuation and capital letters to the following sentences. If in doubt, try reading the sentence aloud; your pauses and changes of tone should help to identify where punctuation is needed. Solutions are provided at the end of this section:

(a) fellow shareholders my comments today are based on fifteen years service to the company i do appreciate your problems and can assure you that the directors want to resolve them as quickly calmly and effectively as possible thank you for your continuing support

(b) its hopeless well never meet our sales target Angela cried as the mornings only customer left the shop she had spent £2.50 a whole week's pocket money on her little brothers third birthday present

(c) the following four depots exceeded januarys performance figures portsmouth aberdeen chester and bath our thanks are due to all the staff concerned it was an exceptional effort well done

Essential punctuation guide

⊡ **Full stop**

A full stop indicates the end of a sentence. If your sentences are over-long, break them up by replacing a conjunction with a full stop and a capital letter. Full stops are sometimes used to indicate an abbreviation (e.g. *B.B.C. Television, U.S.A., Dr. Jeckll and Mr. Hyde*). However, as noted in Chapter 8, 'open punctuation' is now widely accepted. Full stops are omitted from abbreviations (as in *BBC Television*) but not from the ends of sentences.

⊡ **Colon**

A colon is sometimes used, as an alternative to a comma, to open a quotation (*As Groucho Marx once said: ' I wouldn't want to join a club that would have me as a member.'*). More commonly, it marks the beginning of a list. It is not good practice to follow a colon with a dash, a colon on its own will suffice.

⊡ **Semi-colon**

A semi-colon indicates a pause that falls somewhere between a comma and a full stop. It is most commonly used to split two clauses in a complex sentence in place of a conjunction (e.g. *Our new product range has been a great success; it has out-sold all of our main competitors.*). Note how this pause acts to balance the sentence, adding emphasis to the words that follow it. In the above example, the obvious alternative would be to replace the semi-colon and the word 'it' with the conjunction 'and'.

⊡ **Comma**

A comma signifies a short pause. It is used to separate items in a list and to mark out a subordinate clause or additional detail that breaks the flow of a sentence (e.g. *The year-end figures, released last Friday afternoon, revealed a dramatic improvement in retail margins . . . The President's five year old daschund, Algernon, ate all the sandwiches . . .*).

⊡ **Single quotation marks/inverted commas**
⊡ **Double quotation marks/inverted commas**

Inverted commas are used to enclose spoken words and the titles of books, films and other publications. The following examples show how other punctuation marks are used within a quotation. Double inverted commas are only used where one quotation contains another item which also requires inverted commas.

> **Asked what he thought of Western Civilisation, Mahatma Ghandi replied, 'I think it would be a good idea.'**

During their visit, they went to see 'A Doll's House', the classic play by Henrik Ibsen.

The sales director commented, 'I thought we could base the new advertising campaign on that "Four Weddings and a Funeral" theme tune. What do you think?'

⟨!⟩ Exclamation mark
⟨?⟩ Question mark

These marks are used at the end of sentences, replacing full stops. They are sometimes over-used in advertising copy and other text, limiting their impact.

⟨-⟩ Hyphen
⟨–⟩ Dash

A hyphen is used to link two commonly associated words, especially where the adjacent letters of each word cannot easily be joined (e.g. *co-operative, pre-election, self-employed, X-ray*). However, once the combinations become widely used, the words are often merged together (e.g. *multimedia, antisocial, cellphone*). Dashes are sometimes used in place of brackets or commas. They do have a distinctive role, however, to mark a break or change of direction in a quotation (e.g. *'Emily said, I know a really great pub we could visit – but perhaps you have other plans?'*). Technically, a dash should be longer than a hyphen. However, most keyboards only allocate one key for both marks, which are therefore becoming interchangeable.

⟨(⟩ Round brackets/parentheses
⟨[⟩ Square brackets/parentheses

Brackets separate additional information or ideas from the main flow of the sentence, including incidental details and references to other publications. Square brackets have a special function, enclosing words that have been inserted by someone other than the original writer in order to make a short extract of text comprehensible (e.g. *As a leading conservationist suggested, 'The [Scottish Highlands] region is surely one of the most beautiful in Europe ...' (Gordon 1995a)*)

⟨'⟩ Apostrophe

The apostrophe indicates possession (e.g. *John's motorbike*). When the 'owner' is **plural**, the apostrophe normally moves to the end of the word. Hence, an individual *athlete*'s performance is distinguished from the team of *athletes*' collective performance. One word which seems to cause particular problems in the business world is 'company'. The full range of alternatives comprises:

Singular:	*Company*
Singular possessive:	*This company's managing director ...*
Plural:	*Companies*
Plural possessive:	*The top five companies' financial results ...*

Apostrophes are also used to show the kind of abbreviations that are common in **spoken** English (e.g. *we're, that's, it's, isn't, don't, won't, wouldn't* are shortened versions of: *we are, that is, it is, it is not, do not, will not, would not*). These abbreviations are not normally used in written English, except when quoting a speaker or when making rough notes.

☐ Omission marks/ellipsis

Three dots are used to signify that words have been omitted from a piece of text that you are quoting (e.g. '*The great masses of the people . . . will more easily fall victim to a great lie than to a small one.*') Without omission marks, the quotation might be open to mis-interpretation.

EXERCISE A1C

Getting to the point – solutions

(a) *Fellow shareholders, my comments today are based on fifteen years' service to the company. I do appreciate your problems, and can assure you that the Directors want to resolve them as quickly, calmly and effectively as possible. Thank you for your continuing support .*

(b) *'It's hopeless, we'll never reach our sales target !' Angela cried, as the morning's only customer left the shop. She had spent £2.50, a whole week's pocket money, on her little brother's third birthday present.*

(c) *The following four depots exceeded January's performance figures: Portsmouth, Aberdeen, Chester and Bath. Our thanks are due to all the staff concerned; it was an excellent effort. Well done !*

Bringing it all together

In this short section, it is not possible to cover the many complexities of the English language. However, the exercises should help to demonstrate the dramatic improvements that can be achieved by a more careful use of words, grammar and punctuation. Additional background material can be found in Chapter 3 and in the Further Reading recommendations. The key to improving your writing style is to be self-critical, re-reading text to ensure that it expresses your intended meaning. The following checklist highlights some of the more common pitfalls.

Drafting better text: a six-point checklist

1. *Is the spelling correct?* Some words are particularly easy to mis-spell (e.g. accommodate, committee, correspondence, embarrass, gauge, manoeuvre, re-

ceive, recommendation, subtlety, unnecessary, wholly, yield). Spell-checks on a wordprocessor may help, but these should never be used to replace words automatically, because they tend to turn some proper nouns into meaningless alternatives. If you think that your spelling is a weak point, make it a priority to get your written work checked. Try some self-improvement by noting down and learning each mis-spelt word. Remember the warning of a certain Leeds nightclub bouncer: '*I turn away people with moustaches, or with facial tattoos that are spelt wrongly.*'

2. **Have I used the correct word?** Some words (called 'homonyms' or 'homophones') sound similar to one another but have an entirely different meaning. Amongst the words most commonly confused are:

affect/effect	alternate/alternative
aural/oral	break/brake
compliment/complement	council/counsel
definite/definitive	dependent/dependant
discrete/discreet	enquiry/inquiry
farther/further	metre/meter
moral/morale	personal/personnel
principle/principal	precede/proceed
review/revue	stationery/stationary

If you are unsure of the differences between these words, check the meanings in a dictionary; spell-checking software will not help with this problem.

3. **Are subjects and verbs consistent?** In a simple sentence, errors in agreement are easy to identify (e.g. '*The video recorders was not stolen, they is only borrowed*'). However, in longer sentences and extended text, it is easy to mix different tenses and to confuse singular with plural forms. It is therefore best to decide at the outset whether, for example, you are writing in the present or past tense, and in the first person ('I think that . . .') or passive form ('It is thought that . . .').

4. **Are verbs being over-stretched?** Do not expect one verb to express both past and future activity, or the actions of different subjects. Consider the sentence: 'Throughout the past year, the charity was well managed, effective in delivery and ready to face the challenges that lie ahead.' To clarify the writer's meaning, an additional verb is needed: 'Throughout the past year the charity was well managed and effective in delivery. It is ready to face the challenges that lie ahead.'

5. **Are sentences overly complex?** As the previous example demonstrated, longer sentences can usually be broken into their component clauses. Shorter sentences increase the readability of text, especially when shorter words are used. This is particularly important if your message is designed for audiences with a range of reading abilities. Documents such as instruction manuals, tax returns and social security forms need to be written using simple vocabulary and sentence structures.

6. *Are certain words or phrases over-used?* Everyone has their own 'favourite' words and phrases, but their repeated use does become tedious for the reader. When re-reading a section of text, look out for frequent repetition, especially where these are located close to one another. Depending on the context, most words can be replaced with equivalents from the thesaurus, whilst pronouns make a suitable substitute for repetitive nouns.

EXERCISE A1D

Editing text

Editing is a useful skill to develop. If you are working in a group, spend half an hour preparing a 'poorly constructed' short report on a topic of your choice (alternatively, your tutor may be able to provide you with practice material). Exchange reports with other members of the group, and spend a further period editing and redrafting the report.

(a) Correct the grammar, punctuation and spelling in the original version.
(b) Rewrite the text so that it is clearer and more interesting as well as error-free.
(c) Compare the 'before' and 'after' versions of the report.

EXERCISE A1E

Drafting text

Select topic of your choice which should involve some specialist technical information (e.g. an economic theory, a medical treatment or an engineering problem). Prepare three extracts (maximum 500 words each) covering exactly the same information, but presented in a format that is suitable for each of the following readers:

(a) a specialist in your subject area
(b) a general reader with no specialist knowledge
(c) a child aged about nine OR an adult with limited knowledge English (specify your choice)

Note how vocabulary, sentence structure and overall style need to alter in order to convey the message effectively.

Appendix two

The personal dimension: preparing a CV

Curriculum Vitae

Course of life

One of the most important *persuasive* communication exercises that most of us tackle is getting the right job, and one of the main elements in a successful application is a well-thought-out CV. Whether you are a placement student, recent graduate or an established manager, your CV is going to be a continuously updated document that needs to be tailored to a specific job opportunity. The keys to exploiting this communication channel successfully are to begin with a fairly open mind about potential jobs, obtaining a large number of adverts and brochures, and then to concentrate your attention on each *receiver*'s individual requirements and expectations. Before constructing or revising your CV, ask yourself two deceptively simple questions: firstly, 'What are these prospective employers really looking for?' and, secondly, 'Am I delivering evidence matching their requirements?' (see Chapter 5 for additional material on persuasive communication).

Q1 What are these prospective employers really looking for?

Some criteria are very specific, and are usually stated in the advertisement or the additional details that you are sent, including education level, professional qualifications and job-related experience. However, others may be less obvious, requiring further research or 'reading between the lines' of the job specification.

Informal discussions and desk research

Find out as much as you can about your target – and do it *before* the application is posted! Some adverts include a contact name and number to call for an 'informal discussion'. This is an excellent opportunity to obtain more information about the job and the organisation, though recruitment professionals express surprise at how few applicants use these facilities. In any event, you should invest some time in desk research. Other sources of information include the organisation's own annual reports, promotional brochures and possibly its World Wide Web site. For an independent perspective, you can also search newspapers and specialist magazines,

EXERCISE A2A

Analysing a job advertisement

Consider the following advertisement for sales personnel which was placed in *The Grocer*, a leading national trade journal.

TWO FOCUSED
SALES PERSONNEL
Dyfed, West Wales

Our client is ready to break the mould of traditional agricultural sales recruitment, by bringing your professionalism in your field of sales, and applying it to their own. Agriculture?! Yes, experience of selling in the rural environment would be a bonus, but what our client primarily seeks is goal oriented people who want a career in agricultural sales.

The company is young, team empowered and expanding; specialising in the feeding of dairy herds. The accent is on premium quality and customer service.

You are young, ambitious, organised and career-oriented. You have a positive personality and show total commitment in all that you do. You have a formal relevant qualification and have already built up a good track record in sales.

Our client offers a rewarding career with comprehensive training and an excellent remuneration package. This includes an attractive negotiable salary, company car, telephone, and the opportunity to grow with an expanding company.

In the first instance send covering letter and CV, stating current circumstance / salary to:

Harper Adams Recruitment Service
Newport
Shropshire
TF10 8NB

(a) List what you consider to be KEY requirements of the job under the headings:

Qualifications:
Experience:
Skills:
Personal qualities:
Age range:
Other factors?:

(b) Have you identified any requirements that are *implied* rather than stated explicitly?
(c) Which of the factors do you see as 'desirable' and which are likely to be 'essential'?
(d) How do you think that the location of the business and its industry sector might influence the selection criteria?
(e) What reasons might the client company have for advertising in a retail trade journal?

many of which are available on CD-ROM. If practical, it is also a good idea to experience some of the organisation's products or services for yourself, along with those of its major competitors. Last but not least, you can try to locate a current or former employee amongst your network of friends and relatives; an informal conversation could provide you with valuable material for the application as well as helping to decide whether the job is likely to be right for you.

'No time wasters please': being selective

Having analysed the job advertisement, plus all of the related information that you have obtained, it is time to make a realistic self-assessment. Firstly, do you meet the majority of the stated requirements? Employers may be flexible on a few of their specifications, but in a competitive job market it really is a waste of time to chase after posts where you have few, if any, of the pre-requisites. Secondly, are you still genuinely interested in the job? Having begun with a wide range of potential employers, you are now ready to conduct your own 'screening' exercise on those opportunities identified. It is better to focus your efforts on fewer, but more carefully targeted, applications. Above all, it is pointless to pursue a job if you lack personal motivation or commitment; this will almost certainly be picked up at the interview stage.

Q2 Am I delivering evidence matching their requirements?

Having decided that you 'have what it takes', the challenge is to generate sufficiently strong evidence *on paper* to get you through the initial 'screening' stage of the selection process (see Chapter 13 for practical advice on job interviews). In most cases, the employer's initial decisions are made on the basis of a CV, covering letter and perhaps an application form. Ensure that your paperwork demonstrates, as clearly and convincingly as possible, that you fulfil the criteria identified in the advert and from your research. As Exercise A2a suggested, these will include:

- Relevant skills, knowledge and experience, both technical and managerial
- Personal qualities, covering anything from creativity to self-discipline
- Other screening factors (e.g. age, current salary, home location)

Sometimes, the search for useful evidence requires some lateral thinking. For example, how can you demonstrate 'people management' and entrepreneurial skills if you have little or no work experience so far? The answer is to draw on other life experiences, such as leading a student expedition to Norway, organising rag week or setting up a gardening venture whilst at school. All sort of non-work projects can provide the necessary evidence. Employers are rarely interested in the activities themselves. Instead, they want to discover what your earlier life says about you as a person *today*. More specifically, they want to know whether you are likely to enhance their organisation in the future.

One infuriating but inescapable reality of recruitment is that items described as 'other screening factors' are sometimes used to reduce hundreds of applications to more manageable proportions. It is difficult to avoid feeling demoralised when an apparently strong application is rejected at the first stage. However, in the case of 'screening', this does not necessarily mean that you failed to provide good evidence. Though it may be little consolation at the time, one of these screening factors might have triggered a rejection *before* your application was reviewed in any detail. Try to remain philosophical – these things happen to all applicants at one time or another.

Writing your CV: layout and other requirements

Keep your CV concise, extending to a maximum of two sides of A4 paper in most cases. The layout and contents should always be adapted to suit the needs of the employer. Hence, the illustration shown below must **not** be seen as a model layout. However, whilst there is not 'one best way' of presenting a CV, some general guidance can be given on the main sections to be included:

- **Name** Include your full name, printing it in large bold type on the first page and repeating it at the top of each continuation sheet. This, after all, is the name you want those selectors to remember!
- **Address/telephone** Many invitations to an interview get lost in student post trays or fail due to unanswered telephone calls to halls of residence. If your current postal address is inaccessible or unreliable, give an alternative one, care of ('c/o') a close relative or friend. Be sure to check with your contact regularly!
- **Education/qualifications** Show your highest qualifications first, including any courses currently under way (with expected completion dates and projected outcomes if available). As you progress through the education system, drop the lowest level qualification; graduates do not normally list their GCSE grades, for example. Give details of any projects, dissertations, field trips or special subjects studied that are particularly relevant to the current application. Names and dates for your secondary schools, colleges, etc. can be incorporated into this section, or listed separately.
- **Employment/work experience** Use reverse chronological order, displaying the most recent job first. Summarise the role and responsibilities of each post in 'active' terms, highlighting factors relevant to the application. For example:

  *As **production supervisor**, I managed a team of 40 night shift workers in the packhouse, dealing with quality assurance and productivity . . .*

  *As **clerical assistant** in the surveyor's office, I was responsible for supporting the company's buildings maintenance programme. Tasks included data input . . .*

Though a previous job may be entirely unrelated to the one you are now seeking, it can often provide valuable indications of key personal qualities such as reliability, initiative and dynamism. If you are short on paid work experience, voluntary work and job placements can be equally useful sources of information.

- **Achievements and interests** Employers are rarely particularly interested in your hobbies, though something very unusual may succeed in catching their attention and making your application stand out from the crowd. The main reason that people scan this section is to seek further evidence of your personal qualities. For example, being a county tennis champion is not – in itself – an essential requirement for most management trainee positions. However, this achievement does suggest the kind of self-discipline and determination that an organisation requires. Never exaggerate your achievements or fictionalise your interests, but be selective in the details that you include. The inclusion of activities like: 'enthusiastic train-spotter', 'television soap opera addict' or 'revolutionary anarchist' are unlikely to boost your appeal.

- **Other information** Include any *relevant* details, such as language skills or clean driving licence, that have not been mentioned under the previous headings. This section is particularly useful for inserting items that reflect job requirements, such as willingness to travel overseas or experience with a particular software package.

- **Referees** Include the name, address and telephone number of at least two people who have agreed in advance to provide references. Recruiters often specify at least one reference from a current or past employer. You may also ask a tutor to provide an academic reference. Always ask permission from the people you include, and stay in touch, thanking them for their support and providing updates on your progress to date.

- **A personal statement** Some recruitment specialists argue that a CV is enhanced by including a brief personal statement. The idea is to summarise, in a memorable way, what you can offer a potential employer. For example:

  A lively and creative junior sales executive, Gillian is ambitious and results-oriented with proven people management skills.

  Ahmed is a hard-working and conscientious finance professional with extensive experience in acquisition and international accounting practice.
  Personal statements are normally placed immediately after the name and address section of the CV (see the 'Jenny Smith' illustration below). They can be in your own words, or you may be able to use a quotation from a previous employer. These statements can help to increase the impact of your CV, but they need to be drafted very carefully to avoid sounding pompous or complacent.

Covering letter

Keep your covering letter short and polite. State where you first heard about the post and focus on the main reasons why you should be considered. Some employers still specify a *hand-written* covering letter (nb: a few may use 'graphology', a controversial technique of handwriting analysis that is supposed to reveal hidden personality traits). However, most people prefer a word processed letter, with the font and paper matching your CV.

Application forms

Many organisations insist that you complete a multi-page form, even when it duplicates much of the information on your CV. The advantage, from the employer's point of view, is that all of the information is in a standardised format. Some may view this time-consuming exercise as a test of your commitment to the job! It is therefore essential to take these forms seriously, writing neatly and answering all of the questions posed. An incomplete or error-ridden form is likely to result in rejection, even if it is accompanied by a 'professional' looking CV and covering letter.

Final points: paper and packaging, typos and feedback

- *Paper and packaging* It is worth investing in a good quality paper to make your CV stand out from the inevitable pile of competing applications (see Appendix 3). Some applicants make considerable efforts to package the material, using spiral binders and non-standard page sizes. Others have been successful using a multimedia CV, submitted on disc. In each case, you need to consider the employer's characteristics, especially its culture, work activities and technologies.
- *Errors and typos* Check and re-check for spelling and grammatical errors (e.g. 'I am hard-werking and conscietus' or 'I has a clean licence and car'). Errors are bound to prejudice your application. They give a negative impression, suggesting that you are either: (a) badly educated, (b) careless or (c) poorly motivated. None of these is an attractive feature in a prospective employee. If in doubt, ask someone to proof read the material you have prepared.
- *Feedback* One of the frustrations of job applications is that you rarely discover the reasons for a rejection. However, if you have reached the final round of selection, or if the organisation is relatively small, it is worth contacting the relevant manager for some informal advice on your strengths and weaknesses. In general, a prompt and polite telephone enquiry is the most effective channel.

"The man we need must have guts, daring and
initiative, Mrs. Hempson! Is your son that man?"

A sample advert, curriculum vitae and covering letter: Jennifer Smith

---

MARKETING EXECUTIVE
Ambitious Expeditions

Manchester, attractive package

Ambitious is a leading specialist holiday company, run by active mountaineers and naturalists and established in 1985. We now offer a wide range of high quality adventure and nature-watch experiences in Eastern Europe, Africa, South East Asia and South America. We have an enviable reputation for innovation and customer service. Due to recent internal promotions, the company requires an enthusiastic marketing executive to support our fast-developing expeditions business. We are looking for a graduate in marketing, or a related subject, with at least three years' experience in the travel and tourism sector. You will need outstanding organisation and communication skills, familiarity with database marketing systems and a good sense of humour. The job will involve extended periods of travel within the UK and overseas. In return, we can offer an attractive salary and benefits package.
For an informal discussion about the post, call Tracy Hughes, Marketing Manager on 0161 222 0000

To apply for this position, send a comprehensive CV and covering letter, including current salary to: **Ms. A Leonard, Personnel Department, Ambitious Holidays, 34 Green Street, Manchester M1 2XZ, quoting reference SIN/271A.** Closing date: 12th June 199X

---

25 Severn Avenue
Ironbridge
Shropshire
TF99 7XB

6th May 199X

Ms. A Leonard
Personnel Department
Ambitious Holidays
34 Green Street
Manchester M1 2XZ

Dear Ms Leonard

MARKETING EXECUTIVE: AMBITIOUS EXPEDITIONS (Ref: SIN/271A)

I am pleased to enclose my CV for the above post, advertised in the Sunday Inquirer (4 May). Following today's telephone conversation with Tracy Hughes, I am very interested in this post, since it offers an excellent opportunity to develop my existing career in leisure and tourism marketing.

In return, I can offer varied experience in hotel management and marketing, backed up by a business studies degree. I am also currently completing a professional qualification in marketing. In addition, I have direct experience of adventure holidays, both as an independent traveller in Nepal and Indonesia, and as team leader on a number of Duke of Edinburgh's Award expeditions.

If you have any further questions, I can be contacted on 01952 777777 (office) and 01952 888888 (home – answerphone). With best regards,

Yours sincerely

Jennifer Smith

CURRICULUM VITAE

JENNIFER LOUISE SMITH

Date of Birth	17th November 1973	25 Severn Avenue
Nationality	British	Ironbridge
Status	Single	Shropshire
		TF99 7XB

Telephone	01952 888888 (evening)
	01952 777777 (day)

Email	jenny—smith@xyz.co.uk

A confident, mature and hard-working marketing executive with varied industry experience and good inter-personal skills, Jennifer is keen to develop her career within the leisure and tourism sector.

• *EDUCATION*

Sep 1990	**THE UNIVERSITY OF BRIGHTFORDSHIRE**
Jul 1994	BSc (Honours) Business Administration and Tourism Studies
	Dissertation Title: *Beyond the Grouse Moor: Marketing a Scottish Estate*
	Class 2:1

Sep 1988	**LODGEVILLE COMMUNITY COLLEGE** (Gwent)
Jul 1990	A-levels:

German	A
English Literature	B
Economics	C

• *WORK EXPERIENCE*

Sep 1994	**HILLYFIELDS COUNTRY HOUSE HOTEL, Shropshire**
to date	40 bedroomed luxury hotel and leisure centre

As **Marketing and Publicity Executive**, I plan and manage the hotel's promotional campaign, drafting press releases and advertising material. I initiated a Christmas 1994 promotion, based on a Dickensian theme, which contributed to a 15% increase in sales over the previous year. I work closely with the hotel's Director and advertising agency executives. I am also a representative on the local rural tourism initiative, working with other hotels and visitor attractions on joint marketing projects.

Jul 1994   **BOOTLES HOLIDAYS plc, London**
Sep 1994   Leading UK travel organisation, specialising in charter holidays

As a temporary **Customer Services Assistant**, I was responsible for dealing with telephone queries and complaints. I also supported the Customer Services Manager, making arrangements for re-bookings and refunds and planning a travel agent's visit which was scheduled for autumn 1994.

Sep 1988   **LODGEVILLE LEISURE CENTRE, Gwent**
Sep 1990   Local Olympic-sized swimming pool and leisure pool

As a part-time **Lifeguard**, I undertook a range of tasks, including supervising swimming sessions, organising special events and running training sessions for adults and disabled children.

- *P R O F E S S I O N A L   M E M B E R S H I P S*

THE CHARTERED INSTITUTE OF MARKETING
Student membership. Currently studying for the Diploma in Marketing (Dip M)

- *P E R S O N A L   A C H I E V E M E N T S   &   I N T E R E S T S*

Whilst at secondary school, I led the winning team in a Bindley's Bank-sponsored business game. I also completed the Duke of Edinburgh's Gold Award, which included community work and culminated in a major expedition to Iceland. I enjoy travelling in the UK and abroad. During the Summer of 1992, I travelled by Greyhound bus across the United States, visiting a number of major tourist attractions including Disneyworld, the Rocky Mountains and the Grand Canyon. In 1993, I spent three months travelling independently in Nepal and Indonesia. I was the county junior swimming champion in 1987, and 1989 and continue to compete at county and national levels. I also enjoy playing golf and tennis and am a member of the Hillyfields Choral Society and the Hillyfields Junior Chamber of Commerce.

- *FURTHER INFORMATION*

Computing   Spreadsheet: *Quattro Pro*; Marketing research survey analysis: *SPSS*.
Word-processing: *Wordperfect, Word;* DTP: *Aldus Pagemaker.*

Languages   German to A-level; effective conversational standard maintained through regular visits. Spanish to GCSE level.

Foreign travel   I enjoy travelling abroad and would be happy to spend a considerable part of the year working outside the United Kingdom.

Transport   Own car and clean driving licence.

- *REFEREES*

Valerie Makepeace MSc BSc (Econ)
Lecturer in Marketing
Faculty of Business & Management
The University of Brightfordshire
Hopton Street
Brightford BZ2 4ZA

Brian Boothby
Customer Services Manager
Bootles Holidays plc
Cruachan House
133-135 Longman Street
London W1E 9XX

Important note: CV layout and contents

There are no universal or 'model' formats for a curriculum vitae. You must always adapt the structure and contents of your CV to the specific requirements of the employer, the sector and the type of work for which you are applying.

EXERCISE A2B

Selling Georgina/George

Task Prepare a CV and covering letter for the person who is described below. He (or she) is applying for various graduate trainee posts. Begin by selecting a suitable job advertisement from a newspaper, and analysing the employer's requirements. Then consider how to **communicate** the information provided by this candidate in a way that is clear and persuasive. What is the **content** of your message? What should you include, what needs special emphasis and what is best left out? You should also consider your writing **style** and **presentation** of the material. Make up your own names / addresses and invent additional material if necessary. Review your rough draft, considering the following points:

- Will your design attract attention and persuade a potential employer?
- What are your key messages?
- Have you covered all the requirements previously identified?

'I am 20 years old, and live in Lincolnshire, but go to college at Northshire University where I am studying for a BSc Honnours degree in International Business. I have eight GCSE passes, including English at grade B and Maths at grade C; also A-levels in Economics (B) and Geography (D). I went to school at St Anne's County Junior and Greyfriars High. I was a school prefect and a bookshop monitor. I was also a scout / guide and then a venture scout and captain of the county tennis squad. I have done a newspaper round from age 14 to 16, and have worked at the local leisure centre every holiday for the past three years. I went to Thailand on a travelling scholarship last summer, and prepared a report for the sponsoring company. This was a prize for an essay competition I had entered and was great fun; the food was fantastic. I am a fan of Nottingham Forest football club, and try to get to most of their matches around the country. I also like watching 1950s detective films on video and have a large collection at home, plus a big CD collection, with lots of American imports. I can use a computer (basic level wordprocessing and spreadsheets) but, to be honest, I find them pretty boring really. I have only worked in a real company for three months on a university placement (Erskines Superstores), but it seemed pretty good. We were sorting out a new pallet loading and distribution system; I visited a number of warehouses and presented a report to some senior managers at head office. I help out with a disabled sports club one evening a week, and spend about three evenings in the Student Union bar, where I am entertainments secretary and president of the 'legalise cannabis' campaign group. I drive an 'R' reg Volkswagen Beetle, which I am really proud of, having done a complete overhaul on it. Whilst at school, I set up a little business with three friends, designing and selling 'customised' T-shirts. We lost a lot of money in the first year and almost gave up, but we did much better in our final year, when I made over £2,000 ! My star sign is Sagittarius, and I am 5'9", fairly fit and healthy, with dark hair and brown eyes. I took a year out before going to college, and worked in the United States (on kids' summer camps) for a while, then spent two months wandering around South America with a mate. We raised most of the money for the trip by selling our collection of T-shirts at festivals and to a few local businesses'.

Appendix three

Paper: the under-rated communicator

Verbal agreements are not worth the paper they are written on

Sam Goldwyn, film producer

Paper has been a medium of human communication since the Ancient Egyptians first used **papyrus** reed fibres to create inexpensive and portable writing materials. Subsequent civilisations made use of cured animal skin ('parchment'), pulped fishing nets and rags. Today's paper is derived mainly from wood pulp and recycled material. Despite the computer revolution of the last two decades, the 'paperless office' seems as far away as ever. Paper remains an important communicator, available in a wide range of types, shapes, sizes and colours. It is therefore worthwhile spending a few moments considering which type of paper would reinforce the message you are trying to convey. For example:

- **Luxury/sophistication**   heavy, embossed or coated paper
- **Value for money**   plain, normal weight paper
- **Environmental concern**   100 per cent recycled and unbleached paper
- **Innovation/creativity**   unusual shape, size or colour of paper

An inappropriate choice of paper could be very damaging. For example, if a voluntary organisation prints the annual fund-raising mail-out on brightly coloured, watermarked 110gsm premium paper, its supporters and sponsors will be outraged at the extravagance. However, if it was used for a CV and covering letter, similar paper might attract the attention of someone who had to wade through 250 applications on a rainy afternoon. As always, the decision needs to be based on an assessment of the receiver and the type of message that is being conveyed. Another point to consider is the size and shape of a document. This applies particularly to promotional literature, where an unusual shape, size or type of folding can help you to secure the attention of receivers.

EXERCISE A3A

The business stationery review

Collect samples of business stationery from the list below. Try to establish the weight and type of paper used and its approximate cost (per 500 sheet pack / box, the normal minimum order size). Prepare a display, contrasting those organisations whose stationery reinforces their image and those who have room to improve. Are colours, typefaces and logos used consistently throughout? Do you consider these to be important factors? Make some alternative suggestions for your under-performers.

Main printed stationery items

Letter paper (and continuation sheets)
Compliments slips
Envelopes (often plain, but sometimes incorporating a company logo and address)
Facsimile (fax) cover sheets
Financial stationery (invoices, delivery notes, statements)
Business cards
Telephone and 'while you were out' message pads

The good paper guide: main features

- **Weight** The weight of paper is measured in grams per square metre (gsm), with heavier papers being considerably more expensive. Some printers and copiers are unable to cope with particularly thick or thin paper.

  70gsm lightweight paper, suitable for airmail letters
  80gsm standard, mid-range copier paper
  100gsm heavier and more opaque paper for letterhead paper
  110gsm premium quality cartridge paper for prestige reports

- **Colour** A wide range of colours is available. Key issues include cost and company's 'house style'. Darker tones should normally be avoided, since these produce poor quality or illegible photocopies and faxes. If, for security reasons, you want a document that *cannot* be photocopied, print it on deep red paper!

- **Size** There are now international standard sizes for paper and envelopes, based on the metric system, though the United States retains traditional measurements. Most business correspondence uses the A4-sized sheet. As the illustration shows, two A4 sheets (placed side by side) are equivalent to one A3 sheet.

Technical   Some papers are unsuitable for particular applications, such as for photocopiers, laser printers, inkjet printers or fax machines. The special coatings required for certain colour printing processes mean that these papers tend to be more expensive. If in doubt, check with an experienced supplier before purchasing office equipment or large paper stocks.

Recycling   Recycled paper is becoming popular with organisations that want to promote an 'environmentally aware' image. Once seen as sub-standard, it is now available in specifications that are suitable for most purposes. However, there is a counter-argument that the de-inking chemicals and additional energy used in recycling make it a less attractive option. An alternative environmental claim states that the virgin paper used is from: 'softwood pulp from managed forests; for every tree cut down at least one more is planted ...' Some businesses also make special arrangements for the re-cycling of their own office waste, including the safe disposal of used toner from photocopiers.

Folding   Leaflets, forms and brochures can be created from single sheets using a variety of folding techniques. When designing a document, it is important to consider how text and illustrations will appear in the final version. Mock-ups can be produced quite easily, with the help of a photocopier.

Paper Sizes 'A' Size Standard Sheets

	SIZE IN MM	SIZE IN INCHES
A0	841 x 1189	$33\frac{1}{8}$ x $46\frac{3}{4}$
A1	594 x 841	$23\frac{3}{8}$ x $33\frac{1}{8}$
A2	420 x 594	$16\frac{1}{2}$ x $23\frac{3}{8}$
A3	297 x 420	$11\frac{3}{4}$ x $16\frac{1}{2}$
A4	210 x 297	$8\frac{1}{4}$ x $11\frac{3}{4}$
A5	148 x 210	$5\frac{7}{8}$ x $8\frac{1}{4}$
A6	105 x 148	$4\frac{1}{8}$ x $5\frac{7}{8}$
A7	74 x 105	$2\frac{7}{8}$ x $4\frac{1}{8}$
A8	52 x 74	2 x $2\frac{7}{8}$
A9	37 x 52	$1\frac{1}{2}$ x 2
A10	27 x 37	1 x $1\frac{1}{2}$

DL 110mm x 220mm

C5 162mm x 229mm

C6 114mm x 162mm

EXERCISE A3B

Promotional leaflet design

Prepare a promotional leaflet for an organisation of your choice. For example, it may be a recruitment drive for a charitable body, or sales literature for a hotel or sports club. You will need to consider the text and artwork, as well as the paper type and size. Prepare a mock-up of your design, showing how it would be folded. Provide a suitable envelope, so that the leaflet can be posted, along with a covering letter (see Chapter 8 for background information on business letter style and content).

Examples of folding

Two-way fold

Gate fold
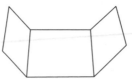

Three-way fold

Further reading guide

The following bibliography includes references from each chapter, plus a selection of recommended texts for readers wanting to pursue specific topics in greater detail. Most of these texts are currently available in both bookshops and libraries.

Chapter 1 ▨ Introduction and overview

Shannon, C. and Weaver, W. (1949) *The mathematical theory of communication*, Illinois University Press, outlined in Gates (1996) – see Chapter 14 below.
Hargie, O. *et al.* (1994) *Social skills in interpersonal communication*, Routledge, London.
Luft, J. and Ingram, H. (1955) *The Johari window: a graphic model of interpersonal awareness*, UCLA research paper, outlined in Hargie *et al.* (1994) – see previous reference.

Chapter 2 ▨ Barriers to communication

Gross, R. D. (1996) *Psychology, the science of mind and behaviour*, Hodder & Stoughton, London.
Hickson, D. J. (1997) *Exploring management across the world*, Penguin Books, London.
Hofstede, G. (1984) *Culture's consequences: international differences in work-related values*, Sage Publications, London.
Janis, I. L. (1982) *Groupthink: psychological studies of policy decisions and fiascoes* (2nd edition), Houghton & Mifflin, Boston, MA.

Chapter 3 ▨ Words: using language

Allen, R. E. (ed.) (1991) *The concise Oxford dictionary of current English*, OUP, Oxford.
Gowers, E. *et al.* (1987) *The complete plain words* (revised edition), Penguin Books, London.
Inman, C. (1994) *The Financial Times style guide*, Financial Times/Pitman, London.
Keane, F. (1996) *Letter to Daniel: despatches from the heart*, BBC/Penguin Books, London.
Orwell, G. (1957) *Inside the whale and other essays*, Penguin Books, London.
Urdang, L. (1991) *The Oxford thesaurus: an A–Z dictionary of synonyms*, OUP, Oxford.
Jarvie, G. (1993) *Bloomsbury grammar guide*, Bloomsbury, London.

Chapter 4 ▨ Pictures: using images

Morgan, J. and Welton, P. (1992) *See what I mean?: an introduction to visual communication*, Edward Arnold, London.

Murphy, S. (1990) *The manager's guide to audio-visual production*, Kogan Page, London.

Ollins, W. (1989) *Corporate identity: making business strategy visible through design*, Thames & Hudson, London.

Richey, T. (1994) *The marketer's visual tool kit: using charts, graphs and models for strategic planning and problem solving*, American Marketing Association/AMACOM, New York.

Chapter 5 ▦ Powers of persuasion: changing minds

Hamlyn, S. (1989) *How to talk so people listen*, HarperCollins, London.

Kotler, P. *et al.* (1996) *Principles of marketing: the European edition*, Prentice Hall, Hemel Hempstead.

Packard, V. (1997) *The hidden persuaders: the classic study of the American advertising machine*, Penguin Books, London.

Pratley, P. (1995) *The essence of business ethics*, Prentice Hall, Hemel Hempstead.

Saker, J. and Smith, G. (1997) *European casebook on principles of marketing*, Prentice Hall, Hemel Hempstead.

Warr, P. (1996) *Psychology at work*, Penguin Books, London.

Chapter 6 ▦ The organisational dimension

Argyris, C. (1994) *On organisational learning*, Blackwell, Oxford.

Handy, C. B. (1996) *Understanding organisations*, Penguin Books, London.

Handy, C. B. (1996) *Understanding voluntary organisations*, Penguin Books, London.

Huczynski, A. and Buchanan, D. (1997) *Organisational behaviour: an introductory text*, Prentice Hall, Hemel Hempstead.

Huczynski, A. and Buchanan, D. (1997) *Readings in organisational behaviour: a self-study text*, Prentice Hall, Hemel Hempstead.

Jay, A. (1987) *Management and Machiavelli*, London: Hutchinson Business.

Moss Kanter, R. (1985) *The change masters: corporate entrepreneurs at work*, International Thompson Business Press, London

Pugh, D. S. (1997) *Organisation theory: selected readings*, Penguin Books, London.

Chapter 7 ▦ Information capture: forms and questionnaires

Bell, J. (1995) *Doing your research project: a guide for first time researchers in education and social science*, Open University Press, Buckingham.

Blaxter, L. *et al.* (1966) *How to research*, Open University Press, Buckingham.

Gilbert, N. (ed.) (1993) *Researching social life*, Sage Publications, London. (chs. 2, 4, 3, 5, 6).

Kinnear, T. C. and Taylor, J. R. (1991) *Marketing research*, Mc-Graw Hill, Maidenhead.

Wright, L. T. (1995) *The marketing research process*, Prentice Hall, Hemel Hempstead.

Chapter 8 ▦ Business letters and direct mail

Janner, G. (1989) *Janner's complete letter writer*, Century Hutchinson, London.

See also: Chapter 3 and 4 references; for direct marketing, see Chapter 5: Kotler et al. (1996).

Chapter 9 ■■ Reports, memos and briefings

Economist, The (1991) *The Economist numbers guide: the essentials of business numeracy*, Economist Books, London.

Flemming, M. and Nellis, J. (1996) *The essence of statistics for business*, Prentice Hall, Hemel Hempstead.

See also: Chapter 3 and 4 references; for research reports, see Chapter 7 references.

Chapter 10 ■■ Making presentations

Janner, G. (1989) *Janner's complete speechmaker*, Century Hutchinson, London.
See also: Chapter 3 and 4 references; for AV materials, see Chapter 4: Murphy (1990).

Chapter 11 ■■ Meetings, teams and negotiation

Adair, J. (1983) *Effective leadership*, Gower, London.

Armour, D. (1995) *The ICSA company secretary's handbook*, ICSA Publishing, Hemel Hempstead.

Belbin, R. M. (1993) *Team roles at work*, Butterworth-Heinemann, Oxford.

Belbin, R. M. (1981) *Management teams: why they succeed or fail*, Butterworth-Heinemann, Oxford.

Fisher, R. and Ury, W. (1981) *Getting to yes: negotiating agreement without giving in*, Business Books/Century Hutchinson, London.

Hiltrop, J.-M. (1995) *The essence of negotiation*, Prentice Hall, Hemel Hempstead.

Martin, D. (1996) *One stop company secretary*, ICSA Publishing, Hemel Hempstead.

Williams, H. (1996) *The essence of managing groups and teams*, Prentice Hall, Hemel Hempstead.

Chapter 12 ■■ Adverts, news releases and displays

Hart, N. (1995) *The practice of advertising*, Butterworth-Heinemann, Oxford.

Harrison, S. (1995) *Public relations: an introduction*, Routledge/ITBP, London.

Riel, C.M.B. Van (1995) *Principles of corporate communication*, Prentice Hall, Hemel Hempstead.

Chapter 13 ■■ Interviews and listening skills

Breakwell, G. (1990) *Interviewing (problems in practice series)*, British Psychological Society/Routledge, London.

Caroll, M. (1996) *Workplace counselling*, Sage Publications, London.

Gratus, G. (1996) *Successful interviewing*, Penguin Books, London.

Sisson, K. (ed.) (1994) *Personnel management*, Blackwell, Oxford.

Torrington, D. and Hall, L. (1995) *Personnel management*, Prentice Hall, Hemel Hempstead.

Chapter 14 ■■ Future communication: the role of technology

Edwards, C. *et al.* (1996) *The essence of information systems*, Prentice Hall, Hemel Hempstead.

Gates, W. H. (1996) *The road ahead* (revised edition), Penguin Books, London.

Gunton, T. (1996) *The Penguin dictionary of information technology*, Penguin Books, London.
Handy, C. (1994) *The empty raincoat: making sense of the future*, Random House, London.
Harvey-Jones, J. (1994) *All together now*, Heinemann, London.
Reid, A. (1994) *Teleworking*, NCC Blackwell, Oxford.
Schumacher, E. F. (1979) *Good work*, Jonathan Cape, London.

Index